Deep Travel

American Land and Life Series

WAYNE FRANKLIN

series editor

Deep Travel

In Thoreau's Wake on the Concord and Merrimack

DAVID K. LEFF

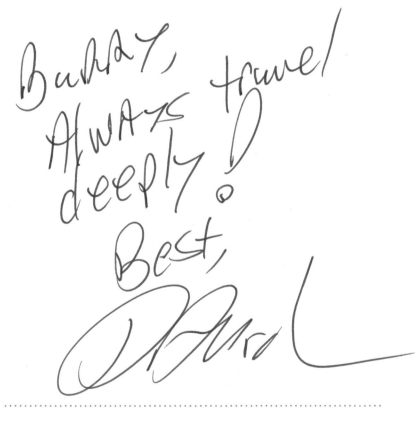

Buddy,
ALWAYS travel
deeply!
Best,
[signature]

University of Iowa Press

Iowa City

University of Iowa Press, Iowa City 52242
Copyright © 2009 by the University of Iowa Press
www.uiowapress.org
Printed in the United States of America

Design by Omega Clay

The University of Iowa Press is a member of Green Press Initiative and is committed to preserving natural resources.

Printed on acid-free paper

Library of Congress Cataloging-in-Publication Data
Leff, David K.
  Deep travel: in Thoreau's wake on the Concord and Merrimack / David K. Leff.
    p.   cm.—(American land and life series)
  ISBN-13: 978-1-58729-789-2 (cloth)
  ISBN-10: 978-1-58729-789-2 (cloth)
  1. Concord River (Mass.)—Description and travel. 2. Merrimack River (N.H. and Mass.)—Description and travel. 3. Leff, David K.—Travel—Massachusetts—Concord River. 4. Leff, David K.—Travel—Merrimack River (N.H. and Mass.). 5. Canoes and canoeing—Massachusetts—Concord River. 6. Canoes and canoeing—Merrimack River (N.H. and Mass.). 7. Travel—Psychological aspects—Case studies. 8. Awareness—Case studies. 9. Thoreau, Henry David, 1817–1862. Week on the Concord and Merrimack rivers. I. Title.
  F72.M7L445 2009   2008036505
  917.42'720444—dc22

09 10 11 12 13 C 5 4 3 2 1

For Alan, Josh, and Pam
Companions for days, a week,
a lifetime

CONTENTS

F O R E W O R D

In the record of famous river odysseys in American history, from that of Joliet and Marquette down the Mississippi in 1673 to the legendary gauntlet of one-armed John Wesley Powell on the Colorado in 1869, the brief excursion of a pair of Yankee schoolteacher brothers down the Concord and up the Merrimack in 1839 ought to have little more than a footnote. Those two rivers, after all, hardly impress one by their size or scope. The Concord, on the shores of which the brothers lived, is hardly a river at all by most definitions of the term. It arises from the juncture of the Sudbury and Assabet rivers in the town of Concord and dozes along a nearly flat course until it loses its name and identity in the Merrimack at Lowell, Massachusetts, a mere fifteen miles away.

Compared to the Concord, the Merrimack is of another order of magnitude altogether. Eight times longer, it drains an area fifteen times as large. Even so, by continental and indeed hemispheric standards, the Merrimack tips merely a thimbleful of New England water into the infinite sea. The Mississippi discharges sixty times the volume of freshwater into the Gulf of Mexico; the Amazon, sometimes called "the river-sea," floods the Atlantic with an amount of water so great that the Merrimack's contribution amounts to merely one-tenth of 1 percent of it. Gertrude Stein to one side, a river is *not* a river is *not* a river.

To be sure, the Merrimack has turned many mills in its day, including those in the junction town of Lowell, as well as in big-named Manchester, New Hampshire, some miles upstream. And for its length the Merrimack does run a significant volume of water down its course. Its floods have crumpled human structures and torn away great swaths of the land and its multifarious life. But it is not the water, or the watershed, that has made the Merrimack and its little tributary loom larger

{ i x }

in the American imagination than they otherwise might. Rather, their notoriety stems from the book that one of those Concord brothers published in 1849 about their short trip. Called *A Week on the Concord and Merrimack Rivers*, it was written by Henry Thoreau while he lived in a one-room cabin by a small pond in the town of Concord, a small pond that, in a more famous book Thoreau published in 1854, would acquire its own Amazonian presence in the national, and indeed international, mind.

Thoreau could grow things by putting them into prose, such was his magnifying skill as a writer. His account of a battle between two nations of ants in *Walden* gives epic, and indeed tragic, scope to the little affairs of their Lilliputian world. Moreover, he had the true naturalist's profound patience, the will to outlast the momentary boredom of many of our instants on earth in order to be there when the extraordinary things do occur. To be sure, in his 1849 book, written as a kind of belated eulogy to his brother John (who cut off his fingertip while stropping his razor on New Year's Day in 1842 and died from lockjaw on the eleventh), Henry Thoreau had not yet fully discovered that patience and its transformative power. *A Week on the Concord and Merrimack Rivers* considered as a structure seems glued or nailed together more than germinated and nurtured. While he and John wait for canal locks to fill, or when the landscape is shrouded in such dense mist that he can see very little, Henry inserts a miscellany of short essays and observations preserved in the formaldehyde of his notebooks. But at its best, his prose in *A Week on the Concord and Merrimack Rivers* does anticipate the bright illuminations of *Walden*. It has, for one thing, an array of subtle atmospheric effects. Its ability to parse mist and cloud and darkness, and to visually calibrate the river world, still can enlighten a postimpressionist mind.

Had Thoreau not been living at Walden Pond when he wrote his river book, I think he would not have been able to recover as finely as he does the sense of water-mixed-with-air that *A Week on the Concord and Merrimack Rivers* exhibits. And that is one of Thoreau's finest effects as a nature writer. When I was teaching literature in Boston, I used to take the Fitchburg train to the city in the morning, and it chanced on various occasions that I would be rereading *Walden* en route in order to discuss it with students later in the day. By a kind of occult mechanism, I might look up half-consciously just as the train made its pass along the west end of the pond, so that the place itself momentarily flashed into a mind saturated but an instant before by Thoreau's verbal evocations of it. What most lingers in my memory from those rich happenstances is a sense of the misty transpiration of the pond, that sunken body of liquid light that empties itself only by slow subterranean losses and, indeed, up through the air. So the true source of the Concord and Merrimack, in terms of Thoreau's writing about the former, was *that* Walden Pond. Thoreau expanded the two modest streams by pouring into them the Ganges—which, as every reader of *Walden* knows, was the secret spring beneath that sixty-one-acre pond.

Many boaters have followed this glow of Walden water out onto our streams and rivers, even in the most unexpected ways. *Walden* will always remain the quintessential Thoreau. Yet when the desert *isolato* Edward Abbey wrote *Desert Solitaire*, in which he dutifully imitates the unnamed Thoreau, he put an account of his descent of the Colorado into the heart of that book as a sort of grudging tribute to the watery magic of *A Week on the Concord and Merrimack Rivers*. Abbey also used a narrative of another Colorado descent as a foreword to his edition of *Walden* in the 1980s. John Wesley Powell lay behind those two Abbey tales in obvious ways, but so did Thoreau. In fact, it is hard for any American writer to push out from any river's bank without gesturing, if only subconsciously, toward the modest Thoreau expedition of late summer 1839. John Graves's *Goodbye to a River*, a splendid Texas narrative published as a eulogy for the soon-to-be-dammed Brazos in the 1950s, took its melancholia and its drifting sense of the land and history from Thoreau.

And then there are the more direct tributes to Thoreau's river trip, ones that openly announce their purpose, including John McPhee's in *Uncommon Carriers* and the unfortunately incomplete collaboration between Ann Zwinger and Edwin Way Teale, *A Conscious Stillness*. I cannot imagine anyone accidentally replicating the Thoreau brothers' itinerary, for it was an implausible route in 1839 and remains, but for the book Henry wrote about it, implausible today. One does not need to hear of Joliet and Marquette to yearn to commit oneself to the Mississippi or read Lewis and Clark's *Journals* in order to light out for the headwaters of the Missouri. But rare indeed are the boaters who would embark on the lazy Concord in search of adventure unless *A Week on the Concord and Merrimack Rivers* ballasts their vessel. Rarer still would be the rowboat owners or canoeists who would turn upstream at Lowell.

In following the Thoreau brothers in their summer-ending trip, David Leff brings to the venture a sharp eye and an adept pen. Those who have read his fine book about his Connecticut hometown, *The Last Undiscovered Place*, will understand that he writes especially well about the spaces of everyday life. Let others climb Mount Everest and rush down the Amazon. For him, the terrain that reaches out beyond our own windows, the terrain that occupies our hearts and minds as we occupy it, will always be the most challenging. To copy the modest undertaking of the Thoreaus in 1839, to be sure, requires that Leff venture somewhat farther from home. But he is well suited to the undertaking. Not only does he understand rivers as complex hydrological facts, he understands even more that they are cultural channels and that river trips therefore move us through time as well as space.

One can rewrite Thoreau's river valleys by copying his trip, much as historically inclined photographers, carefully reshooting original images, have learned how to make old pictures yield new insights (into, for instance, Robert B. Stanton's Colorado canyon). Leff does some of that, showing us how much the postindustrial riverscape of Lowell or Manchester has changed, or stayed surprisingly the same. Yet what he does best of all is to imbibe the spirit of the Thoreau venture, that love of the everyday and the ordinary that helped Thoreau see these little rivers as big things. An adventure, Thoreau reminds us, can start in our own backyard if we are ready to commit ourselves to the large energies that flow through it. David Leff decidedly agrees. Let us push off and join him!

Wayne Franklin

Headwaters

To follow a creek is to seek a new acquaintance with life.
Peter Steinhart, "The Making of a Creek"

Whoever owns the real estate and its constituents, the
explorer owns the landscape. And the explorer owns all the
insights, all the magic that comes from looking.
John R. Stilgoe, *Outside Lies Magic*

Canoe and Time Machine

We hear so much said about the mighty Missouri, the great
Ohio and other tributaries of that king of rivers that we feel
almost ashamed of our own comparatively small rivers.

Boston Courier, August 30, 1839

Invigorating Climate of NH Creates Boom

Manchester Union Leader, August 31, 1969

FBI joins probe of Iraq

Lowell Sun, September 1, 2003

I dug my paddle deeply into the river, pulling hard along the canoe's stern. Each stroke seemed more difficult than the last, as if the water had become viscous, slowly solidifying like concrete. My shoulders and arms throbbed. My back ached from fighting a stiff wind that pushed the boat sideways.

"Brace yourself for another damn speedboat wake," Alan shouted from the bow. His voice seemed distant, almost lost in the breeze as he gestured toward a broad open boat with fishing rods standing at attention like antennae and huge twin Johnson outboards hanging over the transom. Unrelenting August sun sparkled on the river, stinging my eyes. I blinked at the powerboat gliding so easily while we struggled for every foot of forward motion. The wake hit us broadside like an ocean roller, and instinctively we each shifted our weight to keep the canoe from tipping.

We passed a tan brick cube of a building cantilevered over the river and marked on our map as a Lowell water department pumping station. Suddenly, I was thirsty. My lips were sun-dried and my throat parched, but I didn't dare let go of my paddle long enough to take a swig from the water bottle. With even a momentary distraction, the wind would shove us against the bank like a hockey player making a hard check.

Nearby, a couch and sink were washed up onshore along with the usual beer cans, plastic bottles, and foam cups. The city undoubtedly treated its water, but at the moment that fact hardly made the thought of drinking it more appetizing. Weren't pesticides and fertilizers running off the lush greens and fairways of the Vesper Country Club just upriver? Hadn't we seen the bubbling geyser of Nashua's sewer outfall in midstream the day before?

As we crossed beneath power lines carried from bank to bank on twin towers, a couple of jet skis whining like giant mosquitoes darted around us, leaving twisted and braided wakes. The left bank immediately above us was dotted with houses and small commercial buildings, and traffic whizzed in and out of the city on Route 113. Railroad tracks paralleled the far opposite shore. An old redbrick mill hunkered in the distance.

Why would two middle-aged guys drive hours to canoe a lakelike impoundment on the Merrimack River in a garden spot like the battered industrial city of Lowell, Massachusetts? Could there be a more peculiar outdoor vacation destination than the tired mill precincts of the Northeast? If we had craved a paddle through settled countryside, the bucolic Farmington River with its treed banks and rollercoaster rapids beckoned just down the street from our Connecticut homes. Like the Merrimack, it passed a few old factories, Indian encampments, and vistas with farms, forests, and hillsides sporting new subdivisions. For adventure, I could have returned to the wild heart of Labrador or the edge of polar bear country on Ontario's James Bay. If vacations were about rest, beauty, a change of scenery, and getting away from it all, what were we doing here?

Was this a dare? Could money be involved? Did it hint at the bizarre twist of a midlife crisis? There had to be an ulterior motive.

No doubt such were the thoughts of friends and colleagues who learned we were off for a few days of canoeing. At first, they approvingly envisioned some remote stream with a thickly treed shoreline and primitive campsites far from paved roads. But when we revealed our destination, an awkward silence often resulted, soon broken by a weak smile, as if we were joking. Then they patiently waited for a punch line.

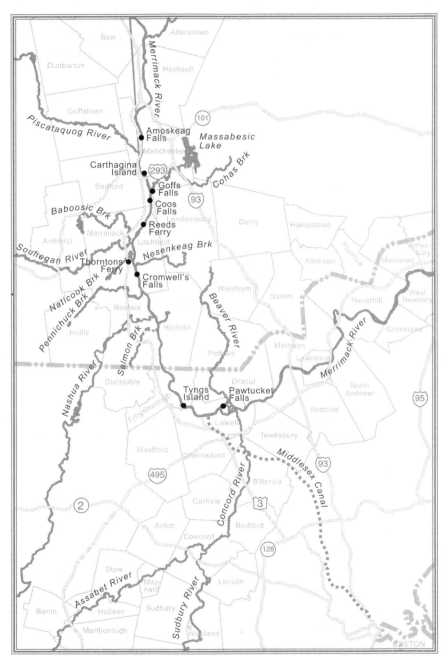

MAP BY LARRY GARLAND

They offered cautionary words of concern for our health and safety. Hepatitis and worse lurked in such garbage-strewn and polluted waters. We could drown at abandoned and uncharted dams. Old machinery and chunks of metal lay in ambush just below the water's surface, ready to tear our small canoe apart. Regardless of positive change over the past thirty years, the Merrimack retained its notoriety as an industrial sewer.

A few explanations seemed to allay most anxieties but could not dispel concern for our sanity. Clearly, we seemed borderline lunatic to people with vacation plans for Paris or the Jersey shore. Why would two people with busy jobs, families clamoring for attention, gardens needing tending, houses crying out for repair, and volunteer activities demanding time spend their valuable vacation days on a river hemmed in with development when they could just as well float Maine's Allagash Wilderness Waterway or kayak around the Florida Keys?

The incredulous faces of friends now seemed to appear in the crests of waves driven by the wind into whitecaps as we paddled ever harder to make even slower progress toward the dam at Pawtucket Falls. The vague images made me feel like Scrooge rubbing his tired eyes at the sight of Marley's ghost. My shoulder was about to give out from an hour of exhausting paddling against the growing gusts, and my back threatened to spasm.

Despite the whistling breeze, I heard trucks rumbling where the road swung close to the water. The landscape grew increasingly crowded with a hodgepodge of structures. Like an ersatz flower pot, a rusting fifty-five-gallon drum sprouting a willow sapling lay at the river's edge, and a suicidal washing machine that had leapt from the steep embankment was just downstream. The whitecaps whispered, "Told you so."

"That's the Rourke Bridge," I yelled to Alan as soon as I saw the span's thin gray line stretched across the water. Rather than turning toward me and missing a paddle stroke, he nodded his head. Being in the bow, he likely saw it first anyway. But I was less interested in a landmark than in voicing my presence and giving a shout of encouragement. I was still pulling with him. We had a definable goal on the horizon.

Alan and I paddled for none of the usual reasons people interrupt their normal routines to slide a canoe into the water. There was no wilderness, whitewater, pastoral countryside, or arresting urban scene. We weren't fishing, hunting, or racing. We were *deep traveling*.

At its simplest, deep travel is about heightened awareness. It is careful looking. It is paying attention to what is around you. Deep travel demands that we immerse ourselves fully in places and realize that they exist in time as well as space. A deep traveler knows the world is four-dimensional and can't be experienced with eyes and ears only.

Deep travel is not so much a matter of seeing sights as it is sight-seeking. It is a searching for the patterns and juxtapositions of culture and nature and delighting in the incongruities left by the inexorable passage of time. Deep travelers revel in the wild, inspiriting call of a kingfisher as it flies over a couple of trolling anglers with Bud long-necks in one hand and rods in the other. They savor the sight of a tree-shaded burial ground squeezed between big-box retailers on a traffic-choked commercial strip.

Deep travelers look not so much for scenery or enchanting objects as for a tapestry of comprehension woven from stone walls, retail establishments, street and topographical names, transportation networks, building styles, plant and animal assemblages, advertising signs, and other artifacts. Each element makes a statement about the landscape as a whole and the relationship of one part to another. Together, they tell a story. Deep travel is an ecological way of looking where everything we see has a function and all the parts are related, no matter how seemingly disparate or contradictory.

Like animals that remain intensely aware of their surroundings and any alteration to them because predation or starvation await the unwary, deep travelers work to be keenly conscious of their environs. They strive for the alertness and acuity of wildland firefighters or soldiers whose survival depends on their knowledge of topography, history, weather, vegetation, and the observance of changes in minute phenomena. Such mindfulness simultaneously enriches experience and makes the voyager worthy of the journey.

Alan and I aspired to being the Marco Polo and Christopher Columbus of the near-at-hand. We were less on our way to a particular place than exploring a means of going places. The river's destiny meant more than our destination. But unlike the great discoverers, our goal was less to look for something different and novel than it was to look in a novel way at something familiar. We weren't trying a new route of travel or exploring new territory. In fact, contrary to the usual dream of outdoor enthusiasts seeking the grail of going where few have been, we were here precisely because others had preceded us.

The archetypal trip on the Merrimack River, as well as on the Concord, was made in 1839 by twenty-two-year-old Henry David Thoreau and his brother John, three years his elder. They left their hometown of Concord, Massachusetts, on the afternoon of August 31, having been delayed by a light rain that morning. Their upstream voyage concluded on the Merrimack in Hooksett, New Hampshire, six days later. Hiding their rowboat in a cove, they took a side trip by foot and stage to the White Mountains, returning after a few days for the voyage home. They were back in Concord on September 13.

It was a time of accelerating change in New England, especially in the Merrimack Valley. Large-scale industrialization was on the rise in cities like Lowell and Manchester, New Hampshire. Railroads were gaining ascendancy over the canals that floated the brothers on part of their voyage.

Thoreau witnessed a still bucolic landscape, but one in which rivers were increasingly harnessed to earn human livelihoods with dams, power canals, turbines, and leather belts to turn machinery. Observing changes wrought by growing industrialism and commercial farming such as denuded forests, barriers to migratory fish, and destruction of Indian artifacts, the young man surely began developing a view of nature different from the one defined by biblical dominion and capitalistic entrepreneurship. He saw the natural world not as an economic resource merely to be subdued for human benefit, but as pregnant with intrinsic value—wildness, beauty, and organic functions. This outlook would percolate in American thought, growing in importance and ultimately providing the philosophical underpinnings in the late twentieth century for the subversive science of ecology and the environmental movement.

Despite our mix of pleasure and frustration in trying to envision the river as Thoreau saw it, ours was no mere Love Boat nostalgia cruise. We weren't paddling for escape or as an armada of reproach at the onslaught of development since his time. But with construction within the river corridor accelerating and "Smart Growth" buzzwords in nearby communities, could there be a more pertinent place to confront contemporary dilemmas at play on the landscape? Its artificial and natural attributes posed questions and offered lessons on the viability of cities, forest conservation, transportation, historic preservation, waste disposal, sprawl, and even global climate change. Being armed with Thoreau's more than a century-and-a-half-old observations as we gazed at today's countryside would give us a more acute perception of change over time, helping us understand the present and anticipate the future. We were not just looking around, but learning how to see.

Floating a small boat away from the routines of daily life, Henry and John Thoreau lived their Concord neighbor Ralph Waldo Emerson's Transcendentalist dictum of self-reliance and an "original relation to the universe." Buoyant with this philosophical energy, they peered past the gunwales in search of universal truths from a mundane slice of the world. With muscle power and keen observation, couldn't Alan and I do the same despite the cluttered twenty-first-century landscape?

Perhaps more instructive to the deep traveler than what Thoreau saw is the Transcendental way in which he looked at things. In addition to seeing worldwide verities in small facts and occurrences, he sought connections among diverse thoughts and phenomena that could make commonplace experiences epiphanic. Most significantly, Thoreau perceived correspondences between the landscape and a person's inner state. Geographical experience was about more than being in a place, more than visual and aesthetic reactions. Emotional resonances tied spirit to topography and gave singular dimension to what he observed. In Thoreau's youthful voyage are the roots of deep travel.

Although Thoreau is most famous for sojourning at Walden Pond several years after his river trip, the "private business" he proclaimed to transact while living there was the writing of his book *A Week on the*

Concord and Merrimack Rivers, which was published in 1849. A series of philosophical musings tied together by a river voyage narrative, the volume is shaped as much by Thoreau's complex friendship with his brother, who tragically died shortly afterward, as it is by the topography of the Merrimack Valley. Though hidden below the text's surface, the outer landscape clearly corresponds to an inner emotional state. At the book's end, Thoreau's inward sentiment about John's death blossoms in the natural world when he uses autumnal imagery, though it is barely mid-September, to describe the last glorious day traveling with his brother.

That Thoreau's travel recollections are heavily colored by his brother's death emphasizes how our viewpoints always depend somewhat on our experiences with companions. Human relationships frequently frame our understanding of the places we travel. However distant or fleeting our connection to an area, we see a place distinctly if, for example, we met a lover or lost a friend in a tragic accident there. Even less intense experiences with a partner often influence our outlook and distinguish a location from the perceptions of others. This effect of companions was manifest as I shared my canoe on the Concord and Merrimack rivers at times with my neighbor and old friend, Alan; my eleven-year-old son, Josh; and my sweetheart, Pamela.

My perspective was shaped not only by personal relationships, but also by the experiences my companions brought with them. Alan's landscape acuity as a veteran city planner; Josh's fresh, boyish inquisitiveness; and Pamela's compassion for people as a professional caregiver broadened my vision and added depth of field to what I saw. Their company would not only mold the journey, the journey would shape and grow our relationships and give further texture to our most routine future interactions. My fellow paddlers, in turn, no doubt benefited from my years as a top government official in natural resources policy, an experience that taught me not only about the connections among diverse and divergent features in the countryside, but about the intersection of places and social politics.

With its perceptive descriptions and emotional resonances, *A Week* was our principal travel guide. No doubt dated compared with the latest Frommer's or Michelin, it remained relevant to our trip as a methodology and a yardstick of progress. The old book enabled us to see things that no longer existed and perceive the tenor of a distant era. Wherever we went, I tried to imagine the world through the eyes of the Concord naturalist. His perceptions allowed us not only to reconstruct and see the past but to measure change and the passage of time. Alert the keepers of *Guinness World Records*! Surely we hold the record for using the oldest travel guide.

Although *A Week* is a bit stale as a reference, its use recognizes that much outdoor travel and writing are inevitably mere footnotes on Thoreau. Indeed, it is nigh impossible to pen an outdoor adventure, however originally conceived or well written, without drawing a comparison. If we inescapably follow in Thoreau's footsteps or paddle strokes regardless of our itinerary, I thought, why not confront that essential fact explicitly, thoroughly, and Thoreauly by traveling the first of the familiar routes he pioneered? Could there be a finer acid test for measuring the Transcendental originality of our own relationship with the universe and the landscape? After all, deep travel is a lot about upsetting expectations of the familiar.

Leaning into the paddle as if the river had turned to molasses, I squinted across the shimmering water. "There's where the old Middlesex Canal entered the river," I said, briefly stopping in midstroke to point a finger far ahead at about two o'clock. "See where the railroad crosses over Black Brook? It was just upstream."

"I'll take your word for it," Alan replied with irritation, again nodding his head without a look back. "At this point, I just want to get off the water and stretch."

The canal once connected Boston with the Merrimack. The Thoreau brothers used it as a shortcut from the Concord River, avoiding dams and rapids and detouring around bustling Lowell, which even then had more than seven textile mill complexes. In doing so, they not only bypassed that shining City of Spindles, but scrutiny of its much-lauded future of economic and moral progress.

Lowell was central to a later voyage on the Concord and Merrimack—that of journalist Raymond Mungo, poet Verandah Porche, and a couple of others in 1969. By then, the city had long been in decline, and its once bright future had grown bleak with deteriorating mills and dilapidated housing, dwindling jobs, ethnic tensions, and polluted waters reeking of sewage, poisoned with chemicals, and tinted with dyes. Mungo and Porche saw in Lowell a symbol of all that was wrong with American capitalism. Workers were left suddenly unemployed and living in grimy slums, once proud cities fell apart, and nature's beauty was despoiled.

In October, the pair left their Vermont commune where they had gone in search of "the New Age." The idea for an excursion "in the vanished footsteps of old Henry D. himself" had come to Mungo during an LSD-induced dream in which he "was floating silently downstream in a birchbark canoe, speechless . . . watching vistas of bright New England autumn open up with each bend, slipping unnoticed between crimson mountains, blessing the warm sun by day and sleeping on beds of fresh leaves under a canary harvest moon by night." The trip "had to be made because there was adventure out there."

Mungo was a leading voice for the 1960s counterculture, having been a cofounder of the Liberation News Service, an agency that sent leftist dispatches to student and underground newspapers around the country. He wrote with a fresh and breathless anger at his "luck for being 23 years old in a time and place in which only the past offers hope and inspiration; the future offers only artifice and blight."

Though infused with romantic Thoreauvian notions of contemplative travel through nature, his mindset was largely political and his true inspiration more likely iconoclastic Lowell native Jack Kerouac. The beat generation icon's legendary cross-country trips had exposed emptiness at the heart of America, with its increasingly alienating political system that demanded conformity and its tawdry middle-class values exalting material goods over spiritual values. Kerouac and compatriots like Allen Ginsberg and Gregory Corso were the godfathers of literate sixties revolutionaries like Mungo. Ironically, Kerouac died a few days after Mungo got off the river, a disheartened alcoholic who angrily rejected those following his footsteps.

The suicide of Mungo's friend and journalist colleague Marshall Bloom shortly after he returned home seems to animate the sharp sarcasm and estrangement imbedded in his writing. Like Thoreau, Mungo wrote in the aftermath of a difficult personal loss, but without intervening years to heal. "Marshall's death was the logical extension of the Concord and Merrimack rivers trip," he wrote. "What bad angel, thus, has elected to sit over our chimney? When your crop don't fail and your house don't burn down, your best friend will leave you stranded and helpless."

Mungo and his companions set out with two canoes and paddled from Concord through difficult rapids at Billerica to Lowell in a day. Canoeing on the Merrimack the next morning, they made it to Nashua, New Hampshire, late in the afternoon. Although expecting to find the "rivers polluted but still beautiful," Mungo and his friends became profoundly despondent over contamination and development. They abandoned the notion of camping near Nashua and drove around both that city and Manchester to Bow Junction, New Hampshire, far to the north of where Thoreau left off at Hooksett. Alternating between the canoe and a Volvo to take them around rapids, Mungo headed north.

By the fourth day they had "so badly botched up Thoreau's itinerary" and found "so much of the original waters were now inaccessible to living creatures," they got off the river. Feeling somewhat defeated, they drove to a place with a television so they could watch the perpetually underdog New York Mets win their first World Series. A year later, Mungo published "Another Week on the Concord and Merrimack Rivers" as a chapter in a book about 1960s commune life titled *Total Loss Farm*.

With more than a century of relentless industrial pollution, sewage discharges, damming, and unchecked paving and construction, the health of the Concord and Merrimack rivers had reached their nadir when Mungo and his companions paddled. In some places, the streams resembled public cloacae with a greasy sheen on the surface and floating remnants of people's bowels. Lowell had hit bottom as textile companies folded and the population declined. Nevertheless, there were signs of hope. The first Earth Day was celebrated the following spring. A few years later, the federal Clean Water Act would begin investing billions in river cleanup and punishing polluters. Within a decade, Lowell's mill district would become part of the Lowell National Historical Park, drawing tourists from around the world.

The fruits of these efforts were evident when another traveler on these rivers, writer John McPhee, made his trip shortly after the dawn of the new millennium, an account of which was published in the December 15, 2003, issue of the *New Yorker*. Enjoying the relatively fresh, translucent rivers, he called the Clean Water Act one of the "highest legislative accomplishments of the twentieth century." Its enactment, he maintained, "owed more than a little to thought set in motion by Henry David Thoreau." This urbane and erudite observer of natural phenomena and human nature launched into the Concord River with his former Princeton roommate on the last day of August. His companion, a college football star with an MBA from Harvard, ran an international sports management business.

McPhee was bound fifty-five river miles north to Hooksett, New Hampshire, and tried to keep as close to Thoreau's schedule and route as possible. Owing to the lack of canals that made passage around rapids relatively easy in 1839, he often portaged by vehicle. Perhaps in deference to his seventy-plus years, he also spent nights at hotels and dined in restaurants rather than camping and cooking over an open fire. Unlike Thoreau, he changed companions and paddled the Merrimack reach of the trip with his son-in-law, a creative writing professor.

McPhee's is a calculated and carefully orchestrated trip, and his piece about it is consummately researched and flawlessly written. Perhaps that is why his writing lacks both Thoreau's almost innocent depictions and refreshingly adolescent wiseacre social comments as well as Mungo's headlong rush of disjointed passion and spontaneity. But he is an exquisitely well-informed tourist, with an upscale voice that speaks to executives who, trapped in the office, are eager for recreation that will soothe the mind and challenge the body. His readers are concerned for the fate of nature and have a nose for history. Like many people, they are searching for context, for their place in time, for meaning larger than their daily routine.

Whereas Mungo and his companions became disheartened by Lowell, and Thoreau maintained a reticent fascination, McPhee barely mentions the city. He also makes little note of the rapid commercial development in the river valley below Nashua. But his affluent outlook will not let the exclusive Vesper Country Club pass without some fairway anecdotes.

Alan spotted the dark apron of macadam at the boat launch and pointed vigorously like a whaler from the crow's nest. Together, we erupted into a cheer, breaking simultaneously into laughter at the outburst. The end of our purgatory of wind and waves was in sight. Every paddle stroke now made a difference, drew us perceptibly closer to our destination. My tired muscles felt rejuvenated by the progress—a personal second wind to beat the breeze sweeping across the water. Squinting toward the ramp, I made out a dark SUV backing down a big powerboat, its white fiberglass hull gleaming in the sunlight.

I felt a slight jolt as the canoe scraped pavement. Nearby, the SUV slid its fiberglass leviathan into the water. A couple of other boats were in the queue. My legs felt rubbery stepping onto land, and it took surprising effort to haul the canoe up the embankment.

In a grassy spot beside the ramp, we sat and snacked on Fig Newtons and pretzels. A college student in a wetsuit readied his sailboard. An Asian man prepared to launch a Boston Whaler while a couple nearby spoke Portuguese as they unloaded fishing rods from the back of a Subaru. We seemed more than just a few river miles downstream from Vesper.

Stretching out on the lawn, I let my mind drift and play shape games with the few clouds cruising overhead. As my thoughts wandered, the cumulous puffs seemed like boats on the blue, watery sky. The boat-clouds became canoes floating the Merrimack over centuries. With truly defiant, nonconforming Thoreauvian conviction, I realized how different my voyage on these rivers had been from the others. To start, my journey during the hot summer of 2004 involved several discrete trips and explored the rivers in fragments. It headed downstream on most of the Merrimack and involved three different companions. Neither the thread of connected days nor the direction of travel mattered most. I wanted an elemental encounter with the landscape, and I wanted to share that experience with my paddling partners.

Regardless of how singular my trip seemed, Thoreau, Mungo, and McPhee had made my voyage vastly more interesting by allowing me to see in multiple layers of time and perspective. They bequeathed a rich inheritance of memory, emotion, thought, and expectation that overlaid my vision of the landscape as clearly as a Mylar sheet on a zoning map. They enabled me to deep travel.

Despite their storied literary history, the Concord and Merrimack rivers remain mundane waterways. The Concord is a sluggish stream, often busy with powerboats, that hardly knows which way to flow. The Merrimack courses through a development-scarred landscape where the whine of highway traffic is omnipresent. Following Thoreau's paddle strokes may have been irresistible, but certainly the Maine woods beckoned with vastly more solitude and natural beauty.

But these waters seduce a deep traveler precisely because they have nothing to do with wilderness, beauty, or testing one's paddling skills. Such a trip is not about sightseeing and camera snapshots. To perceive truly, you need to forget the grocery list approach to travel promoted by most guide books and agents with their "must see" agendas. The Concord and Merrimack beguile and intrigue deep travelers because they flow like an aorta through the heart of three centuries of American social ferment. They cradle a landscape fully engaged in the nation's three great revolutions: political, industrial, and suburban.

The "shot heard round the world" to overthrow British rule was fired on the banks of the Concord, and the first planned industrial community in the United States, Lowell, was built at its confluence with the Merrimack, whose waters later powered the world's largest complex of textile mills at Manchester, New Hampshire. These river valleys have witnessed suburbia's inexorable progress with all its promises and broken dreams, from the development of commuter railroads to the advent of interstate highways. A paddler on these waters takes a journey on the current that created today's America.

There is no magic formula for deep travel, but it requires preparation as surely as you need to remember a toothbrush. Still, in little more time than it takes to pack a suitcase, a person can be good to go. Just as Thoreau carried his gazetteer, a deep traveler's first step is to devour everything about a place from tourist brochures, travel guides, books, and the fruits of an online search. Deep travelers pore over maps that show not only roads, but topography and landmarks. To induce a new perspective, they investigate alternatives to automobile travel, such as boats and trains. Deep travelers look for museums, especially quirky local ones that display bizarre items like two-headed cats and fast food wrapper collections. They take overnight accommodations that link to the story of their destination, such as a bed and breakfast in an old house. In a factory town, deep travelers might eschew the usual fast food fare and find a restaurant in a rehabilitated mill or a diner where locals gorge on Yankee pot roast and political gossip. Inevitably, patterns will be revealed, and the museum visit will relate to the restaurant meal and what is seen from behind the windshield.

Looking carefully, deep travelers soon discover connections among the diverse phenomena that catch their gaze. There are serendipitous, electrically charged moments when they feel as if they've completed a picture from a thousand-piece jigsaw puzzle. In places they've never been, deep travelers find themselves overcome with déjà vu as what they've read, remembered from a high school science or history class, seen in another place, heard someone tell about, or otherwise recalled from a different context suddenly becomes real. They find personal connections to places they've never been because they discover that geological, historical, and other forces molding their destination have an underlying commonality with where they live.

The canoe had been our time machine, I thought, as Alan and I hoisted the sixteen-foot-long boat on top of my pickup. Never mind those Hollywood images of complex machinery with lights and dials, a sudden whir, and a flash. The canoe was a methodology as well as a means of travel because deep travelers' discoveries depend not just on what they see but on *how* they see it.

Travel is a form of communication where the medium is essentially the message. In our case it wasn't just that a river requires a boat but that its current, eddies, bends, obstructions, and shoreline attributes highlight subtle landscape nuances that induce the traveler to feel them bodily. Slower travel also gave us time to think as we absorbed the images, sounds, smells, and textures around us.

"Shit!" I yelled, breaking out of my philosophic reverie in a momentary primal scream. Something greasy and cold was sliding down my shirt, and I felt the boat slip off the edge of the truck.

"What's with you?" a startled Alan shot back. "You almost made me drop the canoe."

"Damn dirty bilge water spilled all over me."

"Is that all?" he asked laconically. "With a scream like that, I thought you'd been bitten by a dog, at the very least."

"You disappointed?"

"Only a little," he smiled.

Deep travelers always return with more than an album of photos, a few souvenirs, or a bilge-stained T-shirt. They find themselves at home with a new way of looking at things, a greater context, and a means of exploring what is just beyond their doorstep. No deep traveler returns unchanged. The synergies of deep travel provoke a person to see new connections among diverse phenomena. The metamorphosis may be subtle and slow to manifest itself but is inevitable. Often we find ourselves and our relationships transformed in unexpected ways, later recalling things we did and saw in new situations and at odd moments. I still feel reverberations from the Concord and Merrimack rivers, as do my companions. The experiences will echo a long time. Like one of Mungo's psychedelic flashbacks, you never know when or where.

Tributary

We were not sent into this world to do anything
into which we can not put our heart.
John Ruskin, *Religious Light in Architecture*

Landscapes are not just material objects, explicable by some
chronology of events in combination with the local climate and soil,
but are presences that matter in human lives; they are experienced
not only visually and kinesthetically, but aesthetically
and emotionally as well.
Kent C. Ryden, *Landscape with Figures*

Concord and Conflict

Passing up the turnpike from Lexington to Concord we were struck
with the vast difference between that which had been subdued and that
which was in its natural state, as they were divided only by a ditch.

Boston Courier, August 31, 1839

Traffic Toll Rising at Rate of 6 Hourly
Manchester Union Leader, September 1, 1969

Hunters may take aim along Concord River
Lowell Sun, September 2, 2003

On a dank, humid July morning, Josh and I launched our canoe into
the Assabet River from a grassy ribbon of land behind the large public works complex at Concord, Massachusetts. Although a few paddle
strokes downstream of where Thoreau began his voyage, it was a put-in
where we could safely leave our pickup, according to local police, who
seemed unsurprised by a request that might have invited suspicion in
some towns. Of course, in Concord they must be used to the eccentric
requests of visitors, many of whom are on a pilgrimage to the haunts
of quirky characters this community has nurtured for centuries.

It being a weekend, the trucks waited quietly behind bay doors.
Stacks of miscellaneous lumber, corrugated pipe, piles of gravel, and
concrete catch basins were unattended. With all the implements and
materials of bustle around us, this construction depot seemed perversely still. I imagined idling diesel engines and the chatter of workers sipping coffee from foam cups as they loaded tools, maybe a few
shovelfuls of cold patch to fill a pothole, or a length of pipe to fix a
culvert. Instead, Josh and I quietly filled the canoe with bright red and
blue packs stuffed with provisions and clothes, our neatly rolled nylon
tent, a tiny gas backpacking stove, and other camping gear. Unlike the
departure of the Thoreau brothers, who fired their guns after passing
some friends downstream, ours was hushed, disturbing only a large
toad resting in the grass.

{ 21 }

No doubt their boat skimmed along the water as silently as ours, though the two vessels, emblematic of their times, differed significantly. Thoreau's was a rowboat handcrafted of wood, whereas my canoe had a hull constructed of a virtually indestructible green plastic laminate. Theirs had cost a week of labor—of sawing, planing, and fitting boards together. Mine required fewer hours to earn the purchase price of about fifteen hundred dollars while working in an office far distant from boats or water.

Such distinctions were less about evolution in boat design and construction than about changes in society wrought by materials technology and about the time average people have for such detailed projects. Before taking a single paddle stroke, I could feel a chasm between Thoreau's era and ours. Still, in deference to the past and the beauty of natural materials, my canoe was outfitted with ash gunwales and thwarts and cane seats. I liked this marriage of old and new. Within the compass of a small vessel were reminders of both where society had been and where it was going. Regardless of the boat's actual power to bridge the past and present, these old-time accents made me feel good.

Even before fully achieving a paddling rhythm, Josh and I were alongside a low granite knob, a bright bald chunk of ledge known as Egg Rock. Here the Assabet River meets the Sudbury and forms the placid Concord. Thoreau and Emerson sometimes perched atop this outcrop, enjoying the calm and contemplation induced by the smooth flowing water. Sculptor Daniel Chester French, best known for the seated president at the Lincoln Memorial in Washington, D.C., is said to have occasionally breakfasted here.

In history-conscious Concord, such an important natural feature cannot go without commemoration. For the town's 250th anniversary in 1885, the rock was inscribed with a few phrases indicating that the Indians were "owners" of the river "Before the White Man Came." Such an obvious statement about the presence of Native Americans and the puzzling reference to land ownership by a people who did not subscribe to such legalisms said more about Concord in 1885 than about the Indians and clearly demonstrated that the authors had not read their native son, Thoreau.

The often swift Assabet and the quieter, meandering Sudbury were Thoreau's headwater rivers and among his principal inspirations. He spent as much time on them as on any body of water. Pulitzer Prize–winning author and naturalist Edwin Way Teale paddled the Concord's tributaries with fellow naturalist Ann Zwinger in the late 1970s, and they would have gone beyond Egg Rock had not Teale died in 1980 at age eighty-one. Though he didn't canoe the Concord and Merrimack, his Thoreauvian insights and river observations published in *A Conscious Stillness*, the book Zwinger finished after his death, are as fitting and fully realized as any ever penned. "In a world of patchy, scraggly, tentative beginnings and inconclusive endings," Teale wrote in echo of Thoreau, "there is about a river an artistic unity, a beginning and a middle and end."

Admiring Thoreau less for his philosophy than for his dedicated and disciplined observations of nature, Teale may well have been the spiritual reincarnation of the Concord native. A founder and early president of the Thoreau Society, Teale felt an empathy for creation and had a facility for seeing connections between civilization and natural phenomena that gave voice to Thoreau's genius into the late twentieth century.

Perhaps there has to be an element of Thoreau in anyone who cruises these waters and then has had the temerity to write a coda to the epic nineteenth-century voyage. Certainly, Mungo shared the incendiary politics of the Thoreau who sneered at materialistic lives of quiet desperation, refused to pay taxes, and supported radical causes like John Brown's attempt to foment violent rebellion in opposition to slavery. McPhee may be the incarnation of the worldly and knowledge-hungry Thoreau, the widely read and meticulous writer, the organized and methodical man who keenly observed nature and society in an economical and precise style. The sage of Walden, though a lifelong bachelor and frosty solitary, nonetheless has many children.

Also among Thoreau's heirs, Josh and I glided easily into the newly formed river. The sun was unrelentingly bright and reflected off the dark surface as if from a sooty mirror. Clumps of purple loosestrife frequently lit the shallows. Silver maples overhung the water and cast deep shadows, the pewtery undersides of their leaves fluttering in a slight breeze that felt like a warm breath.

The aptly named Concord River moves quietly and unperturbed. Classic nineteenth-century author Nathaniel Hawthorne lived on its banks three weeks before realizing which way it flowed and called it "the most unexcitable and sluggish stream that ever loitered, imperceptibly, towards its eternity, the sea." I would have remained as perplexed as Hawthorne save for telltale grasses growing just beneath the surface that revealed the current's direction. These grasses are also emblematic of the area's Indian name and the river that runs through it: Musketaquid, Grass-ground River. In thrall to both his home stream and Indian culture, Thoreau christened his boat *Musketaquid*.

Among both native peoples and European settlers, the river was famed for its broad, grassy meadows, which lured colonists to form Massachusetts's first inland settlement in 1635. Concord's name signifies the peaceful purchase of the land from the natives for hatchets, knives, and cloth, a deal sealed by smoking a pipe of friendship.

Thoreau speculated that the river's barely perceptible and gentle current may have produced "the proverbial moderation of the inhabitants of Concord." This imperturbability can be felt in the handsome and prosperous village center, lively with commerce, and along the tranquil, leafy streets that radiate into Concord neighborhoods. Described by the Depression-era Federal Writers' Project as "predominately residential, retaining much of its quiet colonial atmosphere," the village today remains a perfect tourist brochure snapshot of suburban repose and satisfaction.

Perfection is perhaps Concord's greatest shortcoming. It seems as if not a blade of grass is out of place, and all the shops and restaurants are fashionable with trendy names. The old houses are well kept and speak of wealth, power, and quaint New England. Not a curl of peeling paint was visible on the ancient clapboards as Josh and I passed through earlier that morning. The roadsides were free of tossed soda bottles and candy wrappers.

Thoreau would surely have railed against today's Concord, with its self-conscious well-to-do ease, probably with greater vehemence than he applied to the town of his own time. In a perverse way, he might have liked the twenty-first century more than his own relatively down-to-earth nineteenth, furnishing as it does greater opportunity for his famous conscience-stinging verbal barbs about the pursuit of goods and status.

My easygoing Josh, with his soft brown eyes and mop of auburn hair, hadn't heard of Thoreau until this morning. He nevertheless had very Henry-like thoughts, complaining about the tourist-town slickness of Concord center. He didn't like the gourmet eateries and well-appointed shops with artfully eye-catching windows hawking kitchenware, clothing, pottery, and other "girly stuff." Fine dining at the Walden Grille seemed a desecration of the converted firehouse. Crafts and clothing displayed at a store called Perceptions were uppity and "boring."

"Dad," he said in a conspiratorial tone as we waited for a map at the Chamber of Commerce, "doesn't this place seem a little fake and touristy? It's sort of like Main Street in Disney World." He rolled his eyes at the woman in front of us who wanted to know where her family could play miniature golf. "It's pretty and everything, but doesn't it seem kind of unreal? All anyone is doing is looking around and shopping."

Precocious thoughts for an eleven-year-old, perhaps, but Josh had seen the onset of gentrification and creeping tourism in our home-town of Collinsville, Connecticut, once a blue-collar manufacturing village where edge tools like axes, machetes, and knives were made. For Josh, the hodgepodge of old factory buildings at home had been more fun before the rusting piles of machine parts and clusters of century-old construction debris were cleaned up to make them look prettier. He was annoyed that the mysterious aisles of the old hardware store he had explored—with its wooden bins of fasteners, plumbing pieces, and electrical parts—had been replaced by the dull displays of an antique store. How could I explain that as much as its rough edges induced me to live there, the very act of moving to Collinsville with my college degrees and books had invited some of the change neither of us welcomed?

In simple terms, I tried to describe adaptive reuse of the fire station and the need for upscale niche retailers to fill small-town storefronts that would otherwise be emptied by the influx of shoppers to Wal-

Mart and Target. Tourism was just another industry, I suggested. It was keeping Concord center vibrant. Like a factory with noise, air and water pollution, or workers subject to repetitive tasks, this industry had its negatives. Jobs and business always invited trade-offs. Thoreau earned his living as a surveyor. It enabled him to be outside learning about the landscape but also helped subdivide lots and develop the town.

Thoreau-like, Josh stood on principle and would have none of my fancy excuses and explanations. Even though I believed the macro-economic implications of what I said, Josh could tell that my heart wasn't in it, that, at the very least, I didn't like it. He listened politely, but oblivious of the adult world of compromises, he looked at me with an expression that urged me to try harder. I felt like a jerk.

Josh is an indispensable companion. Having few answers and many questions, he constantly forces me to think and rethink. Like Albert Einstein, he is "passionately curious." Although I sometimes longed for a bit more quiet, his gap-toothed smile and galaxy of summer freckles made it hard to be peeved by the constant barrage of queries. Besides, my job as his dad was not so much to deliver answers as to provide information that fueled more questions. Without ever hearing the term, Josh grasped the very essence of deep travel: asking questions about the obvious.

It hadn't previously occurred to me, but Josh was right: there was a remote but discomfiting likeness in Concord center to Disney's Main Street. More troubling was trying to discern which was the copy and which the original. Clearly, Disney mimicked some of the warmest and most heartening aspects of a classic village center like Concord's. But hadn't many authentic main streets been corrupted with the flavor of Magic Kingdom marketing savvy? Isn't that what "improvements" like brick sidewalk pavers and gaslight-looking street lamps in so many downtowns were about? Colorful banners were increasingly sprouting from utility poles, and organized programs had sprung up to promote festivals and coordinate marketing among main street shops. It often looked nice, but it could engender an atmosphere of forced authenticity.

Of course, this was nothing new. The colonial revival and village beautification movements that thrived for a couple of decades on either side of the onset of the twentieth century did much to visually cleanse rough old New England towns and make them attractive. White paint, handsome monuments, large shade trees, and manicured town greens were a marketing invention of their time. This prettification was an aesthetic statement that not only made the past more pleasing to the present but established a quaint idyll where visitors could escape a rapidly changing world.

With the town facing some dilapidated structures and traffic congestion in the 1920s, a serious proposal was floated to demolish much of Concord center and construct new colonial-style buildings. The architectural firm that re-created Colonial Williamsburg, Virginia, drew up plans. The community admired today for its unplanned patchwork of building styles and civic spaces married and grown together over three centuries came close to becoming a carefully managed make-believe stage set.

A village center vibrant with commercial activity is the heart of authenticity. That is what Concord and other such places are all about. Despite being gussied up, perhaps they were more real than commonly thought. The nature of commerce and the people whom the stores served had changed, but not the essential function of the place as a locus of business and a spot where people meet. Perhaps Josh and I were nostalgic for local political chatter at the tavern or for farmers sorting through bins at the hardware store. Can there be any greater danger to an authentic place than nostalgia? What good is a perfect architecturally preserved town center lacking busy stores and restaurants? It may be beautiful taxidermy, but like a trophy fish affixed to a wall, it is drained of all vitality.

Josh and I had a weird sense that Concord had become a kind of performance. Many people seemed to wander the streets in a voyeuristic haze. Had Concord succumbed to its own postcard charm?

Nevertheless, tourism was not some planned entrepreneurial invention or government economic development program. It was Concord being Concord. Even in the early 1840s, Hawthorne remarked on the "many strangers" that came in summer to view Concord's Revolutionary War battlefield beside his home. Pilgrims to Walden Pond appeared even before Thoreau's death in 1862. By the mid-1880s, "barge loads of sight seers" were observed in town daily, and shops selling Emerson, Thoreau, and other souvenirs became common.

We weren't entirely immune from visiting a few stores for our own souvenirs, and fortunately the Concord Book Shop and Brine's Sporting Goods stood side by side on Main Street. I bought a new copy of Emerson's essays, and Josh found a wool Red Sox cap on sale. It was a fitted model in a precise size, exactly like the players wear, without an expandable band or a plastic mesh back. It was the real thing, the genuine article.

On the river, Josh proudly wore his cap with the big stylized red and white B. As we paddled, his thoughts were far from Concord center or Disney World. He pointed out a great blue heron stalking fish among arrowhead and loosestrife clusters growing thickly at the river's edge and spotted a red-tailed hawk overhead. Clearly, there was some Thoreau in him.

The current drew us lazily downstream, and we became lackadaisical about paddle strokes. Watching cloud shadows move over nearby hillsides, we relaxed. The stress of packing and getting the house in order and then the dull car ride were finally behind us. We were on our way and life felt grand. "Something in all men," wrote Mungo, "smiles on the idea of a cruise up the planet." We were ready for adventure. It wouldn't be long in coming.

Around a slight bend, the rustic wooden arch of the old North Bridge came into view. Ironically for a town whose name evokes its peaceful founding, this humble stream crossing marked the violent beginning of the United States of America, the first armed resistance to British rule. Here was fired "the shot heard round the world."

Tourists armed with cameras ambled across the bridge as we approached, pausing to snap photos of the river and the monuments on either shore. "Dad, some of those people are taking pictures of us," Josh warned, as if we were being spied upon.

"I guess we're just part of the scenery."

Josh shrugged, removed his cap, and leaned over the gunwale looking for fish, his hair burning brighter red in the sun. "Tell me again about the minutemen at the bridge," he said.

"Church bells rang the alarm," I began, the battle story fresh in my mind from a pamphlet I'd fallen asleep with the night before, "calling minutemen from their homes just after midnight on April 19, 1775. British troops were marching from Boston and had shot into a crowd of militia in Lexington the previous day. Eight Americans had fallen. When the redcoats arrived in Concord about 7:30, they went foraging for breakfast and . . ."

An abrupt rhythmic thrumming and loud boom reverberated in the heavy air. I stopped paddling. Thunder? A car with a bad muffler? Startled out of fish gazing, Josh looked up and turned to me with a mixture of puzzlement and alarm. The beating rhythm began again.

"You hear drums?" he asked incredulously. I nodded. Was it possible to conjure sounds? "You're telling a good story, but I don't think the British are coming again," he smiled.

At that moment a squat stone boathouse with a gambrel roof came into view on the right. Perched beneath the spreading canopy of a massive tree, it looked to us like a Hobbit home.

"Let's paddle to shore and check out the drumming," I suggested.

"Sure," he agreed readily, "but you've got to finish the story."

"The redcoats searched for military supplies in the village," I resumed, angling the boat toward a low dock floating among stalks of loosestrife and other vegetation. "With the town's liberty pole and some equipment, they built a bonfire. The militia, meanwhile, had fallen back to Punkatasset Hill," I said, pointing beyond the opposite shore. "From that height they saw smoke rising in town. Fearing their homes were being torched, the minutemen hurried down the hill with muskets at the ready. Near the river, they encountered three companies of redcoats, and the British withdrew across the bridge with the colonials in pursuit . . ."

Just as we pulled alongside the dock, an unmistakable booming erupted and echoed down the river. "That's rifle fire!"

"I smell gunpowder," Josh said excitedly.

"After the militia crossed the bridge," I continued, hurriedly tying the boat to the dock, "the British fired a volley, killing two minutemen."

I grabbed my camera and notebook, and we started up the bank. "At that point," I said, raising my arm for emphasis as we charged up the slope, "Major John Buttrick of Concord shouted, 'Fire, fellow soldiers, for God's sake, fire!' Two redcoats dropped dead and the war began."

Reaching the top of the embankment, we came upon a broad lawn alongside a large old colonial house. But there weren't any redcoats and militia in tricorn hats. Instead, we found ladies in long, shaped dresses and soldiers outfitted in blue wool coats with brass buttons. Paddling in 2004, we had been talking about 1775. Now we had crossed into 1861. I felt a little like Alice at the bottom of the rabbit hole wondering where I was and which way to go next. The serendipitous wonderland of deep travel beckoned.

About a dozen soldiers were lined up on the grass, in unison loading their muskets and positioning them in response to orders barked by a sword-wielding officer. Rifles in front of them, butt on the ground, each man bit a paper tube filled with gunpowder and poured it down the barrel. They tossed the empty scrap on a lawn littered from previous volleys. Raising muskets to their shoulders, they cocked the hammers and placed a firing cap on the tip.

Josh was transfixed. In his eyes I saw him dreaming himself among the blue-coated soldiers on some distant battleground over a century and a half ago. If this were like other reenactments, he would talk vividly about it for days.

On the officer's command and with a deft motion of his sword, the soldiers aimed at an elevated angle and fired. Josh and I jumped slightly at the echoing boom though we knew it was coming. A cloud of bluish gray smoke acridly reeking of gunpowder floated toward us.

"This is *really* cool," Josh said, looking at me with a wide grin. "I thought this place was about the Revolution."

I shrugged. "Just because a place is known for one thing doesn't mean time stops. Life went on here during the Civil War, just as it's going on right now. We're part of it."

The officer continued shouting orders and the men moved in a rigid choreography. We watched another round of rifle fire. Then came the command to fix bayonets.

"They didn't charge with bayonets very often," said my son. He'd been bitten by the Civil War bug after seeing the movie *Gettysburg* at age six. Sharing his name with battle hero Colonel Joshua Chamberlain had captivated him. "They mostly used them as candleholders in camp."

Still a little boy with a small voice in a Union blue kepi and carrying a wooden musket when we first visited the Gettysburg Battlefield a year after the film, he had charmed an antique shop owner with his knowledge of soldiers' gear. Josh's grasp of the battle so impressed the elderly man that he reached into a glass display case and gave the kid a bullet excavated on Culp's Hill, site of some fierce fighting.

Josh watched in rapture as the men drilled with bayonets. Their movement in heavy wool uniforms under bright sun and deadening humidity was amazing. I was sweating just standing still in shorts and a T-shirt, remembering a Gettysburg reenactor telling me that people wore wool all year long in those days, were used to it, and paced themselves differently. "If wool uniforms breathed," he had quipped, "it must have been because they were moth-eaten or had bullet holes." We could never truly appreciate what those soldiers endured, no matter how well a volley of rifle fire grabbed our attention. There were limits to understanding the past.

With drill over, the men leaned their rifles together teepee style. Removing their leather cartridge boxes, they pulled off their coats and stripped to shirtsleeves. After a few canteen swigs, several soldiers regrouped with fifes, banjos, a washtub bass, guitar, and spoons. They began playing "Bonnie Blue Flag," a lively song Josh remembered from the film *Gods and Generals*. "That's real Civil War music," he informed me.

We joined briefly in the singing before wandering through the encampment of white canvas tents where small fires were smoldering below sooty pots of boiling potatoes or simmering stew. Josh peered into the tents with their wool blankets and straw bedding. In one I spied a plastic cooler poorly camouflaged beneath a frock coat. Fortunately, he didn't notice. Battlefield visits, movies, and endless books he had consumed were converging in his imagination with the smell of gunpowder and the sight of uniforms. He was deep traveling and didn't need to know the trip could be fragile.

A handful of other tourists toting cameras were strolling leisurely through the campsite. Most people grasped white programs, often using them as hand fans. Having come by water rather than road, we hadn't been given one on entering the grounds. Josh quickly found one discarded on the grass.

"A soldier here today is playing Lieutenant Ezra Ripley," I said, scanning the brochure. "He was born in that house called the Old Manse." I pointed my finger across the encampment to the gambrel roofed structure with its uneven white clapboards and big twin chimneys. "Before he was sent south, Ripley returned home with some men from his regiment. He said goodbye to his family and then got the guys psyched for battle with a visit to the very spot where America's first fight for freedom began."

"So this place really *does* have something to do with the Civil War. It's not just about the Revolution." Josh looked at me expectantly. "You've decided I can be a reenactor, right?" It was a question he had repeated often over the past year, more emphatically each time we encountered a Civil War demonstration, his tentative query morphing almost into a sure statement.

I shrugged my shoulders. "Let's take a look at the house," I said, walking toward the foursquare old building. It seemed to slumber in the sun while activity buzzed around it. The uplifting rhythm of "Battle Hymn of the Republic" wafted across the field.

Even beyond the cost of equipment and schlepping hundreds of miles from event to event, I was queasy about battles without bloodshed, hunger, cold, and mud, absent the fear of death or the uncertainty of an end. Was this sanitized playacting a desecration of the sacrifice made by those who fought? Did these events with thousands of participants and cavalry and cannons say more about how we amused ourselves in the twenty-first century than about war in the nineteenth?

"What about being a reenactor?" Josh insisted.

"I'll think about it," I said without much conviction, a bit annoyed as he dawdled toward the Manse.

"It's not even a real house. It's just a museum," he sulked.

"The house was built five years before the battle, and a lot of famous people lived here."

"Like who?" he demanded.

"In this very house, Thoreau's teacher and friend Ralph Waldo Emerson wrote a book called *Nature* that changed many people's lives, including mine. Also, remember that haunted House of the Seven Gables you saw in Salem a few years ago? That house is famous and people think it's scary because Nathaniel Hawthorne wrote a novel about it after he lived here." Josh rolled his eyes. "This is a real historical house. It's not some made-up thing. Stuff actually happened here."

As we made our way to the front door with its transom window over the entry, I thought of Emerson scribbling his controversial essay in the cramped second-story study, and Hawthorne thumbing through dusty books in the cobweb-strewn attic on a dismal rainy day. What to Josh appeared as just another old house seemed to me a sacred space. It had not only witnessed the battle but nurtured the writings of men who had given me hope and joy and had long influenced my life. He couldn't see what was so palpable to me—like something beyond the visible spectrum of light. And I couldn't seem to find the right angle of focus by which he could gaze into the prism through which I looked.

As we stepped inside from the sunlit lawn, the house instantly seemed as dim and claustrophobic as a cave. A cheerful, young docent in a bright print dress greeted us. I looked at Josh's face, scrunched nearly as tight as a fist, and decided we didn't want a tour. Still, she let us peek quickly into a few rooms.

"There can't be any children living here," Josh complained. "It's too neat and smells like old people."

Josh was right. Everything was orderly and arranged to perfection—chairs, china, a clock, and some books on a table. I took a sniff. Old newspapers and furniture polish, I thought.

Homes are in large measure their daily mess, from mail on the counter to kids' drawings on the fridge, wrote journalist Howard Mansfield. Museums, however, are about controlled and cataloged environments. This means that "a house museum [by nature] is in conflict with itself."

We experience a posed portrait of a moment, not a candid snapshot in the midst of daily chaos. It's like a theater scene where we forever wait for the actors to arrive.

"How can there be a house where no one lives?" Josh asked. "Maybe it was a house once, but a house has to have a family."

Again Josh was right. Still, the Old Manse was an authentic place. Sure, it might be less entertaining than a theme park reproduction, but here was a place that actually concentrated time, absorbed it. How could the reenactment, an acknowledged performance, be more compelling than a real place? Shouldn't we crave authenticity above all else?

Once outside, Josh dashed toward the encampment. He stood enthralled as a soldier wearing a bright striped shirt and white suspenders, his wool coat tossed on the grass, described the parts of his musket—lock, stock, and barrel. The infantryman showed how to carry it and shot a couple of rounds. He related battle experiences so vividly that Josh could hear cannon boom, see flags flapping in a breeze, and smell mud and sweat. He evoked the odor of bacon in the morning and the extremes of hunger that drove men to chew maggoty hardtack.

Stories make a difference. Well-told stories hold people's attention and stick with them like a late afternoon shadow. Seeing a musket in a museum case, looking at a diagram of gun parts, or reading about a soldier's dinner wasn't the same as listening to a tale while a man in uniform took apart his firearm or poured coffee from a campfire-blackened billy.

Not having planned to stop, I hadn't told Josh anything in advance about the Manse and the characters it had sheltered. Maybe I should have given the docent a chance to make the house come alive through her stories. Maybe a family *should* be living there. With so many high-tech means for conveying information, perhaps we underestimate the power of oral tradition. Stories keep places alive. They foster a geography of imagination. Without stories, Independence Hall is just a well-proportioned brick building and Arlington a bucolic cemetery. Telling and listening to stories connect us with places, join us to distant lands and long-ago people.

These story-filled reenactors and their compatriots at Gettysburg, Antietam, and elsewhere had ignited Josh's interest in history, an unusual passion for a fifth-grader. Their theatrics birthed his deep traveler's understanding that places exist temporally as well as spatially.

Everyday places are a distillation of time, regardless of whether they become historical sites like the Manse. Rivers, buildings, and roads are shaped by the passage of years. As historical artifacts like colonial homes become increasingly juxtaposed with the present, perhaps we shouldn't merely lament modern intrusion but seize the opportunity to better grasp the continuum in which we exist. Deep travelers crave stories of both the unusual and the commonplace, they listen for them, they learn how to tell them.

Walking across the lawn toward the famous North Bridge as the notes of Stephen Foster's "Oh! Susanna" hung in the air, I pointed out women dressed as the daughters of Nathaniel Hawthorne, Harriet Beecher Stowe, John Brown, and Henry Wadsworth Longfellow.

"Is that the same John Brown who came to Collinsville to buy knives on poles for a slave revolution?"

"Yeah. They're called pikes. John Brown probably walked by our house in the late 1850s when he was buying them." Josh looked at me with saucer eyes. History was getting personal.

"What did John Brown look like?

"He was in his fifties, tall and muscular with a farmer's tan and a leathery face. They say he had fiery eyes that could look right through you. Later, he grew a long white beard." Josh was in a momentary fugue of imagination, undoubtedly envisioning the "terrible saint" from his bedroom window overlooking Collinsville's Green and Main Street. "The program says that an actor playing Thoreau will give a lecture on John Brown this evening."

"Thoreau was in the Civil War?"

"No, but he was against slavery, met John Brown, and gave speeches defending him."

"I guess this is a good place for us to be at a reenactment. We're finding Thoreau everywhere."

We slipped into the trees, past a stone wall, and headed down the shaded path toward the water. It was cooler and damp beyond the sun's reach, and moisture condensed on rocks embedded in the ground as if they were perspiring. I resumed the story of the battle.

"After the colonials fired, the British realized they were outnumbered four to one. With half their officers wounded, they retreated to town and rested before marching back to Boston. Over much of the route they ran a gauntlet of colonial musket fire from militiamen stationed behind buildings, trees, and stone walls. The redcoats took casualties at curves and on hills where the colonials had good position. The British thought the Americans were sneaky and didn't fight fairly."

Josh had an enfilade of questions for which I had no answers. He wanted to know what the soldiers ate, how much they slept, and what they told their wives and children when leaving home. Were their shoes comfortable for walking? Where did they get their water? Were there any doctors with the troops? This was the kind of information that couldn't be found in most books and brochures or on signboards. Such odd little details could render history more vivid by enlivening cardboard images of the past with the daily trivialities ordinary people have cared about for centuries. Good reenactors are fluent in such minutia.

"This monument," I said, as we stood before the tall stone obelisk planted at the entrance to the bridge, "was dedicated on Independence Day in 1837. A choir that included Thoreau as a college senior sang a poem Ralph Waldo Emerson wrote in the Old Manse." I pointed to the first stanza, which is carved in stone:

> By the rude bridge that arched the flood,
> Their flag to April's breeze unfurled,
> Here once the embattled farmers stood,
> And fired the shot heard round the world.

We stepped onto the bowed wooden span stretching across the river. Stopping at the apex of the arch, we leaned over the rail and gazed into water seemingly as still as time appeared to most tourists. Wands of magenta loosestrife, a fleecy cloud, and shadow-dappled tree reflections were painted on the surface. Current was visible only in the slight ripples ringing the pilings.

From this vantage, we looked upstream at our canoe tethered to the dock with its cargo of brightly colored stuff sacks, backpacks, and life jackets. The boathouse was the perfect landing spot. It had been a center for nineteenth-century river tourism during an age of elaborate river events that might draw as many as eight thousand spectators. We were just two more in a long line of recreational boaters that early on included Thoreau.

A steady flow of sightseers combed the area, firing more shots with cameras in a few minutes than were discharged by muskets that whole first day of war. Did these visitors envision the confrontation between ragtag farmers worried about their homes and the well-trained British troops tired from a long march? Were these just some "must see" monuments and an old-fashioned bridge commemorating some famous event best described in history books? What you saw depended less on what was there than on what you looked for.

Apparently, this is where Mungo launched his canoe, describing it as "a park full of monuments and walkways, grass mowed as if with a Gillette Techmatic, but a lovely spot notwithstanding." Even considering his annoyance at the poor directions he received from a surly gas station attendant, how could such a politically astute individual concerned with the Vietnam War, corporate greed, and the perversion of American values not realize he put in at ground zero of the American Revolution? Instead, he fretted about the legality of launching a boat as a friend took pictures of dorky tourists. Just as he was shoving off, a flock of Canada geese flew overhead, "enough to make you believe in God." Unfortunately, it wasn't enough to make him see the significance of where he was.

We crossed to the far side of the bridge, the direction from which the militia had come after descending Punkatasset Hill. On a stone pedestal was Daniel Chester French's bronze minuteman in tricorn hat, grasping his Brown Bess low on the barrel while standing beside his plow. Dedicated at the 1875 centennial, this image is seared into American memory as the archetype of the citizen soldier, though its first official day was inauspicious. Emerson and President Grant spoke at a ceremony plagued by downpours, collapse of the speaker's platform, and overcrowded tents, railways, and hotels. Except when reenactors are caught in a downpour, history seldom remembers rainy days.

Musket fire boomed as we made our way back across the bridge's rough planks. Josh glanced at me. "The shot heard round the world probably sounded like that." He seemed lost in thought for a moment. "Can you believe we're walking on the same bridge the soldiers crossed?"

I shook my head. "Actually, it's not the same bridge."

"Well sure . . . they've probably replaced a lot of boards but . . ."

"There have been several bridges here. When Thoreau passed, there was no bridge at all. He saw only the pilings."

The bridge the minutemen crossed was built in 1760 and replaced in 1788. It was taken down in 1793 when the river crossing was moved upstream. In 1874 a new bridge was constructed for the centennial. Since then, five bridges have "arched the flood."

"This bridge isn't real?" He eyed me suspiciously, like a kid's first hint that Santa Claus is make-believe.

"It's real in a very important way," I insisted. "It's just not the original. It's a reproduction. Supposedly, it's in the same spot and looks just like the one the minutemen crossed. A newspaper I saw says that the one we're standing on is almost fifty years old and will be closed later this year so it can be rebuilt again."

"It's not fair," Josh said indignantly. "I'll bet most people here are fooled into thinking that this is *the* bridge."

"They're only fooling themselves. You can't just look at something. You've got to learn about it." I paused momentarily, searching for the right words. "Bridges don't last forever. But sometimes an object becomes a symbol." I hesitated again. "Do you know what I mean?"

"Sort of like what we studied in school about the Statue of Liberty?"

"Exactly. And just like the statue, this bridge symbolizes ideas like liberty and freedom. It probably doesn't get any more real than that."

Seeking Refuge

Shoving our paddles into the soft, mucky river bottom, Josh and I pushed away from the dock through clumps of yellow flag iris and spikes of violet pickerelweed. In an instant we passed beneath North Bridge and left the Revolution and Civil War behind. For the moment, at least, they would have to continue without us.

The Concord flows a little more than fifteen miles from its confluence with the Assabet and Sudbury rivers at Egg Rock before the Merrimack swallows it up at Lowell. Its 360-square-mile watershed includes at least part of thirty-six Massachusetts towns. The first two-thirds of the river's course has a generous floodplain winding through extensive wetlands in the minuteman towns of Concord, Bedford, Carlisle, and the lower part of Billerica. Several road crossings excepted, the river's marshy margins keep most development at bay in this densely suburban countryside. Where houses and other structures come close, especially in the lower reach, they pay the price of flooding during spring freshets.

Though we were headed downstream, we needed stiff paddle strokes to make any progress because the dark river was little better than a lake in moving us along. Although the Concord has a gentle average gradient of four-and-a-half feet per mile, its pitch is ever so slight until reaching the Fordway Bar, an area of erosion-resistant granite just upstream of nineteenth-century brick textile mills in North Billerica. Once the river arrives in Lowell a couple of miles later, it undergoes a sudden personality change. It sluices through a narrow valley lined with houses and other buildings, dropping fifty feet in a mile over three waterfalls.

As the sun rose and heated the moisture-laden air, Josh and I plotted a zigzag course that kept us in the cool shadows of overhanging trees. Although we would have welcomed a little more current to ease our labors in the tropical heat, I couldn't agree with J. W. Meader, a nineteenth-century booster of industrial waterpower whose 1869 biography of the Merrimack and its tributaries censured the Concord for its "idleness and stupidity." Despite its languid flow, this has always been a hardworking river.

From a commercial perspective alone, fishing and boating poured millions into the watershed's economy. More importantly, the river and its tributaries were essential to carrying away the cleansed sewage of several municipalities, including Concord and Billerica, and two prisons. Several industries, including Minuteman Missile–maker Raytheon, discharged treated industrial waste. Furthermore, Billerica withdrew about five million gallons per day for household drinking, cooking, cleaning, car washing, lawn watering, and the myriad other uses people make of tap water.

"Want to hear something interesting?" I asked Josh.

"What," he said flatly. I was clearly interrupting a daydream.

"The stuff we flushed down the restaurant toilet this morning gets cleaned with bacteria and chemicals in a special facility before being piped to the river."

"So?"

"And water from a faucet in Billerica where we'll fill our canteens tomorrow also comes from the river."

The look on my son's face couldn't have been more incredulous if I had told him he'd have to sip his urine. "You mean we're going to drink our own poop?"

What I thought would be an edifying parable about the grand cycling of water was, in his adolescent mind, a scatological horror. My primitive knowledge of sewage treatment was no match for his imagi nation. The logic of chlorination and ultraviolet light disinfection fell on deaf ears. Sometimes deep travel evokes contradictions and layers of understanding that we can't accept.

"Drink all the water in Billerica you want," Josh said, shaking his head like I was a fool. "Don't even tell me how it tastes."

Complain as we might, the river's lethargy was probably its principal virtue, allowing generations of people to enjoy ruminative moments contemplating their lives and the natural world. Perhaps its ability to induce meditative states had spawned so many naturalists and philosophers, famous and obscure, along its banks. "This is the finest, most peaceful, tranquil, quietwater paddling in the metro-Boston region," observes the Appalachian Mountain Club's *River Guide*.

The Concord flows in obdurate defiance of our frenetically paced existence. It forces us into a tempo that can restore psychological balance to our lives, just as certain hot springs and natural mineral waters are said, for various reasons, to have healing or medicinal qualities. The river has, wrote ornithologist Roger Tory Peterson, "a hundred ways to soothe nerves jangled by the pushes and pulls of human pressures." More than ever, we need to "go with the flow" of the Concord.

Flint's Bridge, with its handsome four stone arches, provided momentary relief from the heat and blinding light. Josh hooted, testing the echo as we passed underneath. He got a tepid response.

Wooded shore alternated with neatly groomed lawns fronting stately homes that bespoke money and comfort. Dozens of painted turtles sunned themselves on rocks and logs. It was so quiet, we could hear them sliding into the water with a "plop," as if someone had tossed a small, flat rock. Turtle spotting became great sport. Whoever shouted "Turtle!" first was credited for the sighting. By day's end, Josh was the hands-down winner, having yelled first twenty-two times from his perch in the bow. At our campfire that evening, I used a stick to knight him with the "Yertle Award," bestowed in remembrance of Dr. Seuss's turtle hero whose exploits had been read at many a bedtime.

"There's a sign!" a startled Josh said with a hint of laughter in his voice, pointing to a modest marker that signaled our entry into the Great Meadows National Wildlife Refuge. "Can you believe there's a sign on the river?"

Although the boundary post was relatively unobtrusive, its appearance was as surprising as an interstate highway might be without signs. We've grown so used to them, we typically fail to realize how thickly forested our roads have become with placards that give direction, impose rules like speed limits, caution us against hazards, and advertise everything from insurance to sex. Rivers may be the only earth-bound corridors of travel offering a free zone from most mileposts, signals, posters, billboards, and signs of any kind. Even backcountry paths far from civilization have marked trailheads, intersections, and campsites. Not so for most rivers.

Devoid of signs, rivers force us to keep alert so we can avoid falls, rapids, and other hazards. They demand that we understand topography and gradient so we won't miss turns or take-outs. Rivers require that we recognize landmarks so we can measure how far we've traveled. Merely by their lack of signs, rivers call for us to pay attention and rely on our own wits. They offer the freedom of not having officialdom constantly telling us what to do in bold print on bright, reflective backgrounds. Rivers are an ideal means of deep travel.

The Concord became dank, twisting, bayoulike, and eerily quiet. The floodplain was thick with red and silver maples, the woods lit by an occasional crimson flare of cardinal flower. Roots exposed by erosion left many trees standing as if on stilts, and turtles lurked on every log, little ones often resting on the backs of their larger brethren. Only Josh shouting "Turtle!" broke the gloomy silence where decaying vegetation smelled equally sweet and sour. It seemed incredible that we were within just about twenty miles of Boston's Fanueil Hall where pavement sprawled, greenery grew in pots and sidewalk cracks, and people and cars crowded the streets. Clearly, we featherless bipeds were among the species of wildlife seeking refuge here.

Established in 1944 with a 250-acre gift from a public-spirited private citizen, Great Meadows is an irregular band of land, part hugging the Concord River and part straddling the Sudbury. The Concord reach extends some six river miles and contains about 1,400 acres of the refuge's 3,600. Most of the protected land is along the east bank until the Carlisle Road crosses the river about three miles downstream. Just beyond the bridge, both banks are within the refuge. Shortly afterward, the bulk of the property shifts to the west, the protected lands ending two miles later as the river slips into Billerica and slides beneath the Nashua Road Bridge.

Not long after passing the refuge boundary sign, we spotted an area on our right where light poured through a thin curtain of trees like sunshine into a darkened room. Glimpsing what appeared to be a broad meadow, I beached the canoe on a mudflat. We stepped out onto soft, gooey ground and took a short trail to a vast opening in the woods of a few hundred acres. Startled with a sudden burst of light and space at the edge of the trees, we spent a moment letting our eyes adjust.

Most of the area was occupied by twin swampy basins of about one hundred acres each, divided by a dike as straight and flat as a drag strip. On the far side, near where our map indicated a parking lot, an observation tower stood watch. How strange that someone with binoculars might be observing our every move.

We had entered the heart of the refuge, the original acreage that had inspired this oasis for wildlife in the affluent, rapidly developing western suburbs of The Hub. As one of the few places in the Great Meadows that was walkable without getting wet feet, it remained the most heavily used part of the refuge. Squinting into the sunlight, we saw a couple of joggers, a clutch of people scanning the upper pool with binoculars, and a pair of dog walkers who looked at us queerly. I realized we were still in life jackets.

The basins appeared largely drained, hardly the wide swath of blue water shown on maps. Instead, we looked at a marsh that seemed to embrace more shades of green than ever dreamed by Crayola. There were bleached greens and hues reminding me of trees freshly leafed in spring. Some patches mimicked the color of pines, others the defiant deep green of Christmas fern in December. Irregular, amoeba-shaped splotches of shallow water sparkled among the greenery. Swatches of brown-headed cattails and soft magenta loosestrife clustered near the water. In the hazy August sun, the area looked like a Monet painting burst from its canvas.

"Look at all those Canadian geese," Josh said, as we began walking down the dike. "I can't even count the ducks."

"Mallards, mostly. The one with the colorful head is a wood duck. Might be a blue-winged teal in there, too." A couple of egrets waded nearby.

"This is like pure nature," Josh said proudly, feeling something profound about his first experience in a national wildlife refuge. "Just like when Thoreau was here."

"It seems that way, I guess. But what you're looking at is entirely manmade."

"How's that? There aren't any houses," he noted, glancing around to make sure. "You told me that all this land is protected forever and that we could see tons of animals and birds here." He was challenging me, but there was also a note of betrayal in his voice, as if he sensed I had misled him.

"It's true about the property being preserved for wildlife, but the land hasn't always looked like this. Animals thrive here not because people have stayed away and let nature alone, but because people are taking care of the land like it was a big garden."

Josh looked at me suspiciously. His eyes told him that this was a wild place. He couldn't see any buildings, roads, driveways, monuments, or flowerbeds. Everything was lush and green, unkempt and untended.

"The ponds were dug in a big hayfield during the late 1920s so ducks and geese and herons would have more places to live. Look at this path we're on. See how it's so perfectly straight and level. Does that look natural?" He gave a lazy shake of the head, and I motioned for him to follow me farther up the trail. "Also, the ponds are divided almost equally. That's not very natural either." At about the path's midpoint, I stopped to show him a culvert connecting the pools. "Refuge managers can change water levels right here. We're walking on what's called a dike. It's kind of like a low dam. It was built with dirt dug out of the holes that became the ponds."

"So this really isn't nature we're in," Josh said, looking down at his sneakers in disappointment.

"Of course it's nature," I reassured him. "There's more nature concentrated in this spot than in most places. Look around you." I gave a wide sweep of my arm. "There's water, sky, birds, flowers, grasses, and, like you said, not a house in sight. See those cone-shaped bumps among the cattails? Those are muskrat huts. You only find muskrats in good natural places. It's just that this isn't pristine wilderness. It's a place where people and nature work together. Most natural places we visit are like that."

Josh's confusion about the naturalness of the Great Meadows wasn't unusual. McPhee observed the area looking "essentially as it must have in 1839," when Thoreau described it as "a broad moccasin print" that had "leveled a fertile and juicy place in nature." But the meadows are vastly different from when Thoreau characterized them as owned by Concord farmers who "get the hay from year to year." Such change wasn't unnoticed by Mungo. "Of course, get the hay!" he wrote. "But the Great Meadows are mostly woods now."

Today's marshes and dense, low-lying forest patches were a natural hayfield when the first settlers arrived, a spacious grassland where a person could walk dry shod in the treeless sunshine. It stretched more than three miles east and north along the river to the Billerica line, more than four hundred prairielike acres.

The refuge we see now is not fresh from the creator's hand, nor was it in Thoreau's time. It's just the latest iteration in a long relationship between human beings and natural forces ongoing since people first arrived here more than ten thousand years ago as the glacial ice retreated. Since then, the meadows have provided food; livestock fodder; home sites; and a place for nature study, recreation, and replenishment of the spirit. Understanding this requires stepping beyond the conventional bonds of three-dimensional vision and seeing in time. We need to deep travel.

Back on the water, Josh and I paddled through a couple of tight river bends between muddy shores. Beyond were lowlands thick with hardwoods. Soon we passed a high bank on the west side that led upwards to a ridge crowned with pines. A large, shingle-style mansion with huge stone chimneys wasn't far away. Not long afterward the shoreline flattened again, the river broadened and sparkled with sunshine. Irregular wetland backwaters meandered on either side, choked with iris, cattails, loosestrife, water lilies, duckweed, and the spear-point leaves of arrow arum.

Benefiting from a slight tailwind, we stowed our paddles and relaxed on a gentle downstream float, pausing to snack on apples and peanuts and splitting a chocolate bar. Turning the canoe broadside with water lapping against the hull, I told Josh the story of the Great Meadows as I had learned it from books and brochures and a telephone chat with Libby Herland, the energetic refuge manager.

The meadows had long nurtured human beings. Indians gathered fish, frogs, and turtles and harvested cattail shoots and arrowhead tubers. They hunted waterfowl and deer and gathered rushes, grasses, and cattails to make baskets, bags, and mats. In autumn, cranberries and wild rice ripened. Later they grew corn, beans, and squash on nearby upland fields.

European colonists were attracted by the broad, treeless margins along the river offering ready hay for animal feed and bedding. With as many as 90 percent of native inhabitants falling prey to Old World diseases such as smallpox by the time Concord was founded, the land was virtually unoccupied. No wonder the Indians accommodated the settlers so peaceably.

Farmers divided the land into long, narrow haying lots. Over generations, they increased yields by improving drainage through dredging, ditching, and cutting weeds. Hay from the meadows fueled Concord's agricultural economy for more than two hundred years, but by the late nineteenth century flooding and prolonged saturation of the ground rendered the meadows practically worthless. High summer water levels left them inaccessible, promoted sedges rather than livestock-nourishing grasses, and drowned the meadow muck once dug to fertilize fields. The milldam downstream in Billerica, release of excess water from Boston's reservoirs, and deforestation by the farmers themselves were the culprits.

Engaged in a protracted legal battle against the dam owners, Concord and Sudbury farmers hired Thoreau in 1859 to survey the river, take measurements, and collect facts that would demonstrate historically lower summer water levels. Although considered more than a bit quirky and odd by his contemporaries, he was nevertheless well respected for punctilious surveying skills and knowledge of local waterways. Over a period of months he frequently cruised the river, not to check on the timing of flower blossoms or the haunts of muskrats, but to sound the river's depth, measure bridges, drive stakes in swamps to determine water levels, and locate shoals.

Unbeknownst to Thoreau, he was witnessing the twilight of the meadows as a hayfield. Not long after his death in 1862, a legislatively appointed commission dominated by mill owners ruled against the farmers. Fortunately, Thoreau was the progenitor of an entirely new interest in and use for the land that would transform its economic value.

With the land no longer actively farmed, trees encroached on fields, drainage ditches clogged, and the meadows became the haunt of hunters, fishers, and naturalists seeking quiet and proximity to nature. Valueless as hayfields or for waterpower, the meadows seemed to many people like Meader's grim assessment of them: "so remarkably level that its waters are sullen, sluggish, and slimy, making out through the numerous depressions of the soil in extensive marshes and lagoons, foul with rank water grasses and filthy reptiles." It became the perfect setting for the rise of ecotourism that now attracts thousands of visitors.

We paddled downstream slowly, sticking our hands in the water between strokes to dampen our foreheads and stay cool in the unrelenting sun. I mischievously flicked wet fingers at Josh, sprinkling his head, shoulders, and back. Looking overhead a moment, he quickly discovered the perpetrator of the sudden shower. Responding by slapping the water with the flat of his palm, he sprayed my T-shirt and left my glasses spattered with droplets. The splashing soon escalated by use of paddles, and in minutes we were soaked, cooled, and convulsed with laughter.

"Now we're as wet as those meadows the farmers couldn't mow," Josh said with a triumphant smile and loud slap on his drenched shirt.

"Unlike wet clothes, which keep us cool in the heat," I said, at the risk of boring Josh with a lecture, "these meadows seemed useless for decades after farming ended. They were considered a wasteland. Long after Thoreau was gone, an avid hunter and fisherman who understood the woods and swamps and the ways of animals looked at the land in a new way and saw its value for protecting wildlife."

Josh looked at me quizzically. "Hunters want to shoot animals, not preserve them, don't they?"

"Wildlife refuges weren't created by canoeists and birdwatchers. They got started more than a hundred years ago by hunters and fishermen."

"Like Theodore Roosevelt?" Josh suggested. "My social studies teacher says he was a big-time hunter, but as president he saved the first bird sanctuaries."

"Hunters like Roosevelt shot lots of animals but also cared about nature. Hunting gets you super aware of what's around you and the slightest environmental changes. These guys saw animals disappearing and did something about it. They ended hunting for money, what was called 'market hunting.' They pushed for seasons and limits on the numbers of ducks and deer killed. They voted for taxes on guns and ammo so the government could buy refuges."

"Thoreau didn't hunt, did he?" Josh asked tentatively.

"When he was young he did. That's a reason, I think, that he understood nature so well. On the Merrimack River in New Hampshire, he shot a bird out of a tree, roasted it over a fire, and ate it for lunch."

"Could we do that?" he asked hopefully.

"Maybe on another trip—unless you make a slingshot." By the flicker in his eyes, I could tell he'd be searching for a forked stick as soon as we went ashore.

"The hunter who started the Great Meadows Refuge," I continued, "was a lawyer named Sam Hoar. In the 1920s, he bought the property where the ponds are." Josh snickered. "What's so funny?" I demanded.

"What's his name?" he asked with a big smile.

"*Not* what you're thinking," I scolded and sighed. "It's spelled H-O-A-R." Though somewhat exasperated, I probably also showed simultaneous amusement at Josh's irresistible adolescent humor.

"Whatever, Dad," he said offhandedly, his smile slowly receding. "It's good he preserved the land."

"He didn't just preserve it. He made it better for ducks and other water birds by digging the ponds and cutting trees and brush. Remember, keeping up a wildlife refuge is a lot like . . ."

"Gardening or farming," Josh interrupted, finishing my sentence wearily. "You've told me a million times."

"You can't just ignore the land and expect lots of different animals," I replied, letting his rudeness slide. "Most people think all you do is let nature take its course. That usually means fewer habitats and species of animals. A refuge should encourage what scientists call 'biodiversity.' That makes a refuge wild."

The breeze strengthened and rippled the river's widening surface, which spread before us in a luminescent reflection of faded blue sky lumpy with scattered cumulous clouds. Large, staid homes in colonial revival, shingle, and international styles punctuated the high ground at a distance from the shore, peering down at the river like castles on the Rhine. A hemlock-dominated ridge appeared on the left.

Issues of ecological adaptation and conflicting access to resources that were once fought in the Great Meadows, notes environmental historian Brian Donahue, today lie hidden "beneath a quiet lagoon and wild marsh." Natural and cultural changes have progressed in tandem. In a more developed landscape, we no longer need hay as much as the wetlands and moist woods that regulate stream flow, sponge floodwaters, recharge aquifers, and provide wildlife habitat. As Teale observed, swamps where humans rarely tread provide essential undisturbed living for animals. Concomitant with society's needs and changes in the land, scythe and hayfork have been replaced with binoculars, fishing rods, and other implements of recreation.

We passed among the creosoted wooden pilings and beneath the concrete deck of the Carlisle Bridge. Thoreau described it as supported by "twenty wooden piers, and when we looked back over it, its surface was reduced to a line's breadth, and appeared like a cobweb gleaming in the sun." An access ramp on the eroded right bank was busy with motorboats and bright plastic kayaks.

Once the bridge was out of sight, the river widened further and the horizon retreated, with marshland occupying both shorelines. We felt remote, in the green heart of a vast everglade, though we were but a few paddle strokes from a paved road. Swallows glided over the water, diving and swooping erratically for their winged quarry. A kingfisher laughed maniacally from a cluster of dead trees at the distant edge of a narrow inlet. Insects buzzed in the heat.

At this point in Mungo's voyage, the river's lack of discernable current seemed to unnerve him. He appears to have lost his bearings. Perhaps the political lens through which he viewed the world blinded him to the quiet beauty of the scene. Without a dam, mansion on a huge lawn, or some industrial insult to the natural world for him to fume over, he became possessed of an angst that robbed him of his gift for acerbic description:

> It was just about standing still and we the only moving things in the landscape. Verandah trailed her fingers through the water from the bow. From my perch in the center, I remarked, "It's pretty but it's dead."
> "Maybe we're dead" was all she said.

Certainly their senses were deadened. At its heart, America has always been about movement, about flow, about forward progress. Despite his radicalization and bitter social criticism, Mungo appears deeply American, unable to tolerate a place that was still and quiet and seemingly going nowhere.

Paddling to shore, Josh and I found some shade at the edge of a cove carpeted in water lilies, a spacious wetland thick with a haze of purple loosestrife behind it. There we lunched on peanut butter spread on Ritz crackers and on granola bars with chunks of chocolate chips. Shielded from the sun, we felt the delicious refreshment of cool air rising off the water.

"Those flowers are everywhere," Josh remarked, taking a swig from a water bottle and wiping his lips with the back of his hand.

"The loosestrife?" It took a moment to launch the words off my tongue, gluey with peanut butter.

Josh nodded. "It's like a purple fog," he said, self-consciously poetic and Thoreaulike. "Did Thoreau write about them?"

"No."

"That's weird. He's so into nature and this flower is, like, all over the place."

"Purple loosestrife wasn't found here until about 1958. Just another thing that's changed in the Great Meadows."

"Too bad for Thoreau. It's so pretty."

"Yeah, but not everything beautiful is good for nature."

Josh shrugged. "It's just a plant. How can that be bad?"

"Botanists call it an alien invasive."

Josh looked at me quizzically, wondering whether I'd made a joke. "Alien invaders? Like from a flying saucer?" Clearly his video frame of reference focused on men in black, not plants in green. I passed him an apple. He waved it off, so I bit into it myself.

"These aren't creatures from outer space," I laughed, "but just the same, they don't belong here. Loosestrife was transplanted from Europe just before the Civil War because people liked its looks. Leaving behind natural competitors and predators—bugs and diseases—there was nothing to stop it from spreading and choking out native vegetation like cattails."

"Like the colonists pushing out the Indians?" Josh wondered aloud. "They came from Europe, too."

I was caught short by an analogy that hadn't occurred to me. "Not exactly," I said after momentary musing. "But it's a good thought." He beamed. I tossed my apple core into a grassy tussock. Josh asked for another granola bar.

"Birds, fish, and other animals can't use purple loosestrife for food and shelter. Cattail seeds and stems, on the other hand, are eaten by those painted turtles we saw. Loosestrife is useless to them. Red-winged blackbirds, swamp sparrows, marsh wrens, and other birds nest among cattails, but not in loosestrife. Grebes, least bitterns, and many ducks mostly use dead cattail stems in their nests. Muskrats build their huts from cattail leaves, and the roots are their favorite food. Beavers eat them too. Certain fish, moths, and other insects also use cattails. They're one of the most valuable plants for wildlife. They don't look showy, but they mean a healthy swamp. Wetlands of purple loosestrife catch the eye, but they're a Sahara Desert for most animals."

Invasive plants are often deceitfully beautiful. Thoreau certainly never heard the term, but as he made his way up the Concord and Merrimack rivers, he recognized how self-deluding people could be about the beauty of their environment. "Nature is not made after a fashion as we would have her," he wrote. "We piously exaggerate her wonders as the scenery around our home."

Teale labeled loosestrife-choked wetlands a "magenta jungle" and feared a "botanical take over." Growing quickly and blooming profusely, each plant of this "hardy, long lived, aggressive perennial," he estimated, could produce as many as three hundred thousand seeds, or twenty-four billion to the acre.

"Loosestrife is everywhere!" Josh said with sudden alarm. "It's taking over, even around Hoar's ponds. Can't we stop it?" His voice had the urgency of a character from a cheap science fiction flick warning of impending doom. Still, he delighted in saying the name "Hoar."

"Sometimes plants get pulled out by hand, but that's hard in big areas. Refuge workers have sprayed an herbicide around the ponds, and that's worked okay. Still, it's best to find natural enemies from the plant's home area. They're experimenting with tiny beetles. Tens of thousands of bugs have been let loose, but it takes time."

Josh seemed intrigued. I think he imagined some tiny Star Wars–like creatures panning out, infiltrating and attacking a derelict loosestrife empire. "Some people volunteer as beetle farmers, growing them in their backyards for release in places like this."

"Let's be beetle farmers," Josh said earnestly, reassured there was something he could do. He took one last swallow on the water bottle and handed it to me.

"Good idea," I said, stuffing our lunch bag into the big pack tucked beneath the boat's middle thwart.

Our meal finished, we paddled from restful shade into full sunshine. The effect was as startling as a light switched on at night. Fortunately, out in midstream we found the heat relieved by a steady breeze. A strong tailwind now pushed the canoe readily downriver. Gliding easily on the surface, we felt as if we were paddling through air.

A big bass boat with a wide, open cockpit whizzed by us. Josh pointed. To his delight, the two older men aboard wore Red Sox caps. Their fishing rods, seated vertically in holders near the stern, whipped in the wind like saplings. Soon we rocked in the vessel's wake, which disturbed us more than it seemed to bother a black-crowned night heron hunched among a clump of rushes.

"Refuge rangers need to do something about the loosestrife in those Hoar ponds," Josh insisted as we passed another infested spot beautifully aglow in magenta.

His impatience surprised me. Maybe I had become too complacent or habituated to the plants. "One of the penalties of an ecological education," I remember Aldo Leopold writing, "is that one lives alone in a world of wounds." Environmental awareness should inspire efforts to heal those bruises and lesions. Josh was pointed in the right direction.

"If it was their only problem, I'm sure the loosestrife would be gone," I replied. "The refuge employees are super dedicated and care about this land like it was their home. I think they're frustrated and overwhelmed because there are so few of them. So much needs to be done."

"Like what?"

"They battle other invasives like water chestnut, which grows so thickly on the river's surface it chokes out all other plants and makes canoeing impossible," I began the litany, like I had at the office so many times when begging legislators for a paltry budget handout. Responsible for managing Connecticut's conservation lands for a decade, I well knew the limitations faced by a refuge where our relationship with nature was complex and resources meager. "The ponds' water levels need to be raised and lowered at the right time of year for the ducks, and dikes have to be mowed and guarded against burrowing woodchucks and muskrats. Snapping turtles have to be controlled so they don't eat all the ducklings. The workers have to keep up with vandals who leave trash, break gates, and slash the ground with ATVs. Conflicts arise between birders and noisy motorboats. A toxic waste dump upstream is leaking mercury and other chemicals that we can't see, smell, or taste, causing a journalist to once call the refuge 'a small patch of poisoned wilderness.'"

"Maybe if people realized all this, more money could be voted," Josh said. "This place is important."

Growing more persistent and urgent with time, environmental threats to the Concord River were not new, and user conflict between farmers and mill owners was not the first. Were Thoreau with us today, he'd likely be surveying the river for invasive species, collecting water samples, counting birds, and helping monitor the river for the Fish and Wildlife Service. Though long gone, he has left in his life and writing a worthy example. We fail to emulate him at our peril.

Our thoughts drifted, and so did the boat. We found ourselves bobbing in the shallows, mesmerized by a complex ballet of dragonflies engaged in aerial acrobatics, landing on the water as if it were a solid runway. Josh likened the big green darners with their clear wings, green abdomen, and purplish thorax to giant cargo planes. The bright red cherry-faced meadowhawks were hot fighters, and the brown twelve-spotted skimmers with their stippled biplanelike wings were bombers. They hovered and darted, landed and dove, endlessly fascinating. I wondered how anyone could paddle these waters without noticing, yet they went unmentioned by our predecessors. New worlds exist no matter how well a place is traveled.

The Great Meadows is a tiny green island, a nature garden, a truncated theme park of a once much larger ecosystem. As a remnant piece of wilderness, it is both less worthwhile because more dysfunctional and more valuable for its rarity. It is a tease, reminding us that more extensive wild places beckon. It is a quick tonic nearby. The Great Meadows challenge us to prove that our urban lives can coexist beside places dedicated to nature.

Perhaps it is less important that the refuge provide wilderness experiences than it offers the possibility of daily contact with nature for millions of people who live nearby. As long as the refuge and places like it exist, the natural world will be proximate to everyday life. Wildness need not be the exclusive province of distant places that release us, guilt free, to poison and pave the rest of the planet. "Our lives," Thoreau wrote in *A Week*, "need the relief of such a back-ground, where the pine flourishes and the jay still screams."

We depend on rules and regulations, bureaucratic mechanisms and administrative structures, and the sweat equity and green thumbs of managers and maintainers. Certainly, this is appropriate in densely settled areas where refuges have become a kind of green infrastructure within urban human habitat. In this frenetic twenty-first century of virtual worlds where we worship daily in the soft radiant light of cathode ray tubes, we must work with unwavering persistence to ensure we will long have the refreshment and replenishment nature offers. Our imperative to protect and nurture such places is rooted, ultimately, in our own desperate needs. The wildlife species benefiting most from the refuge is *Homo sapiens*.

Father of the Man

....

A physician in France, recommends as a preventative to cramps
the placing of a bar of iron about an inch square, under the
mattress upon which you sleep, crosswise of the bed,
and as high up as the calves of the leg.
Boston Courier, September 5, 1839

Cross into Cambodia
Manchester Union Leader, September 5, 1969

Lowell parking clerk charged with embezzling $40G
Lowell Sun, September 5, 2003

....

Wind whipped the river to whitecaps. Water slapped against the boat. The distant Nashua Road Bridge was a mere filament, a thin tightrope stretched from shore to shore gaining texture and substance with each paddle stroke. Soon we were alongside a cluster of small houses as colorful as mushrooms and, after traveling miles along swampy banks without human habitation, just as surprising, popping up on their neatly trimmed lawns stretched to the river.

Beyond the houses was a marina with large, bulky buildings and docks. A broad macadam ramp reached like a dark tongue into the river. The Riverview Restaurant, a white shoebox of a structure, squatted just before the bridge. Only its parking lot abutting the water seemed to take advantage of the view. Just below the grills and headlights of a parked Mercedes and two Fords, a couple of boys Josh's age fished with worms out of a foam cup on the muddy shore. A great blue heron wading near the opposite bank seemed indifferent to our concerns and unperturbed by our presence.

The Depression-era concrete bridge had a handsome balustrade heavily spalled from decades of salt and winter freezing. Though to traffic above, the bridge formed a connection, for us it was a portal leading to a low marshy area that soon gave way to more small houses on our left. The cluster of cottages had all the markings of an old-time summer refuge for middle-class city folks that had gradually become a year-round neighborhood.

Most of these humble structures looked battered by time, weather, and busy lives. Some were daringly close to the river on flood-prone ground and surrounded by bright green grass. Canada geese congregated on one of these close-cropped expanses, and another hosted a henhouse with a fenced run from which a rooster crowed repeatedly though the sun had passed the meridian. A dog barked a few streets back from the river.

Many homes had odd-angled additions in various styles and contrasting materials, indicating growing families and changing tastes over generations. Buildings with peeling paint and leaning sheds were cheek-by-jowl with those so carefully maintained they appeared newly built. Yards were often strewn with old toys and garden tools. There were small stacks of lumber and clusters of plumbing fixtures. These were well-lived-in places teeming with children and people who liked to tinker with their homes and gardens. Pontoon boats were tethered to warped and broken docks.

Labeled "Rio Vista" on the map, the neighborhood clearly offered the river view promised by its Spanish moniker. I searched vainly for a spot to land so Josh and I could stretch our legs, but it was impossible to disembark without, essentially, stepping onto someone's front lawn. The river itself seemed like an extension of the yards, and even from the canoe I felt guiltily like a trespasser. Nevertheless, the temptation to get out was hard to resist. For some unaccountable reason I was drawn here with the powerful, dreamy magnetism of déjà vu. This unassuming hodgepodge of a shoreline community had an indescribable and irresistible charm. I'd be back.

Not until Josh and I were long off the water did I realize that my fascination was steeped in nostalgia for a similar place where I once lived. In early adulthood, I had spent a few years on a dirt road in a twenty-by-twenty-eight-foot cottage about six paces from a large lake at the edge of suburbia. It was an insular and eccentric neighborhood of independent characters that included stiff-lipped Yankees, refugees from the sixties counterculture, and young families. Although sometimes it seemed as if neighbors spoke different languages, the lake was a centripetal force pulling us together. Its moods were our moods. The neighborhood was a place apart, with recurring stories and an odd web of relationships suggesting we held shares in a common enterprise rather than just living in proximity. Ruddy faces around winter bonfires on an icy shore and the plush texture of voices carrying over the water on hot, languid evenings remained bodily in my memory.

With the road now paved and many of the cabins and cottages torn down for palatial lakeside mini-mansions, it was a home to which I could never return. At Rio Vista that world within a world beckoned once again. Deep travelers bring along all manner of baggage, including suitcases stuffed with remembrance and emotion they never recall having packed.

Continuing downstream, we felt as if we had entered into another country. Gone were the grand houses with well-sculpted gardens peering at the river from hilltops. Gone was the federally protected wildlife refuge with its broad margins of dark, densely forested floodplain and wetlands refulgent with unkempt vegetation. Here the river was not something sacred and pristine, but accessible to locals whose humble residences might be within a canoe's length of the water.

A quick look at the map confirmed what the landscape already revealed. We had indeed crossed a boundary. Having passed out of Concord and into its sister towns of Bedford and Carlisle a couple of miles back, we were now in Billerica.

Had we been on a road, no doubt signs would have emblazoned our passage from one jurisdiction to another. But municipal boundaries were the playthings of politicians, surveyors, and cartographers with little actual bearing on the landscape. The signs and boundaries Josh and I witnessed were embedded in the countryside. The nature of houses and businesses and the condition of roads had signaled a social divide as surely as a waterfall indicates a change in geology. Although Billerica had its beauty spots, it lacked the postcard picture New England charm that entices tourists to Concord. It was a borderland between well-heeled Boston suburbs on one end and the rough-and-tumble city of Lowell on the other. Where Concord had a median household income north of six figures, Billerica's was about seventy thousand dollars and Lowell's roughly forty thousand dollars.

Billerica's website proudly proclaims that no other town in the nation bears its name, derived from Billericay, England, where several of the town's first inhabitants originated. As a result, when you are in Billerica, you have no doubt where you are.

The town certainly makes a unique impression on visitors. Thoreau enjoyed the loud gong of its meetinghouse bell, saw handsome groves of elms, and likened the community to an old English town that nurtured poets. Mungo, however, portaging through a burned-out factory in North Billerica after paddling a sewage-laden reach of river, compared the town to firebombed Dresden or a scene from World War III. Aware that Thoreau's name could be accented on the first or the second syllable, the ever-literate McPhee wandered around Rio Vista and randomly knocked on the door of a house on Thoreau Street to ask a woman how she pronounced the name of her road. Locked inside against some imagined assault from this lexical stranger, she shouted "Thor-OH!" from safely behind her door.

The face of Billerica has changed as much as the faces of itinerant river travelers. Thoreau passed through a traditional agricultural community of a few thousand souls, though its isolation had been dissolving for more than a generation because the Middlesex Canal cut across town as it efficiently moved freight and passengers between Boston and the navigable Merrimack River. Soon afterward, small, water-powered textile manufacturers along the Concord River in the north of Billerica expanded rapidly, constructing large brick mills after the mid-nineteenth century. In 1912, the Boston and Maine Railroad decided to build a major train-repair facility that employed thousands of people and catalyzed suburban development. Trolleys, automobiles, and improved roads further fueled suburbanization during the first half of the twentieth century and enabled the town's many lakes and its rivers to be developed into vacation spots and cottage communities like Rio Vista. With the town's current population of about thirty-eight thousand, sprawling residential and high-tech industrial growth continues, fostered by Billerica's proximity to highways and its rail connection to Boston at the old repair shop site. Deep travelers know transportation is a community's destiny.

In the few times I had passed through the center of Billerica on various errands over the years, it felt like a small town bloated by growth, like a person who had put way too many pounds on a once-youthful, athletic frame. The heart of Billerica features an old-fashioned green now encircled by swarming traffic and buildings ranging in age from colonial times to the twenty-first century. The structures are juxtaposed in a jumble that illustrates both the town's passage through time and the present's hunger to prey on the past. An old clapboard roadhouse, a modern shopping center with its expanse of parking, and the handsome new brick library echoing classical features tell in a single glance much about the town's growing pains over decades.

Billerica reflects the fate and fortune of many towns in the Merrimack Valley and throughout southern New England whose sense of community is outpaced by growth. Unlike Concord or Lowell with their well-formed identities, the Billericas of the region struggle for distinction in a climate of sprawling homogeneity regardless of how well they market a unique name.

"Dad, I really think I get it about Billerica," said a bored and somewhat irritated Josh. "How can you talk about this stuff when it's so hot out?"

Little more than an hour on the Internet had made me an artesian well of information. Historical anecdotes and statistical data points flowed from me involuntarily. Poor Josh was drowning in this flood of oracular intelligence.

"Are we almost at our campsite?" he repeated for about the tenth time. Exhausted from the unrelenting sun and humidity, I was as eager as he was to get out of the boat and lie in the deep, leafy shade onshore. I'd promised several times that we weren't far from pitching the tent, and we weren't. Only my endless patter made it seem so.

After the last cottage at Rio Vista, we paddled to the left of a small, rocky island. Beyond the island, the western shoreline changed abruptly. Rising steeply from the water with gray ledge outcrops, it was thick with oaks and other hardwoods and punctuated by clusters of pine and hemlock. The ground also rose on the opposite shore, though less dramatically.

"There's the Route 3 Bridge," I yelled, like a sailor spotting land after months at sea. A massive concrete span with steel beams, it monumentally dwarfed all else in the landscape. "We're camping just before the bridge."

"You mean we're almost there for real!" Josh cheered. Revived by the news, his paddle strokes regained their bite.

We landed beside a rocky shelf near a small clearing at the base of a wooded slope. The spot was shaded by pines and oaks. A battered fire ring, a few bits of foil, and a shriveled orange peel testified to previous use. Unloading the boat, we collapsed in exhaustion on our modest pile of gear, the weather, more than the paddling, having sapped our energy.

Henry and John Thoreau also made their first camp in Billerica, "on the west side of a little rising ground which in the spring forms an island in the river." Having traveled seven miles, they called it a day and came ashore where they pleased. Our spot was equally pleasing and seemed similar to the one the Thoreau brothers had chosen, but we were there not simply because it was a good place given the time of day, our energy level, or its suitability for pitching a tent. We were there because we had gotten a permit. And our trip downriver wasn't nearly as fatiguing as obtaining permission.

It took more than a month and the involvement of a federal agency, a nonprofit organization, and three local governments to find a site and secure the appropriate permit to camp there. Assisted by the ever-buoyant Libby Herland, I scoured sites in Concord, Bedford, Carlisle, and Billerica. Most were too wet. The high ground typically had a structure or some other facility, or was too visible and might suggest to the public that camping was encouraged. We investigated Two Brothers Rock in Great Meadows and Dudley Park in Billerica. At last we found a slice of town-owned land on the west bank of the Concord just south of Route 3, a busy limited-access highway that, like the Merrimack River, connected Lowell with Nashua, New Hampshire.

With ample persistence and a bit of persuasion, I tracked down the town agency having jurisdiction, and after a few false starts reached the right contact. Eventually, I signed a nine-condition permit with the Town of Billerica Recreation Department that included prohibitions on the use of alcoholic beverages and motor vehicles and a clause voiding the document for "inclement weather." I also contacted the fire department for permission to have a campfire.

Everyone was helpful and wished me well, but I had no doubt that navigating the channels of bureaucracy was more difficult than paddling the river. Apparently, such a request was quite novel, and often it was hard to make myself understood because no one could believe that I would want to camp along the Concord River. There were a lot of noisy motorboats, I was warned. Houses and traffic sounds were never far away. More than one well-meaning official tried steering me to a commercial campground some miles distant.

Arising with reluctance from our torpor, Josh and I set up the tent with the front flap facing the water and the fire ring just a few feet away. The land rose steeply behind our flimsy nylon home, the trees sheltering lichen-encrusted chunks of ledge and clumps of bright green ferns. Several flocks of Canada geese flew low over the water as we went about our work, a reminder of why we were here despite the leaden heat that had us yearning for air conditioning.

"Dad," Josh ventured tentatively about fifteen minutes after the tent was up, "I'm kinda bored." Clearly, he was missing the television and computer, but he also knew that his father believed the natural world was interesting and provided plenty for a boy to do. It wasn't that Josh spent all his time indoors playing video games. Little League, scouts, and other activities frequently got him in the sunshine and fresh air.

"There's always your summer reading for school," I teased. He looked like he'd swallowed something bitter. "Why don't you collect some firewood? You could see if there are any animals around here. I'll bet you could catch some frogs or even a turtle." Josh shrugged listlessly. "Rig up your fishing rod, or take a swim, if you want." None of my suggestions generated a watt of excitement, but I was glad he was restless.

One reason we had left early and camped at midafternoon was to induce a little of what Richard Louv, the apostle of getting kids outside, calls "useful boredom," the "loose, unstructured dreamtime" that enables a child to slow down and explore. Louv warns against "nature deficit disorder," maintaining that children need nature as much as good nutrition and sleep lest "their senses narrow, physiologically and psychologically."

As a kid I played in vacant lots, in swamps, and on waste hillsides. My parents had a hard time getting me indoors at dusk. I took more scolding for not hearing them call me inside than for failing to finish homework. But unless it's for something defined like a bike ride or a game of catch, my children don't venture out much. Gone is the delicious indirection of aimless wandering, of messing around in wooded spots, at construction sites, or on abandoned rights-of-way. After organized activities like Little League and scouts are over, most kids retreat inside where DVDs, MP3 players, and the Internet provide sedentary and vicarious experience that keeps them captivated in dimly lit rooms where their exercise is clicking a remote or dancing their fingers across a keyboard. Maybe it's our own fault as fearful parents in an unsettled world. We feel more comfortable knowing our children are indoors or engaged in team sports.

For too many kids, nature has become an abstraction without direct experience. Schools teach them the environmental functions of wetlands, but they have no idea which flowers are blooming in the local swamp, what a muskrat hut looks like, or where to find snakes. At Josh's age, I had never heard of ecology, but I had an emotional attachment to the semiwild places in my neighborhood where I spent much of my time. The woods seemed secret and far from adult intrusions. They were places of freedom and fantasy where I could be my own Lewis and Clark. Though I had less knowledge than Josh of how those places actually contributed to sustaining life, my affection for them led to an adult passion for learning and exploring. Eventually, I dedicated a career to their protection. When nature is reduced to just another video entertainment on *Animal Planet* or a textbook explanation, can we expect kids to care?

"It is not half so important to know as to feel when introducing a young child to the natural world," wrote Rachel Carson, whose 1962 exposé on pesticide abuse, *Silent Spring*, birthed the environmental

movement. Perhaps I'm selfish, but it would take only a single generation of indifference to reverse the progress in cutting pollution and
protecting natural habitats that my cohorts and I have made since the
publication of Carson's book. Nature needs our kids as much as they
need nature.

After simultaneously assuaging his homework guilt and succumb-
ing to his summer's day lethargy by briefly reading, Josh set out with a
small folding saw and a hatchet to collect firewood. Tools in hand, he
seemed to gain a sense of mission as he marched up the trail with that
look of grim determination he remembered from the faces of actors
given weighty tasks in the war movies he watched.

Returning about ten minutes later, he proudly pulled a large old
spruce limb that rustled loudly as he yanked it with some difficulty
through the brush. "This pine tree is good and dry, like you wanted.
All the needles are brown," he announced triumphantly.

"It'll burn great," I said, with conscious enthusiasm. "But it's not a
pine. It's a spruce of some sort." To some people, every evergreen is a
pine, but nearby saplings enabled me to give Josh a quick botany lesson. I also pointed out the red oaks and sugar maples growing around
our tent.

"You can show me more later if you really want to," he interrupted
impatiently. "I need to find more wood. We've got to keep a campfire
going even after we're done cooking." He looked at my face expectantly, searching for a smile or other indication of approval. "I'll bet Thoreau had a campfire," he added pointedly.

Josh lingered longer on his next foray, returning with an armful of
small logs, some of which he had sawn. He dropped them in front of
the fire ring. Sawdust clung to his sweaty forearms.

"Guess what? I saw an owl! A little one! It was sitting on a branch
staring at me. Can you imagine? In the daytime. I laughed and it flew
away."

"You laughed?"

"An owl out in the day? That's crazy." Josh appeared out of breath,
but it was just exuberance. "And then, I picked up this log and found
a few red salamandery thingys with spots on their backs that looked
almost like eyes, and the fattest slugs you ever saw."

After I'd determined he'd probably seen a saw-whet owl and some red-spotted newts in their eft stage, Josh was up the hill at a gallop. Pausing momentarily on the trail, he turned toward me. "You wanna come?" he asked excitedly. I gave a negative shake of the head. "You could miss some cool stuff, like another owl or something." He shrugged his shoulders and turned into the woods, leaves crunching underfoot.

Josh's accidental discoveries were exactly what I'd hoped he'd find. Maybe it wasn't hard to catalyze an interest in nature if you just let a kid loose without batteries, far from any electric outlets.

I had nurtured Josh with food and hugs, made sure he was clothed for the weather, and got him to school on time. I had administered medicine when he was sick, and chauffeured him to ballgames and scout meetings. But at some point, fathering is reduced to cheerleading. I was now sitting increasingly on the sidelines. I felt both helpless and exhilarated.

Josh returned the third time with a couple of large, white birch logs tucked under each arm. Clearly saw cut, they must have been tossed aside in trail clearing. One of the logs was a little punky and adorned with a cluster of white bracket fungi looking like fat little pancakes.

"Will this burn?" he wondered.

"If the fire gets hot enough. They're a kind of mushroom."

"Like the ones you sometimes burn on the grill?" he grinned.

"They're related," I said, returning his smile, "but you can't eat them. Actually, the fungus is sort of eating the wood."

"Right, Dad," he said, in a tone usually reserved for scolding my bad jokes.

"If you don't believe me, feel this," I said, picking up the chunk of wood. It was soft and moist to the touch and fell apart in my hand. "Funguses make logs decay. At first, the wood gets soft and spongy and eventually it disappears into the soil. Without these funguses we wouldn't be able to walk through the forest, it would be so choked with dead limbs. Most people don't notice them, but if you look, you'll see."

Josh took a quick glance around, registering a fungus-infected oak stump at the edge of the campsite. "At least I got a few good ones," he said earnestly. "I know birch makes good firewood because you always see it in fireplaces."

He was so proud. I didn't have the heart to explain that birch was all show and little glow, an easily rotting, quick-burning species that left few coals. It often got laid in the shadowy maw of unused fireplaces because its bark was bright and handsome. I just nodded and smiled. For a campfire, it would be fine.

Josh lay down in the tent and resumed reading while I unpacked the cooking gear and began breaking up sticks for kindling. At the first snap of a twig, he was propped up on his elbows looking out through the mosquito netting.

"You should make a teepee fire," he advised. "Be sure to have the smallest pieces on the inside and then build it out with your larger sticks." I gave him a thumbs-up and he broke into a big smile. In his words I could hear the voice of his scout leader, a gentle but meticulous man. "And don't forget to put a big heap of dryer lint at the bottom of the teepee," he added. "The stuff lights like you've soaked it in gasoline." Josh basked in an emerging self-confidence, glorying in his ability to teach Dad something. He would never know how much I shared his delight.

As dinnertime drew nigh, by the calculus of our growling stomachs, I summoned Josh out of the tent to strike a match. Despite shifting twigs and frantically blowing on the nascent flames as they consumed the nest of lint, the fire fizzled, as Josh had predicted.

"I told you there wasn't enough small kindling," he announced with a newly found, almost smug assurance. Master fire builder or not, I summarily exiled him to the woods for more twigs.

We soon had a roaring blaze, the flames licking hot dogs skewered at the end of long sticks. Perhaps fire brought us as close to the Thoreau brothers as we were likely to come. There was something elemental and enduring in the hypnotic fluctuation of the flames, and the smell of smoke mixing with sizzling food momentarily, at least, could have found us in 1839 as easily as 2004. Henry and John feasted on "bread and sugar, and cocoa boiled in river water." With hot dog rolls as our bread, we shared a common meal with them, though in deference to changing times, we heated tap water from canteens and poured it over instant cocoa mix conveniently placed into our cups from foil packets.

My belly full, I grabbed a fishing rod and began casting from a small wedge of rock jutting into the river. After I had hooked two small perch and a sunfish in five minutes, Josh stopped poking the fire and joined me.

"Don't forget to pull back the bale and keep your thumb . . ."

"I know how to do this," he interrupted.

I was pleasantly surprised when he made some remarkably long, if ungraceful, casts. He needed no further instruction from me, and though I was proud of him, I felt somehow cheated of my paternal right to instruct.

In fewer than a dozen casts he hooked a yellow perch worthy of the frying pan had we not already enjoyed dinner. I leaned out over the water as Josh raised his bent rod, netting the fish quickly in case he jerked it loose in his excitement. Thoreau found in perch "one of the handsomest and regularly formed of our fishes." Its scales sparkled with dark vertical bands against a golden background, the bottom fins bright reddish orange. Josh's face glowed like a lantern in the dimming light. Wetting my hand to avoid damaging the fish's protective slime, I slipped the hook from its mouth and tossed it back for another day.

Regardless of a river's economic value, scenery, or the transparency of its waters, we most readily gauge a river's worth by the variety and abundance of fish. Perhaps a creature spending its lifetime in the water best reveals the virtues and infirmities of a river. Maybe we enjoy a special relationship with a wild animal that anyone can capture for a meal. In an age where satellites can detect what we're barbecuing for dinner, we may relish the mystery of a nearby, yet unseen world below the surface. As the water reflects the sky, so fishing mirrors our attitudes toward rivers.

Observing a man fishing with a silvery birch pole inspired Thoreau to launch into a long essay about fishing and fishermen in which he described shiners, dace, perch, horned pout, pickerel, and other fish.

He mixed Latin names with personal angling experiences, references to Shakespeare, and concerns over dams and factories that stifled the runs of salmon, shad, and alewives. On this same stretch of water, Mungo encountered several fishermen, "and though we dutifully inquired of each what he had caught that morning, we never found a man with so much as a catfish to show for his efforts." Consistent with the despoiled nature he saw around him, Mungo surmised that they were "fishing for old times' sake and not in the hopes of actually catching anything." By contrast, McPhee found fishermen who had just caught a fourteen-inch pickerel, a fish Thoreau described as having a "voracious eye, motionless as a jewel set in water." One of the men had caught a thirty-inch northern a week earlier.

Despite Thoreau's exhaustive analysis of Concord River fish, he doesn't mention today's most sought-after species because, although now naturalized into the river's ecology for well over a hundred years, it wasn't introduced until later in the nineteenth century. Regardless, the Concord now has a large-mouth bass fishery of considerable renown and annually yields trophy-sized catches. As we angled from shore, several bass boats cruised slowly up and down the river, the fishers casting tirelessly into weedy shallows.

Earlier in the day, we had paddled past a man in chest waders wielding a fancy cane fly rod, and a couple of barefoot boys lounging on a spit of sand, their spinning rigs resting in forked sticks. No avocation is as ancient and universal as fishing. It cuts across economic strata, from the wealthy sports traveling the globe seeking salmon or bill fish, to the immigrant urban dweller hooking carp for dinner. Fishing knows no political boundaries. It transcends ethnic, age, and gender differences. It's a hot topic in blue-collar barrooms, and great writers have waxed eloquent since Izaak Walton published *The Compleat Angler* in the 1650s.

Fishing stretches the poles of personality and experience. It combines a gambler's chance with arcane skill and an intricate if only accidental knowledge of entomology, riverine ecology, weather, geology, folklore, and other esoteric topics. It mixes the refreshment of the outdoors with indoor pastimes such as fly tying, library research, and fireside boasting. On a river, an individual's intensity of concentration meets the hypnosis of moving and reflective water, punctuated by an adrenalin rush of exhilaration when a fish strikes. Camaraderie with fellow anglers is juxtaposed with a secretive strain that protects hidden trout pools and special lures. Always wondering what lies below mirrored surface reflections, fishers are natural deep travelers.

"I think I've got a big one this time!" Josh exclaimed. "It's really fighting. Get the net!" Holding his bent pole at a steep angle, Josh rapidly reeled. With about ten feet of line left, his catch was splashing frantically on the surface as I bent down to capture it.

"Got it!" I shouted. Looking into the mesh pouch, my body tightened in anticipation of the disappointment I knew would envelop us like a cold fog.

"How big is it? Did I catch a bass?"

Carefully, so as not to lose my balance, I walked back from the water's edge and opened the net. Smile-puffed cheeks deflated like a pinpricked balloon, and Josh looked up at me, almost pleadingly, as if I could somehow change the result.

"It's just a sunfish," he said flatly.

"But it's good size," I replied in a poor attempt at consoling him. "And look how the colors sparkle on its scales."

A long silence fell between us, though it actually lasted but a moment. He seemed at an emotional tipping point. I could tell he was fighting tears, perhaps less of disappointment than embarrassment at having made such a big deal of the fish.

"So this is Moby fish," he finally said with surprising mock bravado, lifting the wriggling creature from the net by an almost invisible strand of monofilament line. Josh looked me earnestly in the eyes, cracked a smile, and broke into laughter. I laughed too, a full belly laugh that he then echoed. We went into giggling fits with the slightest glance at each other. I laughed not just at the fish, but with relief that I wouldn't have to spend the better part of the evening comforting a little boy. Still, I was saddened that that boy wasn't with me, and that save for flashes here and there, he might never be with me again.

"I think I actually had a bigger fish at first," Josh joked as I leaned over the water loosening the hook. "The fish I caught was swallowed by a ginormous bass which spit it out just as I landed it." We were instantly convulsed again with laughter, and I almost fell into the water. Josh clearly excelled at one of the most important parts of fishing: storytelling.

We resumed fishing, and time seemed to disappear. As the day wound down, the air became still and quiet, the humidity draped on our shoulders. Only the buzz of mosquitoes and the quickening click of crickets could be heard. Our bobbers plopped in the water and we waited. We got a few nibbles, reeled in our lines once in a while to check the bait, but a hard strike eluded us. Occasionally, I'd catch Josh's eye, and after a few stifled snickers, we'd erupt again into laughter.

Rods in hand, Josh and I were on equal terms. No fish was more likely to take my worm over his. It was a lottery, fate. All the years of measuring and monitoring Josh's progress, of teaching, helping, and nurturing seemed to be fading in our relationship as much as the light was now leaking out of the day. Here beside the river, we weren't just father and son bound by the lotto of life—we were companions.

"Dad, check out the water! Look's like an oil slick rainbow spreading over it."

Recognizing not an impending environmental disaster, but the reflection of a shifting kaleidoscopic sunset, Josh awakened me from a single-minded focus on the rod and bobber. Suddenly I noticed the air itself glowing with a reddish-orange light so palpable I reflexively moved my tongue across the roof of my mouth to see if I could taste it. The sky was littered with a few cumulous puffs, a shelf of stratus just above the horizon, and contrails arcing overhead. All were suffused with yellow, orange, and red that gradually deepened and then faded and flattened to indigo and gray.

"This is better than the planetarium," Josh said, recalling a school trip earlier in the year. I was awestruck, not just by the theater of the sky, but by the Thoreauvian observations of my son. Wasn't this the kind of thing *I* was supposed to point out to *him*?

Noticing I was lost in thought, Josh tugged my forearm. "Might as well call it quits. It's getting hard to see."

"Sure thing," I replied vacantly.

At its best, angling is less about catching fish than it is about the act of fishing. In *A Week*, Thoreau recalls an old, brown-coated man for whom fishing was neither a sport nor a means of subsistence, "but a sort of solemn sacrament and withdrawal from the world." Indeed, fishing is more than a means of idling time. Its serendipity reflects the moodiness of a world in which our finest efforts are not always rewarded and the best results are often accidental, circumstantial, a mere residue of tenacity and design. Patience, persistence, and passion make for success in fishing, as in life generally. They could fill Josh's heart as well as his creel, and were the big catch of the day—of any day.

Josh busied himself rebuilding a fire sunken to embers. He snapped small twigs, strategically laid them on the coals, and blew the breath of life into the smoldering pile, which erupted in jagged flames. From the goodly stack of firewood he had collected, he carefully selected ever larger pieces, favoring birch with its incendiary bark.

Perched on a large log, we sat transfixed by the flames, as if we were the only beings on the planet, the darkness cloaked around us, our world limited to the penumbra of the fire's flickering illumination. Long laid-back minutes passed, my muscles slackened, and I felt a comfort and communion I hoped Josh shared. This was one of those domestic moments that might resonate unexpectedly down the years and refresh some distant hour. The memory would conjure dank summer river smells, perch tugging on the line, and laughter. A father often fishes for such rare instants, feeling lucky to reel one in. They are keepers, no matter how small.

Neither of us moved until Josh poked the fire with a stick, sending up a shower of sparks like evanescent fireflies. He turned toward me, his face half clothed in darkness, the other side ruddy with firelight. "This is a really cool place," he said in a rare moment of adolescent gratitude. "I like being here with you." With a heart suddenly full, I was glad my moist eyes were indistinct in the wavering light.

"You're my buddy, Josh," I said squeezing his shoulder. "You're my best bud."

"You're my Bud Lite," he replied with a grin, referring to the beer that was made on the banks of the Merrimack less than a couple of days' paddle away. Perhaps loons were reported on the Concord that evening, for our chorus of laughter was enough to rival an entire flock's maniacal, quavering cachinnations and weird falsetto wails.

Once in the tent, Josh fell quickly asleep, breathing softly as he lay on top of his sleeping bag dressed only in boxer shorts. Sweltering humidity conspired with a restless mind to keep me awake. Traffic droned from the tall Route 3 Bridge, while rushing wind rustled leaves and gave voice to creaking tree branches. Somewhere upstream a stereo blared heavy metal, which waxed and waned with the breeze. Bullfrogs filled the quiet when the recording grew dim. The Thoreau brothers heard the footsteps of foxes and a muskrat fumbling with the produce in their boat. They also were disturbed by distant fire alarm bells in Lowell and a chorus of barking dogs.

I tried to imagine Josh growing into his teens. I could easily envision him towering over me and his voice getting deeper and sounding more authoritative even as life's questions began plaguing him. But picturing the kind of person he might be or what experiences might go into the mix strained my imagination. How could I predict his personality when I wasn't sure how the cocktail of my own teen experiences had produced the person I became? Would his wry sense of humor grow more subtle? How would his native inquisitiveness withstand the urge for social conformity? Could his naturally sweet disposition survive the disappointments of growing up? Would he retain the earnestness of purpose I so cherished?

Restless to distraction and overtired, I flicked on a flashlight and reached into my knapsack for my copy of *A Week*. Fumbling through the pages a few minutes, I came to a passage I had underlined. "We linger in manhood," Thoreau wrote, "to tell the dreams of our childhood, and they are half forgotten ere we have learned the language."

Here I lingered in middle age, caught between two icons of my adolescence. Halfway between Lowell and Concord, I felt the gravitational pull of Jack Kerouac and Henry David Thoreau, two men whose stories of rebellion against authority and promise of creative artistry fueled my teenage lust for independence and a voice. How I wanted to live alone in the woods. How I yearned to take off across the country with nothing but a brakeman's manual stuffed into the back pocket of my

Levi's. How I wanted to be a writer, but not just any writer. I yearned to be someone with an original style that would stir kids like me.

Maybe that's why I was here now with my son, the closest encounter I might ever have with my youthful self. As he entered the travail of adolescence, I was returning to a landscape that had illuminated my own teenage imagination and played midwife to my individuality. Aware of it or not, we all go through a Thoreau period of hunkered-down introspection when we build our inner resources and search for a sustaining philosophy of life. We also enter a Kerouac time of expansiveness that urges us to travel, experiment, and be gregarious, hip, and edgy.

Was I trying to show Josh something by bringing him here? He wasn't yet old enough to hear my stories, the ones inspired by the words of the dead men who enlivened my youth. Someday I hoped he would find his own *Walden* and *On the Road*, as I had found mine.

I had not merely read these books, I had dreamed them. I had become invested in their landscapes though I had never been to the places they described. They were emancipating landscapes of romance, nonconformity, and do-your-own-thing. I imagined Thoreau alone in his waterside cabin writing *A Week on the Concord and Merrimack Rivers*, and Kerouac ensconced in a small rented house in the Denver foothills imagining himself a latter-day mountain Thoreau as he wrote his masterpiece. Someday, I knew, I'd have my own solitude and my own book.

At sixteen, I had a vague notion that Walden Pond was somewhere in Massachusetts. If challenged, I probably would have been doubtful as to whether it was a real or imagined place. At the end of a long summer day of Kerouac-style hitchhiking, I asked the pony-tailed driver of a Wonder Bread delivery truck careening down I-495 if there was a place nearby to camp. He wasn't an outdoor type, he confessed, but we'd be passing an exit that had a sign for Walden Pond. "Thoreau camped there," he said matter-of-factly, "so I guess it's okay."

One ride took me from the highway exit to the pond. I walked past the concessions, bathhouse, and beach where people still baked in the sand and splashed in the water though the day was waning. Thoreau had written nothing about such facilities. As I hurried by, they seemed a desecration of something sacred. I walked down the well-worn path, entranced by the silvery water that seemed a pure elixir of freedom and revolt. On my way to the site of Thoreau's hut, I imagined the great man's spirit in the woods, the melody of his flute on the wind.

At the stone cairn marking the home site, I was disappointed. I didn't know whether I expected an epiphany, to see the cabin still there, or to somehow be transported back to the nineteenth century. It was just a pile of rocks.

It was dinnertime. Not having eaten since breakfast, I badly wanted to find a campsite. I would have liked to sleep where Thoreau slept, but was afraid park rangers or police might discover me.

I found a hidden bivouac on the far side of the railroad tracks that have run near the pond's western shore since Thoreau's time. On this relatively flat spot obscured by brush, I rolled out my mat and blanket. With a compact Optimus 8R gasoline stove, I heated a can of soup, enjoying it with hard rolls and cheese.

I wanted to fully feel the spirit of the place, completely open myself to it. This being the dawn of the 1970s, still the age of hippies and yippies, free love and altered consciousness, I took off my clothes and wandered the near shore of the pond, walking around like a youthful Pan, a wood sprite. I imagined myself absorbing the spiritual vibes of Walden in every pore. My nakedness seemed holy to me and wholly right. Reflecting today on this extreme exposure to a literary landscape, I realize I had no idea what I was doing, but it seemed true at the time and I can't say as I have ever again been so intimate with a place.

Perhaps I was more on the mark than I knew, for more than two decades later I read Thoreau's journal entry for July 10, 1852, describing a sensory walk "up and down a river in torrid weather with only a hat to shade the head." Almost naked, he walked along the Assabet in two feet of water, then up to his armpits and into soft mud amid lily pads. Walden itself attracted many intellectual swimmers in the late nineteenth and early twentieth centuries, including some who bathed in the altogether. Among them was Frederick Turner, America's first landscape historian, who enjoyed skinny-dipping off the railroad embankment.

The following year I inhabited the landscape of *On the Road*, living my Kerouac fantasy by hitchhiking across the belly of America from my home in Connecticut to Los Angeles and back. In an age without pagers or cell phones, it was the ultimate freedom from parents, teachers, and authority figures of all types.

I went where rides took me without planning to be any place at any time. I slept in an Ohio cornfield, in a remnant patch of Nebraska prairie, at a church in Denver, in an elderly couple's retirement trailer in New Mexico, and on the bone-hard desert among saguaros in Arizona. I ate roadkill roasted over a campfire, dumpster dived for breakfasts, and let missionaries try to save my soul for a meal of meatloaf, mashed potatoes, and green beans.

I was picked up by a Vietnam vet missing a leg, and a middle-aged man who took me home to his wife because I reminded him of their dead son. There was a shoe salesman on the plains who was lonely, couldn't keep his mouth shut, and repeatedly told me how he liked looking up women's skirts when he fitted them. An old man behind the wheel of a pickup in Arizona drank a beer every twenty miles or so and tossed the empties out the window. A pervert revealed himself while driving, and a young man from North Carolina worried about my soul because I wouldn't give myself to Jesus.

I saw the tight, green hills of West Virginia and the darkest soil I'd ever seen in Indiana. Oceans of sky in Kansas made the expanse of water seen from an Atlantic beach seem parsimonious. Colorado's mountains were like the breasts of the world, and the red, wind-sculpted landscapes of the Southwest were a Disney fantasy. Larimer Street in Denver wasn't the jumble of bars and whorehouses Dean Moriarty described, and I had no crazy Cassady as my companion, but this was the real deal. It was the big trip of people, places, and road miles. I lived the dream. I was never the same.

A loud splash broke my reverie. It might have been a bullfrog leaping or the slap of a beaver tail. Past midnight, the wind had finally died completely, the silence amplifying the slightest noise. Josh rolled over, still sleeping soundly, comfortably unaware of my late-night recollections. Somehow, it seemed as if these memories had been hoarded for

this moment, on this stretch of riverbank, with the malleable boy image of me by my side. I didn't know what it meant. I was just trying to
do my job as a dad, hoping that this journey along the quiescent Concord might deepen my relationship with my son.

Perhaps Josh would come to forget this day. Or maybe it would grow
in meaning as he grew. Something, I hoped, had bound us more tightly
together though the effect might be no more discernable than my visit
to Walden or my cross-country adventure had appeared at the time. I
could only stand by and await the long journey of watching Josh grow
up.

Bewitching Ditch

More Smuggling Discovered
Boston Courier, September 6, 1839

Unfortunately, in the present day people who should know
better and should take a stand have been taught to be tolerant
of EVERYTHING, including evil and swinish behavior.
Manchester Union Leader, September 5, 1969

Palestinian leader quits, threatening
peace talks with Israel and U.S.
Lowell Sun, September 7, 2003

After a restless night dreaming of thumbing cross-country with Kerouac and Cassady and running naked around Walden Pond, I awakened even more tired, it seemed, than when I had put my head to the sweatshirt I used as a pillow.

"Are you up?" Josh's voice penetrated my drowsy lethargy like a distant echo. "It's been getting light for a while now," he said eagerly, leaning over me with a wide jack-o'-lantern grin. "It just started raining."

The word "rain" hit me like a bucket of ice water and I sat up instantly. Drops were lightly pattering on tree leaves and dimpling the river. The air was so heavy and saturated with moisture that rain seemed less a disappointment than inevitable, and I resigned myself to a day of wearing ponchos, struggling to keep firewood dry, and feeling general damp discomfort. But by the time I pulled on my clothes, stepped out of the tent, and met the immediate call of nature in some nearby bushes, the shower had stopped, barely dampening the ground beneath the thick canopy of trees. A thin veneer of haze shrouded the sun, the countryside brightening or dimming as the opacity of clouds passing in front of it varied from moment to moment. Heavy fog hung along the river, obscuring the opposite shore.

It felt as if we were witness not just to a new day, but to the very dawn of time. Yet this misty Billerica morning was not unlike the one that greeted the Thoreau brothers more than a century and a half earlier. Fortunately for the Thoreaus, before they had gone "many rods, the sun arose and the fog rapidly dispersed." I hoped for the same good luck.

Picking up where he'd left off the night before, Josh took charge of the fire without a word from me. He sprinkled the warm coals with dryer lint and kindling, blowing the flames to life. Soon I had bacon and eggs sizzling in a cast iron skillet while he busied himself readying the boat for a day's paddle.

With little conversation, our routine went smoothly, and once again it felt as if we were just old camping pals. We seemed simultaneously closer and more distant. The transition in the way we were together became almost palpable, and I was both wistful and anxious. But I was grateful for this voyage of few distractions where we could merely be together, for otherwise I might have missed this subtle change in our relationship until left suddenly and unexpectedly abandoned.

Once we were on the river again, we passed beneath the gargantuan Route 3 Bridge in only a few paddle strokes. It was so prodigiously out of scale with the river and our Lilliputian canoe that it seemed the grand entry to another world, like a portentous passage in a fantasy film. Above us the whoosh of traffic was distinct despite the morning's sound-hushing humidity. The bridge was relatively new and the stone riprap around it still light colored. A few black plastic silt fences and hay bales remained in place along the steep embankment.

We quickly paddled by the ancient earth and fieldstone abutments of a predecessor span topped with a luxuriant growth of trees and shrubs. The steep banks flattened, and areas of swampy lowland alternated with thick clusters of houses. As it had for Thoreau, the fog melted as the sun climbed higher, the day growing steamier with the dissipating mist.

The houses were generally simple structures, slightly down-at-the-heels places crouching hard by the shore. Often they bore the mark of converted summer homes, a reprise of Rio Vista. At first they were mostly on the west side of the river and then on the east, their location tuned to the subtleties of topography and the location of roads. Makeshift docks, a few small motorboats with old fishing rods lying in them, upturned canoes, and an occasional inflatable raft or tire inner tube perched near the water's edge spoke loudly of the river's attraction to residents.

Many of these low-lying houses looked easily flooded and beyond the reach of modern requirements protecting stream banks, establishing minimum lot sizes, setbacks, side yards, and other zoning requirements. They were outlaws by current standards, bearing the stamp of a more laissez-faire time that permitted river lovers to snuggle the object of their affection.

By their very proximity to the water, these houses well illustrated the need for regulations. Lacking them, the whole river might have become a corridor between closely packed buildings, the banks stripped of trees and other unruly greenery in favor of orderly lawns. The remaining tree-shaded banks kept the water from getting too warm and losing oxygen that fish and other organisms needed. Vegetation stemmed erosion and absorbed floodwaters. Lawns, on the other hand, inevitably introduced fertilizers and pesticides to the river while runoff from nearby roofs, driveways, and roads added oil, salt, and other chemicals. It wouldn't take much more development to alter the Concord's character, making it more homogeneous and canal-like, a seminatural ditch.

Having traveled hours to enjoy the river, I was glad for, and somewhat envious of, people living so close. But I was equally pleased that such development was now limited. If you knew what to look for, you could read a trend in the balance between development and stewardship of the river by the age of buildings, their distance from the water, and the nature of docks and seawalls. Along this reach of the Concord, the progress of shoreline protection measures burst the bonds of legal texts, site plans, and architects' renderings. They were of the landscape itself.

"Look at all the water lilies!" Josh shouted, pointing to a low, marshy area along the left bank. While I ruminated over houses on the opposite shore, he had focused on an area that appeared wild and remote. "I'll bet Thoreau would say they look like hundreds of white eyes staring at the sky," he proclaimed with self-assurance. I nodded a proud father's grin. Were regulations all that kept the bulldozers from filling this lowland and planting houses?

From Josh's hunger for discovery of the natural world to his independence around the campsite and his poetic observations, this trip seemed to inspire some native talent, played to an emerging aptitude that fostered his confidence. I dearly wanted to ensure that this budding interest would be forged into a long-lasting character trait, but at his age I was increasingly reduced to mere encouragement. "Our job now as parents," writes environmental studies professor Terry Osborne, "was to be their stewards—not to *make* them into who they would be, but to help them discover and become the best of who they already were."

At some point, perhaps, stewardship of the landscape and stewardship of children converged. A synergy between human and natural relationships was embodied in the truism that we are shaped by the places we live even as we shape those places. I couldn't care for Josh without caring for the places where he spent his time. I couldn't care for those places without thinking of my son there in the future.

For a couple of miles the river wound lazily, taking us beneath tripartite arches of spalled concrete at Bridge Street and then past a small redbrick box of a building with intakes sucking Billerica's drinking water. Shortly afterward, the east bank was busy with houses. We went under another bridge, flat and angular, and emerged on the far side where the Concord narrowed, was rocky and littered with cobbles. We had hit the Fordway Bar, a formation of erosion-resistant rock underlying the river for about half a mile until it tumbled eleven feet in North Billerica. In the Fordway reach, the Concord "becomes swifter and shallower," Thoreau noted, "with a yellow pebbly bottom . . . leaving the broader and more stagnant portion above like a lake among the hills." Rocks covered with and reeking of duck guano frequently protruded above the surface.

"Look! It's like a castle," Josh sang out as we entered a fat, amoeba-like millpond dotted with lily pads and duckweed. Ahead was a dam just beyond which stood the imposing brick industrial elegance of the Talbot and Faulkner mills. A cluster of buildings that grew through-

out the 1800s, their sudden appearance on the flat millpond right after we passed a beaver lodge and turned yet another bend in the river
lent them a magical, Oz-like quality.

The Faulkner Mill was five stories tall with a central stair tower rising above the factory to a gilt domed belfry. Across the roiling river
the Talbot Mill was another strong brick structure, with its stair tower
topped by a handsome cupola sporting a weathervane. Since about
1708, the site had hosted grain and saw mills, a fulling mill, dye works,
and a carpet factory. By the end of the Civil War, the plants were textile
powerhouses, with Faulkner producing twenty-seven hundred and
Talbot three thousand yards of flannel daily.

As the twenty-first century dawned, the fates of these two former
cloth-making competitors had diverged, one continuing the manufacturing tradition and the other given over to ritzy offices and gal-
leries. In the old Talbot Mill and a variety of newer buildings around
it, the Cambridge Tool Company now made aluminum, magnesium,
and zinc pressure die castings and did precision machining. Recently
renovated to its original splendor, Faulkner housed a law office, craft
shop, the Middlesex Canal Museum, and the New England Baseball
Museum.

With sometimes grimy bricks and windows gray with dirt, the Talbot buildings seemed a little worn and unkempt from generations of
hard use. The Faulkner Mill, however, sparkled like new, its doorways
neatly painted and windows reflecting light. Divided now by more than
the river, the two complexes in a glance told the story of New England's
industrial development.

With the churning falls sounding in our ears, I answered an endless
battery of Josh's questions. He seemed both fascinated by the mills
and annoyed that they disrupted his pastoral and Thoreauvian expectations for the Concord River.

"I don't know much more than you do," I told him, as we landed the
canoe at the edge of a rough parking lot across from the Talbot Mill,
"but there's a lot the buildings can tell us just by looking."

With one hand on his hip, Josh cupped the other to his ear. "I'm listening real hard," he said with a smile, "and I don't hear the buildings
saying anything."

"Don't be a wise guy," I replied, pointing my finger in a mock scold.

We walked across the street and stood where the river came out from under the road, frothing over rocks and ledges. The stone dam was behind us.

"These rapids tell us this was an ideal waterpower site. In an area settled as early as Billerica, the first mills probably ground flour or sawed lumber. They might have burned, been flooded, or made a part of what's here now. The brick buildings with central stairways are a sure sign of textile making in the mid-nineteenth century, and the Faulkner even has '1884' carved on its tower, telling us for sure when it was built. But that's only the fancy part. Other buildings here are simpler and built differently, so you get the idea that they started making cloth or something else well before the tower was constructed." Examining old mill sites on the Assabet with Teale, Zwinger observed varied brick colors that "bespeak different days, different firings, different building periods."

I pointed Josh back toward the falls. "Even the dam tells us it was built in the heart of the 1800s because it's made of big stone blocks, not old-time rubble or wood or twentieth-century concrete."

"Is this Sherlock Holmes and the brick building mystery, or what?" Josh wanted to know. "I guess the case is solved. Besides, it's getting hot and I'm hungry."

As we retraced our steps to the canoe, I pointed out the newer, boxy buildings attached to the Talbot Mill. Their shape and style indicated that another kind of manufacturing resumed here when textiles went south. The Faulkner Mill, on the other hand, demonstrated yet the newest change in the New England economy—upscale retail and tourism.

We sat beside the boat enjoying the deep shade of a decrepit two-and-a-half-story brick building with granite lintels. I handed Josh crackers and cut slices of cheese and salami with my pocketknife.

"So what's this building about?" Josh asked.

"No idea. Storage, maybe. That's the kind of thing you have to ask old-timers about or look through photos in a library or museum."

"Something you don't know?" he teased. "Gotcha!"

"Okay, smarty pants. I've got a question for you. How did Thoreau get around the dam?"

Josh shrugged. "He portaged, I guess."

I took a few steps toward the edge of what looked like a narrow slack-water stream alongside the abandoned building. Overarched with silver maple and Japanese knotweed, it was choked with aquatic vegetation and quickly disappeared in a culvert beneath the road.

"We're standing as far as Thoreau paddled on the Concord. He made it to the Merrimack, about seven miles from here, by going this way," I said with a sweep of my hand down the marshy channel. "It was part of the Middlesex Canal, as busy as a highway in its day, carrying passenger vessels and big freight boats."

Josh looked incredulous. "We could hardly get our canoe down there."

"In 1839 the water would have been up to your neck and the channel almost as wide as two canoes end to end."

Completed in 1803, the canal was a quick, smooth thoroughfare that could move vast quantities of material between the Charlestown section of Boston and the Merrimack River at Lowell. Along with smaller canals bypassing rapids on the Merrimack, the Middlesex Canal vastly improved transportation between the coast and Concord, New Hampshire, which otherwise was reached by an agonizingly slow and rough trip on rutted roads that were either dusty or muddy.

Josh and I followed the old canal alongside the brick building and the parking lot to where it passed beneath the road. On the far side of Faulkner Street, it was visible only briefly before disappearing again in the Talbot millyard under a concrete platform supported by steel beams.

Where the canal flows underground, a dilemma arises for adventurers following Thoreau. Although in his time the Middlesex Canal was the most modern and efficient means of travel, much of the route has long been obliterated, paved, or filled. Even where a section remains and retains water, it has often been reduced to a shallow, linear swamp.

McPhee portaged from the Concord to the Merrimack in his wife's

Odyssey van; he was picked up one afternoon on the tributary and deposited the next morning on the main stem. The ever intrepid Mungo and his companions braved the Concord's difficult rapids and falls all the way into Lowell. They passed old tires, appliances, and cars. Their small outboard motor went missing in the tumultuous flow, they lost control of their boat, and they had to wade over slimy rocks and scale banks thick with burrs and trash. Their provisions and gear got soaked. It was an exasperating passage—dangerous even.

Not only was it impossible to canoe in Thoreau's wake, it would take some sleuthing to even find remnants of the old waterway. With the boat now useless, Josh and I headed for home, our journey together over. Just as Thoreau abandoned the river for the most up-to-date means of travel, so would I. The next portion of the trip—to explore what ruins of the canal remained—would be largely behind the wheel of my pickup, and with a new companion.

Josh had rightly invoked the spirit of Sherlock Holmes. Deep travel was a Holmesian process of piecing together shards of information to deduce a coherent story. So while Josh was later away at summer camp, I returned to the scene of the North Billerica canal mystery with Holmes in tow—at least the closest I could come to the Baker Street sleuth.

Although Alan wore neither a deerstalker cap nor smoked a calabash pipe, his decades of experience as a city planner gave him a sixth sense about topographic logic that would help us find where the canal carved its way across the countryside. A person of meticulous detail and scrupulous attention, he could superimpose a mental map on the landscape as he searched for underlying order in chaos. Such are the vices of a man who doesn't smoke, imbibes little, never gambles, and rarely has so much as a cup of coffee. As long as I could withstand the annoyance of his good example, I was optimistic we could find as much of Thoreau's route as possible.

A sun-splashed, breezy summer day found the two of us peering at the waxy canal waters just as they passed into darkness beneath the concrete apron at the Talbot Mill. Armed with topographic maps, a compass, and a guidebook published by the Middlesex Canal Association, we were ready for traveling deep.

"See the stone blocks on either side of the passage where it looks like a small hole has been hollowed out?" Alan asked, pointing a flashlight into the shadows. After a moment I finally made out a couple of barely noticeable notches in the granite.

"Yeah. So?"

"Look in the guidebook. I'll bet there was a lock here and that's where they seated the gate posts." Adept at crosswords, Alan loved puzzles and had a way of making tedious details fun. His analytical approach to changes in the land would be leavened by the game of uncovering what time had hidden in the countryside. As he expected, the guidebook confirmed his hunch.

As giddy as teenagers finding an anonymous wallet full of money, we excitedly hopped into the truck and took a quick right onto Lowell Street. I drove slowly. Alan had the guidebook and some maps on his lap. Once the street passed the squat concrete fire station housing Billerica Engine 2, it was lined with simple gable roofed houses on one side and woods on the other.

"That firehouse was built over an old canal basin," Alan said, reading from the guidebook as we cruised methodically enough to be taken for burglars casing the neighborhood. "And by this map, the canal should be in the woods over to our . . ."

I suddenly hit the brakes. The car lurched to a stop, and Alan's papers went flying as instinctively he reached to steady himself on the dashboard.

"Sorry," I said.

"Cat run in the road?" he demanded.

"No, but I'll bet those stone benches and that sign have something to do with the canal," I replied, pointing just ahead. "Let's check it out."

"You're on your own," he replied brusquely. "I'm picking up this mess and figuring out where we are."

A little more than twenty-seven miles long with twenty locks and eight aqueducts, the Middlesex Canal was a transportation marvel and an engineering conquest of topography in the uneven Massachusetts landscape, with its hills and swamps, ledges and streams. Built by the sweat of men wielding shovels, picks, and wheelbarrows and using gunpowder to blast ledges, it was called "the greatest work of the kind which has been completed in the United States" by Secretary of the Treasury Albert Gallatin in 1808.

The canal was typically twenty feet wide at the bottom and more than thirty feet at the waterline. Banks were constructed a foot above the water with a ten-foot-wide towpath on one side and a five-foot-wide berm on the other. The system was fed from its high point at the Concord River in North Billerica and required raising the dam three feet, thus destroying meadows, Teale observed ruefully, not only along the Concord but far up the Sudbury River as well. Though the canal's water was supposedly three-and-a-half-feet deep, it rarely exceeded three feet because of siltation.

I peered briefly at the sign. It merely memorialized the canal that had once passed behind it. Surrounded by benches and a few planted flowers wilting from summer heat and drought, the sign seemed a precious, self-conscious memorial for what was once an industrial landscape. Still, it was nice to know the canal was not wholly forgotten in this swath of residential repose.

From the roadside I descended to a ditch of shallow water and fought my way through brush before climbing to the towpath that ran like a railroad right-of-way high above the surrounding land. Where horses and oxen once trod was now overgrown with trees, some quite large. Pines, which like well-drained soils, were common on this manmade berm above the water table. Below the towpath the canal had been reduced to a wide, elongated wetland, dank with green algae. Clumps of yellow iris bloomed.

The canal was neither destroyed nor retrofitted for another use. The ditch hadn't been filled, nor had it been restored as an outdoor museum demonstrating the past for the amusement of the present. The towpath hadn't been blazed for hikers or paved for cyclists. Left unaltered, this was the precise space the Thoreau brothers had passed through. One of them had stepped where I stood.

Despite sweating in the day's heat, I felt a chill, as if I had entered a crypt unopened for a century and a half. Here were bones of the old canal, its banks gradually eroding, its flowing waters become stagnant, vegetation obscuring its once sunlit route.

This unnatural river, built as an engine of commerce, established a new relationship between people and nature. A suburbanizing world had grown around it, and where Thoreau saw nary a home, today you could hardly follow the route without seeing many homes at once. Though still largely an artificial landscape, the canal was now the most natural space in the area. Was nature healing? Regardless of the well-tended sign and benches, most people passing by probably didn't even know the canal was here or what its remnants looked like. To them, it was just some woods, a vacant lot.

Fabricated of oak and pine, canal boats were typically nine feet wide and seventy-five feet long, with a flat bottom and a cargo capacity of twenty tons. Pulled by a horse tethered to a short mast just ahead of the center, the boat had a crew of two, one to drive the animal and the other to steer by means of a long tiller. Salt, iron, raw cotton, cement, coal, leather, and manufactured goods typically went upstream. Lumber and bricks most commonly came down.

A horse on the canal could pull twenty-five tons of coal as easily as a single ton on the road. With a toll of six-and-a-quarter cents a ton per mile, it was the cheapest transportation in Massachusetts and thus a hit with businessmen, lumbermen, and farmers. Colorfully painted passenger boats, known as "packets," were also popular with travelers, who remarked on the comfort and cleanliness of the vessels and the beauty of the passage. Landowners liked the canal because it increased property values.

I returned to the truck and we drove down Lowell Street to its end at a tee intersection. Proceeding straight ahead, we pulled into a small shopping center behind which the canal entered the woods. Though it had seen better days, the small plaza with a post office, coffee shop, pizza parlor, and the New Dragon Restaurant would have made an excellent packet stop.

Running about half a mile to the next paved street, the towpath became a low-lying, rutted woods road passing between a large, reedy wetland on one side and alder-choked canal remnants on the other. As we walked westerly toward the Merrimack, the water grew shallower and so green it appeared solid in places. To the north, the grassy backyards of Alpine Street sloped steeply toward the abandoned waterway and the narrow band of unkempt woods in which it was hidden.

"What's a canal when its life's blood of water is drained away?" Alan mused aloud as we walked down the grassy towpath, dodging an occasional small tree growing where draft animals once had trod.

"Or when it becomes segmented," I replied, slapping a mosquito. "Isn't continuity the very point?"

"We've come to view the remains of the deceased," he said sarcastically. "The only canal is in our imaginations."

"But without this truncated and overgrown remnant of a canal, there'd be nothing for our imaginations to feed on. This," I said theatrically gesturing toward the pea-colored water where an old tire was lodged in the mud and a few foam cups floated, "enables us to envision ol' Henry and John cruising by in their skiff, or a barge loaded with coal on its way from Boston to New Hampshire."

Alan nodded. He bit his lip reflectively with typical exhaustion at my enthusiasms. "I suppose," he said at length. Then, under his breath he added with a smile, "What drugs are you on?"

"What?"

"Nothing. I just think the articles and books you've read and visiting the canal museum were the only feed your imagination needed."

This *was* a geography of imagination. The mind's eye encountering the landscape had crafted a story. Photographs we had viewed, descriptions we had read, and artifacts we had seen allowed us to experience not just rocks, trees, soil, and a half-pipe depression of murky water, but a logical argument laid out in the countryside.

Marriage between what we knew and what we saw enabled us to read a story where most people saw chaos or drew a blank. This was forensic observation, the heart of deep travel. We strove to see the landscape as a coroner saw a body, or as a fire marshal viewed charred factory remains. From the slightest detail, whether a scratch on a fingernail or a smoky smudge on a wall, we could deduce causes and uncover motives. Knowing how to look, we were confronted not merely with facts and images, but with interpretations and explanations. Whether canal fragments, stone walls, cellar holes, trash piles, old dams, abandoned roads, or a large tree growing among pole timber, the landscape was rife with allegories and deductions awaiting only capture by our imaginations.

But the canal wasn't just about the past. In the twenty-first century, the canal corridor featured many uses unanticipated by its builders, from house sites and roads to recreational trails and historic exhibits. Even in the canal's heyday it was quickly integrated into daily life and found a variety of unplanned purposes. Its waters were utilized for swimming, fishing, washing horses, ice skating, and even baptisms. Among the unexpected uses was recreational boating, including a voyage in a small private vessel by two brothers. Their passage was surreptitious, for at fifteen feet long, their boat violated canal company regulations that established a forty-foot minimum.

Getting to where the canal was again visible required a circuitous route by car three times the distance it once took the Thoreaus to travel. At River Neck Road in Chelmsford, in a mixed neighborhood of houses and low institutional buildings, we found a stubby canal remnant with steep banks covered by trees and weeds. The clear water might not have floated a fully loaded canoe, but it seemed to satisfy a few noisy bullfrogs, painted turtles, and several geese. At roadside was a small granite slab with a plaque describing the old waterway.

"Looks like a gravestone," Alan said, bending over to scrutinize the inscription.

"Appropriate. The canal is six feet under in most places." Alan softly hummed a funeral dirge.

We crossed the road and walked back in the direction of Billerica for a quarter mile along Canal Street. Built on the old towpath, the road was close to water level along a wooded swamp that had once been the canal. A flotilla of mallards cruised and several frogs were resting in the shallows at the pavement's edge. The woods were rich with songbirds. I spotted a rufous-sided towhee and heard a veery's melodious call.

It seemed an odd irony, a strange twist of the decades that this one-time transportation artery had healed into a de facto nature refuge. Once a means of taming nature for commercial ends, the canal now provided pockets of plant and animal habitat in a region largely paved and developed. Once a linear machine for moving waterborne traffic, it was now a disjoint series of green ribbons in a macadam jungle. It survived in waste spaces and as forgotten slivers of land. Its failure was, perhaps, its greatest triumph.

Returning to the truck, Alan plopped down in the passenger seat without a word and began scrutinizing the guidebook. In prayerful concentration, he studied one map and then the next. I didn't dare interrupt.

"Near as I can tell, the canal is obliterated for the next couple of miles or so," he said solemnly. "You've got three limited-access highways converging over the old route—I-495, the Lowell Connector, and Route 3. A cloverleaf and tangle of access ramps make it hard even to figure out how we're going to reach the golf course in Lowell where the route is visible again."

"There's nothing to see until we're in Lowell?"

"All bulldozed as far as I can tell, including an aqueduct over Meadow Brook and a passing basin in an area called Great Swamp." Alan took a deep breath and, lost in thought, pursed his lips. "Just another case of newer transportation modes wiping out older ones," he noted. "This may be the most realistic thing to see on the canal route."

The Thoreau brothers turned into the canal with the North Billerica falls rumbling in their ears and made the six miles to the Merrimack in just over an hour. One of them ran along the towpath pulling the boat by a rope while the other used a pole to keep from bumping against the embankment. Henry found the younger vegetation alongside the canal in disharmony with surrounding forests and meadows, but he felt relieved that "in the lapse of ages, Nature will recover and indemnify herself." Though he abandoned nature's meandering beauty for the canal's straight line, he felt comforted knowing the canal was fed by the Concord River and that "we were still floating on its familiar waters."

Safe canal operations required a plethora of rules, from maximum and minimum boat sizes to speed limits of four miles per hour for packets and two and a half for freighters. Boatmen were penalized for blowing their horns on the Sabbath. A bounty was paid on muskrats and mink because their burrowing damaged the banks.

Thoreau no doubt took an iconoclast's adolescent pleasure in violating several canal regulations. In addition to a boat well below minimum size, it failed to be pulled by horse or oxen and bore neither a name nor number, as required. Furthermore, the brothers exceeded the four-miles-per-hour speed limit and traveled away from home on the Sabbath. Luckily, they hit it off with the "liberal minded" lock tender at the Merrimack, who took a "visible interest" in their excursion "though his duties, we supposed, did not require him to open the locks on Sundays."

After careful navigation around an obstacle course of highways and several turns on quiet streets with sidewalks and single-family homes, Alan and I arrived at Mount Pleasant Golf Course. From the parking lot beside the clubhouse we could make out the faded line of the canal and a stretch of Black Brook as it wound among the emerald greens and meticulous fairways in a low area of the course.

With an eye out for flying balls and club security, I walked across the soft carpet of grass to a prettified bridge just large enough for electric carts to cross. Standing at the apex of the span's wooden arch, I gazed at the hypnotically dark brook whose channel the canal had once appropriated. The water moved swiftly between banks that now were far too narrow for a canal boat but that might have floated a canoe during spring flooding. McPhee imagined "John and Henry all but visible hauling their skiff from the second tee and the third green to the second green and the third tee among the putting golfers, the swinging golfers, the riding golfers in their rolling carts." I saw it too, and laughed.

Between the golf course and the Merrimack, the canal has been filled, built upon, or paved. Its path ran along Montgomery Street where tiny ranch houses face the road on shallow lots, then along the south side of Baldwin Street under more houses. The invisible canal then bisected a stone wall–enclosed park known as Hadley Field. In this rectangle of scruffy grass dotted with a few trees, the route passed by shortstop on a baseball diamond and skirted a playscape. Near a low stone commemorative marker, it crossed Middlesex Street, a busy commercial artery of fast food joints, gas stations, drugstores, and chain retailers. It then went between an Advanced Auto Parts Store and the Sterling Company, a moving firm, before joining the Merrimack.

"I now see why Thoreau took this route," Alan observed, as we enjoyed a break from the heat with any icy drink in the air conditioning of the Middlesex Street Dunkin' Donuts.

"How's that?" I asked, figuring I was about to receive some pearl of topographical wisdom.

"They could've gotten one of these," he said, holding up his Coffee Coolatta, "and anything else they might have needed for the long trip up the Merrimack, from canned food to razor blades."

After cooling off at the Dunkin', we spent more than an hour looking for a way from Middlesex Street to the Merrimack in hopes of finding exactly where the canal entered the river. We drove behind businesses where chain-link fences topped with razor wire blocked our way. We walked into a junkyard. We probed a dead end street. Finally, we found a shopping center under reconstruction where neither fences, nor dogs, nor security guards blocked our way. At one time a flight of three stone locks stepped the canal down to the river.

While Alan waited by the truck, I walked down into a swale through waist-high grass and up an embankment to the railroad. How appropriate, I thought, that the railroad should be the canal's final barrier blocking any connection to the river, ensuring that there was no public access for so much as a memorial tablet. After all, trains killed the canal even as railroad construction materials were floated on its waters. The railroad ran faster on a more precise timetable, operated even when the canal was frozen, and required fewer repairs.

Although I walked for ten minutes alongside the rails or stepped awkwardly from creosoted tie to tie, I couldn't find the abutment stones that are said to mark the spot where a railroad bridge once spanned the canal entrance. I even may have passed them unsuspectingly since trees were thick along the river. Only briefly through the branches did I glimpse the expansive water, sky, and light that must have greeted the Thoreau brothers as they left the narrow, wooded canal corridor.

Third American Revolution

The monthly list of prisoners in Boston Gaol shows at
this time but ten debtors in prison; of this six
are at the suit of their tailors.

Boston Courier, September 6, 1839

British Troops Fire Tear Gas Into Irish Mob

Manchester Union Leader, September 8, 1969

9/11 families find support in each other

Lowell Sun, September 7, 2003

On a day originally set aside for exploring the Middlesex Canal, Alan
and I found ourselves on Hampstead Avenue in North Billerica. A quiet, tree-shaded street, it passed through an ordinary neighborhood of
modest houses sitting amidst small lawns. The Billerica Garden Suburb was situated on a low rise behind the Faulkner Mill and bounded
by the Concord River to the west with railroad tracks on the east. Neither of us had heard of the place until accidentally stumbling upon references to it while tracking down Thoreau's route to the Merrimack. A
mere shout from where the canal slipped under the Talbot millyard,
the Garden Suburb struck us with a curious fascination.

Though the old canal passed close to the suburb and kids living
there once skated on its remains, the defunct waterway and the housing development were most closely linked by the railroad. As sure as
trains killed the canal, they gave birth to the community above it. Billerica Garden Suburb was conceived in 1912 after the Boston and Maine
Railroad decided to build a $3 million train-repair shop on six hundred
nearby acres. The need for workers was expected to double the size of
the town, then with a population of about twenty-eight hundred.

It was hard to believe that this development, an unassuming back-
water, would win the same prestigious award granted by the American Planning Association to New York's Central Park, the Appala-

chian Trail, and Yellowstone. Without passing pretentious gates or gilt-edged signs that mark many contemporary subdivisions, we had entered a National Planning Landmark. Even more surprising was the way in which this middle-class enclave unsuspectingly induced long-forgotten childhood memories of similar neighborhoods in which Alan and I had grown up. Billerica Garden Suburb may have been unknown to us until middle age, but it had affected our lives from the beginning and gave rise to the crabgrass frontier in which we spent our formative years.

Deep travelers are often sidetracked. One observation leads to another, and questions beget tangents and delicious distractions. Suddenly you find yourself engrossed in an ordinary place like Billerica Garden Suburb. It's an affliction inherent in the ecology of deep travel where parts reveal patterns, and seemingly unconnected landscape elements are spliced to others in unexpected "aha" moments. We find things by getting lost in them—both the bane and joy of deep travel.

Though we had almost missed it, this tiny neighborhood was essential to understanding the surrounding landscape. Josh and I had paddled past the flashpoint of America's political revolution at the Old North Bridge. The brick mills of North Billerica gave us a foretaste of the Merrimack, heartland of the nation's industrial revolution. But though its effect was all around us, I'd been blind to the third American revolution, one in which we were still engaged and fully involved.

Perhaps the suburban revolution eluded me because I'd grown up in suburban environments and they seemed unexceptional, dull, and normal. As a kid during the late 1950s and early 1960s, I had lived in a neighborhood of tiny new houses cheek by jowl, each with its lawn and stamp-sized vegetable patch. Dads drove the family car to work and moms unabashedly called themselves housewives. The milkman delivered every few days, and fresh vegetables were sold weekly off the tailgate of a truck. On summer evenings, the Good Humor Man sounded his bell. The ringing not only meant ice cream, but signaled that workmen had left the construction sites a block away where houses were being built to the thruway fence. With other neighborhood children, I would bicycle to the partially built structures and explore until dark.

As Alan and I walked down Hampstead Avenue, only a basketball's rhythmic pounding as a couple of kids dribbled in a driveway and the chirp of a cardinal broke the silence of deeply shaded yards. A few houses up the street, two teenage boys were washing an old Ford Econoline while chatting to an anorexic-looking girl in a ponytail. We passed old bungalows with inviting porches, Craftsmen-style houses with exposed rafter tails, and other places that had been built between the world wars. There were also small, cozy ranches and capes dating from the 1950s and 1960s sheathed in clapboards and shingles, some in brick.

As we walked, my mind kept flashing on the street-ball games and cookouts of my old neighborhood. Suddenly I was overcome with longing for return to a place I hadn't seen for decades.

"Not much to look at," I said, sighing with disappointment, "at least not for something that's a big-deal landmark. It just kind of reminds me of growing up."

Alan removed his baseball cap and thoughtfully ran a hand through a few wispy strands of gray hair. Sweat had beaded on his forehead. "I guess that's the point," he said. "If it was innovative eighty-something years ago, it's probably not looking particularly special today."

"Anyway, it wasn't just the design that made it unusual, but its affordability for working families."

"Looking at the size of these places and the lots," he said, with a sweep of his hand, "I'd say it's still serving that purpose compared with the McMansions going up most places. And with the railroad station over where that repair shop once was, you can walk to public transit. It's perfect."

"Sometimes I just don't get it. Almost a century later, we still haven't learned to build enough affordable homes, even with good examples like this."

Alan raised his eyebrows and gave a trademark wry smile. "I drag myself to planning conferences around the country and wonder if we ever learn anything from good planning. The crappy stuff gets repeated endlessly."

Under the direction of Charles Williams, minister of the North Billerica Baptist Church, small, single-family cottages were built on fifty-six acres set aside by the town for rail workers. The houses averaged fourteen-hundred square feet at about five to an acre. With assistance from the Massachusetts Homestead Commission, created to help workers find housing, a special corporation was set up, and laborers earning twelve dollars to twenty dollars a week could afford their own homes by purchasing shares in the corporation and effectively becoming their own landlords.

We took Ilford Road to Seven Oaks and then Letchworth Avenue. Many of the houses sported new windows, additions, porches, garages, decks, and swimming pools, demonstrating the love, money, and energy people had poured into customizing their homes. Some yards had the curb appeal of a real estate ad, while a few were littered with unregistered vehicles, mattresses, and construction debris. Some houses appeared freshly painted, and others seemed under continuous renovation.

"Did you notice," Alan said, "all the British street names like Letchworth and Hampstead?"

"No different from today's subdivisions. Developers worship those prestigious-sounding British names."

"Actually, from what I've gathered, it's homage to the late-nineteenth-century English Garden City Movement, which pushed for environmentally compatible compact communities. The cities these streets are named for inspired what we're looking at."

"Sounds like century-old smart growth."

"Exactly. We're back to the future."

From the outset, there was great optimism about Billerica Garden Suburb. At a time when overcrowding in industrial cities like Lowell resulted in disease, poverty, high infant mortality, and other social ills, the *Boston Transcript* called the site a "Worker's Paradise." As the project was under construction, promoters speculated that it might be "the birthplace in America of a new era in civic life."

Ever the planning maven, Alan had Googled "Billerica Garden Suburb" and found interesting scraps of information, including a preliminary site plan dated from before a single shovelful of dirt was turned. Map in hand, we were now looking for an odd-shaped parcel labeled on the old map as a park at the intersection of several streets.

"This is definitely it," he said, with the triumph of a boy who's found the spot marked X on his pirate treasure map. "See how the streets angle toward this site? Look at the configuration of the lot."

"Not exactly parklike," was all I could say, facing the vacant lot.

Without the plan, we might have wondered why this empty place hadn't been built upon but would never have guessed its original purpose. Overgrown under the dense shade of Norway maples, the lot was littered with piles of brush, grass clippings, and leaves that had been dragged from nearby houses.

"Based on my state park experience, the piles of yard waste are a sure sign of public land," I quipped.

"Another tragedy of the commons," Alan uttered sarcastically. "In some ways this subdivision is a good example of a plan undone."

"I guess a garden suburb needs tending—like a garden."

Strolling down Mason Avenue, we soon came to the pavement's end at the Concord River. More yard waste had been tossed down the bank, which was thick with scrubby trees obscuring the water. Save for a rough, eroded path, there was little evidence of public access to the river though the topic was vigorously discussed in 1912.

"Here's another lost opportunity," Alan said caustically. "Another case of good planning never executed."

The river wasn't always ignored. On a visit to the hushed and spacious Billerica library, I found a typescript of an interview with an elderly Mabel Buker who moved here in 1923 as a young woman. She recalled swimming in the river and skating on its frozen surface in winter.

Mabel lived in a tight-knit community where residents got together for socials and church fairs. The Talbot Mill maintained a library over the post office to which people walked for their mail. Milk and ice were brought by horse and wagon daily, and a grocer came two or three times per week. There were fish, produce, and fruit vendors. I read Mabel's story and saw the descendant of her neighborhood in the one that had nurtured me. Billerica Garden Suburb was appropriately universal in its obscurity.

Billerica's rivers, as well as several lakes, were ignored less and less as trolley and rail service increased, roads improved, and cars became more common during the first half of the twentieth century. The town's bucolic atmosphere and easy accessibility made it a summer destination for both the middle class and those somewhat more well-to-do. Summer cottages on tiny lots sprang up along shorelines, giving birth to new communities with boathouses, dancehalls, and roller-skating rinks. There were small stores and ice cream parlors. A summer development on Nutting Lake in the south part of town was called "The Breton Woods of Massachusetts." By the time the Garden Suburb was conceived, nineteen subdivisions were under development, with more than ten thousand lots. Three of these were at Nutting Lake. Of the remaining sixteen, more than half of them involved a body of water.

Not far from Nutting Lake, Rio Vista claims its stretch of the Concord River. Though Josh and I had easily seen it from the water, along the road it's tucked behind a low rise and is all but invisible to the thousands of cars hurrying daily between Chelmsford and Bedford on busy Route 4. Alan and I missed the narrow Edison Lane entrance a couple of times though it is marked by twin pillars of mortared cobbles in which is embedded a concrete tablet bearing the community's name.

Intrigued by this jumble of small, homely and homey homes since paddling past them, I had been interminably blabbing to Alan since we had left North Billerica. I sensed something proudly and defiantly insular about the community's ability to resist years of high water, architectural fashion, and the latest building and zoning regulations.

Comfortably disheveled with scattered toys, weather-beaten lawn furniture, and sheds, additions, and decks revealing years of amateur-hour devotion, this was anything but the postcard-perfect waterside community. Mixed with my nostalgic lakeside cottage memories, these images left Rio Vista a talismanic and mythic place in my mind. That neither the town planner's office nor the library's historical collection could shed light on the place only captivated me further. Even McPhee had been drawn by the magnetism of Rio Vista, wandering around there a couple of months before his voyage, "ingesting information."

By the time we found ourselves on Thoreau Street, Alan must have been fascinated more with my Rio Vista obsession than with the actual neighborhood. Cruising slowly along the narrow road, we stared through the pickup's windshield. Close to the water, several places retained the look of hastily built summer cottages, buildings that weren't expected to last. Nearby houses often had big, ungainly additions overshadowing the original cabins. Vinyl siding covered molding details and abutted faded cedar shingles. Old roofs were sway-backed, porches a little off-kilter. A few large new houses with fresh concrete foundations dwarfed their neighbors on the tiny lots where small summer retreats once stood.

We stopped beside a small yellow cottage at 28 Thoreau. The yard was busy with rusting garden tools, every manner of battered sports paraphernalia, plumbing fixtures, outdoor statuettes and knick-knacks, construction materials, and machine parts. It seemed the accumulation of generations.

"It may look like messy junk, but I'll bet every piece is filled with family memories," I said.

Alan took a quick accounting. "I suppose," was his deadpan reply. "Anyway you look at it, there's a lot of crap in search of a dumpster."

We crept farther along Thoreau Street as tree-filtered light reflected off the river from behind the cottages. "It's a humble kind of neighbor-hood by today's standards," I said, feeling self-consciously sociologi-cal, "but it's the real American dream."

"Definitely different from the dreams on Letchworth Avenue," Alan observed. "That was about families affording their first home. This place was about getting away from crowded neighborhoods and enjoy-ing the countryside and nature. When you think about it, each of these Rio Vista places was a Thoreaulike hut. They were get-away cottages that gave people what your buddy Henry had—time of his own and a chance to enjoy the outdoors."

"And then the neighborhood slowly changed when people were able to commute to work from here and go to New Hampshire and Maine for summer vacations."

"Bingo," he said pointing his index finger. "Look at this street. The building renovations aren't just physical. You can actually see the growth of families and the transition to year-round homes."

"I guess that's what makes the houses so interesting. They're not just sitting here, they're telling stories."

"So this is deep travel?" Alan tweaked me after a momentary quiet. I nodded. "Seems pretty simple. Just knowing what to look for. You mix a professional planner with someone who's lived in a waterside summer cottage, and here's what you get."

We drove slowly along the hillside roads above Thoreau Street, past small lots sporting solid ranches, capes, colonials, raised ranches, and Dutch colonials. We played a game of dating the houses by checking out utility connections; foundations of stone, brick, or cement; whether steps were wooden or poured-in-place or precast concrete; the size of picture windows; the presence of porches; and whether a garage existed, was detached or built into the house. Set apart from the other streets, Sherwood Drive and Cobblestone Way were new and wide with underground utilities; the houses were much larger. They seemed like aspiring mansions with their multiple gables, fan windows, big doorways, and two-car garages. Rio Vista at the turn of the twenty-first century had strayed far from its origins along the river.

Parking on Thoreau, we walked to Pelham Street, a narrow dirt stub leading to the water. Given the reaction McPhee received strolling around the neighborhood, it shouldn't have surprised me that two men from a vehicle with out-of-state plates and armed with a pen, notebook, and camera would arouse suspicion in this private and quiet community. We hadn't taken a dozen steps toward the river when a large red pickup pulled up beside us.

"Whatcha up to, guys?" a big man asked in a Jack Webb, just-the-facts tone of voice, his beefy tattooed arm leaning out the window. He looked in his mid-fifties, barrel-chested and muscular, his hair in a bristling gray Mohawk, several studs in his earlobe.

"Just walking around and looking," I said. The man furrowed his brow and checked us out as if trying to get descriptions for a future police report. His eye caught Alan's camera. I braced myself for a confrontation.

"I don't mean to be unfriendly, but we don't get many tourists around here," he said in the flat, nasal accent of eastern Massachusetts. There seemed something menacing in his tone, an unspoken threat.

"He's a writer," Alan said a little nervously, explaining our presence. Often, people get defensive thinking they'll be written about, but this turned out to be the right move. After I had elaborated a bit, the man, Joe by name, smiled and extended his brightly tattooed arm, giving us each a firm handshake.

"Over there's my place," he said, pointing to a long, low house with a deck and big windows at the corner of Pelham and Thoreau. "And all this is mine," he added with a sweeping gesture toward a large area behind his home, "right down to the river and including that little yellow cottage that floods on me every time we get a half-decent storm."

Joe maintained a family compound of sorts, including a large picnic pavilion supported on telephone pole posts and emblazoned with a sign reading "Iron Horse North." There was a huge woodpile, several trailers, some horse fencing, and a structure labeled "The Pigpen," a tiny cottage he'd converted into a "party house." He'd been in construction, and it appeared the home grounds were a never-ending project benefiting over the years from odds and ends left over at job sites. "We've had some wild times in that pigpen," he said with a smile. "Big barbecues. Real wild."

"Hope we weren't trespassing," I said apologetically. "We thought this was a public street."

"Gotta be straight with you. You're in your rights. In fact, on paper the street goes clear to the water, so close to that yellow cottage you could probably hear people whispering in the living room." Joe paused. "I don't usually tell people that," he said with a gleam in his eye, "but seeings how we've been regularly introduced, you go on ahead and walk down there if you like."

Joe became genial. He was a guy who enjoyed life by partying hard and working hard. This was his kingdom, and he grew expansive. "Bought my first piece of property here in '77 and I've added more whenever there's opportunity. I've got five hundred feet of river frontage," he said proudly. "It's a good neighborhood. No one bothers you if you don't bother no one. Over the years I've had dogs and I've had horses, but it's no big deal to folks around here. No one puts on airs. We're just plain people," he said with an arch smile.

"Rio Vista started about 1921 as summer homes for middle-class folks from Cambridge, Somerville, and burbs like that." he said. "At least, that's what the old-timers used to tell. Now there's hardly a seasonal cottage left, and a bunch have recently seen the business end of a bulldozer. Lots get consolidated and big houses go up." Now frowning and shaking his head, he added, "With the sewers finally finished, property values are skyrocketing. This place is gonna change big time. New folks with money might not like it so wild and woolly down here. Too bad for them." He let out a deep breath and briefly scanned his domain through the windshield. The truck idled softly.

You might think a man who'd worked so hard assembling parcels of property would see sewers as a gold strike. But Joe was more concerned about his way of life than real-estate resale values. He couldn't just sell out and rebuild what he wanted elsewhere. His Rio Vista paradise was something that could only be built with the sweat and toil of years. It was made of forever unfulfilled dreams that inspired his next move. He had created something that couldn't be bought. It had to be imagined and worked at.

"Gotta run," he said suddenly, as if he'd revealed more than he'd intended. "Lemme know if you need anything else." He scribbled his phone number on my pad. "Go ahead and walk down to the water, if you want. No one'll bother you. It's beautiful." With a wave of his hand, he backed the pickup to Thoreau Street and was off.

Walking to the water, we passed the empty yellow cottage where Joe had ripped out muddy carpets more than once after a flood. We'd gone from skulking strangers to guests of the manor. I wanted to linger, but the heat and our growling stomachs urged us on.

"Residents may be year-round now," Alan chuckled, "but I guess there's still plenty of vacation home spirit."

"I'd love to be here for one of his barbecues. What a hoot! It'd be like stepping back into my twenties at the lake."

The smooth river reflected shoreline trees and a couple of lumpy clouds. There were no wind riffles like the day I had canoed past with Josh. Water striders scooted on the surface and dragonflies hovered. It was indeed a beautiful spot, but it seemed empty without Joe.

We tend to think of suburbs as a twentieth-century phenomenon, especially following the explosive growth of car-oriented developments after World War II. As Alan and I pulled out of Rio Vista and drove down Route 4 to Bedford, hanging a right onto Route 62 toward

Concord, a casual windshield survey seemed to confirm that notion. Outside of village centers, the vast majority of homes appeared to have been built in the last half century. There were occasional center chimney colonials, Greek revival farmhouses with elegant pilasters, simple gabled houses with Victorian gingerbread, and bungalows from the first half of the twentieth century, but both along the state route and down side streets as far as we could peer, the age of houses rarely exceeded the average American's lifespan.

Regardless of the sheer number of houses constructed since the baby boom era began, American suburbs have been developing for more than 150 years. "By the 1830s," writes Harvard's John Stilgoe, "that determination to live in structures surrounded by open lawns that invite light and air . . . caused Americans to build in suburbs and commute to work." Among them was Ralph Waldo Emerson, who, in the middle of that decade, left the noise and hurry of Boston, choosing Concord for its softer-paced life and natural surroundings even as it provided easy access to the city where he lectured and enjoyed intellectual stimulation.

Known for good roads as early as 1775 when the town served as an armory and headquarters during the Revolution, Concord was, perhaps, destined to blossom early as a leading suburb. A market town since the eighteenth century, it developed a self-sufficient metropolitan character with stores, hotels, and a county courthouse that drew people from surrounding areas.

The railroad's coming in 1844 cut Emerson's Boston commute to an hour, a quarter the previous time. Trains not only facilitated travel, they changed the pace and nature of life in Concord. Farmers were "impatient if they live more than a mile from a railroad," Thoreau confided to his journal in 1851. People "had become too well aware what is going on in the world not to wish to take some part in it." Ever the critic of train noise, soot, and the tyranny of timetables, even Thoreau benefited from the railroad; Teale noted increasing demand for his surveys as property values grew.

While closer ties to Boston made life in Concord more cosmopolitan—with fancier homes, the latest fashions, and civic improvements such as sidewalks—they also meant stores were relegated to local trade, hotels and related livery businesses closed, and the courthouse moved to Cambridge. The railroad ended subsistence agriculture as the economy focused on Boston's needs. Tourism became a major business as sightseers increasingly poured into town, giving rise to new enterprises and a new community identity.

Even before Thoreau lived at Walden, the wooded silence was shattered by locomotives several times a day. By 1866, four years after his death, the railroad was increasingly bringing the world to Concord, including the pond where Walden Grove amusement park featured concessions, a fairground, pavilions, a convention hall, picnic areas, sports fields, and a beach of soft sand. Thousands thronged for swimming and boating where Thoreau once sought solitude.

Concord's role as a crossroads and transportation hub still shapes this prestigious Boston bedroom community, a haven for highly paid professionals. Four-lane Route 2 bisects the town, several state routes converge in the center, and trains run daily to the city.

Building styles, architectural details, road width, and the placement of utilities enable deep travelers not only to gauge the age of houses, as Alan and I had done at Rio Vista, but to read a community's growth during various eras, just as dendrologists can decipher a forest's history by inspecting tree rings. A short drive revealed that a few side roads had opened for small subdivisions and some streets were extended in the 1930s and 1940s, but most of the town's residential development merely expanded existing neighborhoods. Then in the 1950s, Concord faced its first large-scale automobile-oriented development. But unlike the orderly rows of houses with tidy lawns on angular streets that characterized most subdivisions of the era, Conantum was a garden suburb for a car-dominated world.

Infused with an idealism akin to that which motivated Thoreau's sojourn at Walden, Conantum was built in the woods at the edge of the Sudbury River. Housing was simple, of modest cost, used new technologies including modular construction, and respected natural site characteristics. People settling there were interested in the outdoors and of prodigious intellectual curiosity. Nonetheless, it was a project unwelcome to many Concord residents, who raised concerns about traffic, water supply, and fire hazards posed by houses in the woods.

But what most agitated them was the project's sheer size and the type of people likely coming into their staid community.

I found Conantum through the kind of serendipitous discovery that often teases a deep traveler. I had never even heard the name until, in the course of ten days, I ran into it three times. At first it seemed just an odd, Native American–sounding term tossed out in a conversation I overheard in a Concord deli. But soon I encountered it again in Thoreau's journal, an entry I read randomly in a fit of boredom. Finally, I uncovered a file on the place at the Concord library. The notion that a hundred houses could be built in one of Thoreau's favorite haunts just a couple of miles upstream from where Josh and I first launched our canoe behind the public works garage and still claim Thoreauvian inspiration seemed too strange to be true. It demanded a visit.

Henry Thoreau and his friend William Ellery Channing once enjoyed exploring the fields and ragged woods of Ebenezer Conant's farm with its large swamp and cliffs along the Sudbury River. They playfully nicknamed the property Conantum because it sounded Indian and exotic. From the cliffs one September day Thoreau saw a "smoothly shorn meadow on the west side of the stream, with all the swaths distinct, sprinkled with apple trees casting heavy shadows black as ink, . . . one cow wandering restlessly about in it and lowing; then the blue river, scarcely darker than and not to be distinguished from the sky, . . . then the narrow meadow beyond, with varied lights and shades from its waving grass, . . . then the hill rising sixty feet to a terrace-like plain covered with shrub oaks, maples, etc., now variously tinted, clad all in a livery of gay colors."

Just south of Concord village on Sudbury Road, Alan and I crossed the river with its broad marshy edges and took our first left onto Heath's Bridge Road. Both sides of the street were briefly wooded, the land to the right opening suddenly with bright sun on a broad, flat lawn.

"That must be the ball field," Alan said, looking up from the map I had copied at the library and pointing across the grass to a simple, rusted backstop and wooden benches. "Looks like community gardens on the far side," he added.

I drove slowly on the narrow street arcing along the river. Waterfront houses clung close to the road, while those opposite were set back be-

hind trees and shrubby growth. Turning inland, we soon found ourselves on The Valley Road and Holdenwood Road, streets winding
slowly over gently undulating terrain.

Clusters of large pines amidst hardwoods towered over us, casting a green shade on houses embowered behind clumps of laurel. Ivy
climbed most every surface. Often hidden by vegetation and topography, and set back at varying angles to the street, each house seemed a
surprise as we came upon it.

"It's like the houses were *planted* in a forest."

"They must have had some big-time heavy equipment digging foundations and grading the roads, but you'd never know that today. Any
excavator or bulldozer scars have long healed."

Begun in 1951, Conantum was the brainchild of W. Rupert MacLau-
rin, an MIT economics professor who dreamed of low-cost homes for
young couples, especially those in academia. He believed that twentieth-century industrial innovations and efficiencies such as group
buying and mass production could be applied to housing. Prospective
purchasers were invited into a cooperative that enabled them to provide feedback on layout, design, financing, and similar details. Ultimately, an association of property owners formed, making decisions
about common land and other matters.

We slowed to look at bright green tennis courts set in a hollow
among wetlands. At a nearby house a couple of kids played catch in
the driveway while next door a middle-aged man stacked firewood.

"The houses are small by today's standards but they seem cozy," I
said. "They're tucked into the landscape, not on top of it, not on display like many built today."

"Definitely of their time," Alan replied, rubbing his chin thoughtfully. I shot him a quizzical glance. "Check out the low rectangular
shapes, the mix of shingles and vertical siding. There's lots of glass,
including the triangular gable windows, but not much in the way of
fancy details. The carports are really telling. Probably saved some
money at the time, but they just aren't done any more."

"Still, the homes don't really seem dated or old-fashioned."

"No. There's something timeless about them. But they are truly of
an era. They're distinctive. But like I said, no one's doing this today."

About 190 acres became a hundred house lots, with 60 acres reserved as common land for ball fields, tennis courts, playgrounds, boat landings, and forest. Economies of mass assembly were achieved while retaining color, floorplan, and window choices. A newspaper ad touted a twenty-two-minute trip from Harvard Square and proclaimed that in Conantum you didn't just buy a house, "you invest in a community."

"As innovative as it was in a time before land trusts and subdivision exactions," Alan said, "the amount of land left undeveloped is typical for a contemporary open-space subdivision, though today a planning commission might want more shoreline protected."

"Problem is, despite successful places like this, open-space subdivisions are still the exception."

Alan shrugged. "Unfortunately. Where Conantum is way ahead of today's developments is not in the amount of open space, but in how developed portions respect the landscape. Conantum was also a recognized social community, not merely a development of houses. That's something you don't see often except in resorts and some senior housing."

Descending into a hollow, we spotted a house that looked untouched since the day it was finished fifty years ago. Not much more than a shoebox with a gable and a little disheveled with a moss-splotched roof, it sat lonely beneath columnar trees and among rhododendrons.

The houses sold for between $10,000 and $16,000, plus another $3,000 for the land when most buyers lived on $5,000 to $10,000 a year. Typical early residents were thirty-something, married, with one or two children. The husband worked in academia while the wife was home raising the kids.

Initial residents were drawn together by professional interests, love of the outdoors, and relative isolation at Conantum. There was a garden club, dinner dances, and Christmas and Independence Day celebrations. There were also common hardships, including the developer's bankruptcy, sometimes hurried and shoddy workmanship, construction delays, shortages of materials such as piping, and confusion over financing. Nonetheless, writing in the mid-sixties, former resident Lili Hnilicka called Conantum "an Ideal community where amiability, congeniality, inspiration, pioneering spirit, Thoreau's belief in symbiotic relation of man and nature, and amenities of good living exist."

"Couldn't you see yourself living here?" I asked.

"I don't know," Alan said cautiously. "Maybe I could, but only in the sense that whenever we're doing your deep travel thing we imagine how we might fit into a place. It's like tasting new food—only something to try."

"It seems a good place to raise a family—private, but you could get to know your neighbors."

"I suppose," a skeptical Alan said slowly.

"Not that I'd trade my house for one here, but I can imagine walking in the woods, launching a boat on the Sudbury with Josh, watching him and his sister play tennis or baseball, digging in the community gardens, and chatting with the neighbors. The homes seem so peaceably settled. They're real. Not some pseudo log cabin or fake colonial." I paused, scanning the houses as we crept past them. "Do you think the neighbors still get together and do stuff?"

"Who knows? Maybe you're so hot on this place because Thoreau hung out here when it was just woods and fields."

The Valley Road wound to the edge of Conantum and we exited onto Garfield Street. Huge houses with multiple gables and fussy conflicting details had recently been erected. Some had garages with more square footage than a Conantum home. They sat perfectly parallel to the street on cleared, flattened lots with manicured lawns. They were *on* the landscape, not *of* it.

"Just look at these places," Alan said sardonically. "Clearly, nothing was learned from Conantum."

With developments like Garfield Street, it's little wonder that suburbs have a reputation as being spiritless, unyieldingly uniform places sprawling with disregard for topography, history, and ecological values. We love them for their privacy, quiet, and green lawns where a garden can reconnect us to the soil. We hate them for a dulling homogeneity, dependence on cars, and their demand for conformity.

Enclaves like Billerica Garden Suburb, Rio Vista, and Conantum are social ecosystems. Unlike the cookie-cutter and McMansion subdivisions we usually associate with suburbia, they neither look nor feel the same.

Deep travelers don't avoid suburbs, they probe them for unique qualities and for patterns that explain who we are and where we might be going. If we could more readily recognize and understand those with distinctive character, perhaps they could serve as inspiration for new developments, and for changes in arid existing ones. Maybe then we would better understand the places most of us live. The ever expanding universe of the third American revolution is not over.

Main Stem

There are in our existence spots of time,
That with distinct pre-eminence retain
A renovating virtue . . .

William Wordsworth, "Lines Written
a Few Miles above Tintern Abbey"

The commonplace is the thing, but it's hard to find.
Andrew Wyeth, *The Helga Pictures*

Art of the Voyage

John Perry, a minor, retracted his plea of not guilty,
and pleaded guilty to an indictment charging him with breaking
and entering the store of Messrs. Harris & Jones and stealing
58 pounds of copper therefrom in the night time.

Boston Courier, September 6, 1839

THE NATION TODAY IS OVERRUN BY AN ATTITUDE OF
"I SHOULD HAVE IT JUST BECAUSE I WANT IT AND I
SHOULD HAVE IT <u>NOW</u> BECAUSE I WANT IT."

Manchester Union Leader, September 6, 1969

High court will tackle campaign finance rules

Lowell Sun, September 7, 2003

On a sun-drenched morning, Pamela and I shoved our canoe into the Merrimack River at Lambert Park, a small slice of riverside situated barely upstream of Hooksett, New Hampshire. Its manicured lawn and careful paving lay just below a low dam, beside which was perched a brick powerhouse. Apparently, it was a popular launch site for fishers in small outboard-powered boats. A few were readying their gear in a gauzy mist arising from the frothy whitewater pouring over the dam onto a jumble of rocks.

I began exploring the Merrimack near where Thoreau concluded his outbound voyage, going southerly with the flow as he did on his return trip. It was nearly forty miles and numerous bridge crossings, several rapids, and the huge Amoskeag Dam to where the river once met the Middlesex Canal at Lowell. Perhaps I could spot remains of their confluence from the water since Alan and I had been stymied by railroad tracks and thick brush when searching along the shore.

As we shoved off, cool air arose from the water, but the bright, cloudless sky held all the promise of summer's heat when the sun reached its zenith. Though the dark reflection-painted river looked smooth and placid, we felt the current's power at once.

Almost immediately we came upon two rusting truss bridges, one an abandoned highway span and the other a railroad crossing with trees growing atop it. Looking simultaneously through the metal fretwork of both created a series of fractured kaleidoscopic images, dividing a coherent landscape of sky and green hillsides into a series of discrete pieces framed by the superstructures' geometry. The moment quickly passed as we found ourselves swept beneath them and then under the modern highway bridge, high and sleek, arching over the river on tall, concrete piers. Still, the notion that even the sky could be compartmentalized in a glance stuck with me, warning this deep traveler to scrutinize details of even the grandest phenomena.

The Merrimack forms at the confluence of the Pemigewasset and Winnipesaukee rivers in Franklin, New Hampshire, and flows 116 miles to the sea at Newburyport, Massachusetts. Though its gradient is a modest 2.6 feet per mile, most of the drop occurs in six short spurts, at three of which arose the textile cities of Manchester, New Hampshire, and Lowell and Lawrence, Massachusetts. Encompassing 5,000 square miles, the watershed extends 134 miles north to south and 68 miles east to west, with tributaries reaching into the steep, forested heart of the White Mountains. The area receives about forty-three inches of precipitation a year, and the river boasts an average daily flow in excess of six thousand cubic feet per second at Lawrence.

The name Merrimack is a corruption of the Indian word *merru-asquamack*, meaning "strong water place." Native peoples gave the river several monikers, this one commonly applying to the reach between Manchester and Lowell. True to its etymology, the river's falls and rapids were prime locations for waterpower development; scholar Theodore Steinberg called the Merrimack the "most celebrated river valley in America's early industrial history." Where the sedate Concord River was the seedbed of original thought and intellectual prowess from the likes of Emerson, Thoreau, Hawthorne, Louisa May Alcott, and others, the Merrimack was a roiling industrial dynamo, a crucible of practical ingenuity. The Merrimack, wrote J. W. Meader in 1869, "surpasses all others in the harmonious blending of the useful and the beautiful," a juxtaposition Pam and I had just witnessed at Lambert Park where the

dam created a roaring falls of foaming whitewater even as it spun a tur-
bine producing as much as sixteen hundred kilowatts of electricity.

A few fishers trolled along the wooded west bank as I scanned the
opposite shore for the spot where the Thoreau brothers stowed their
boat "at the mouth of a small brook." Leaving their vessel in Hooksett,
they continued by foot and stage to the White Mountains, returning a
week later for the journey home. Henry gives short shrift to their adventures on land in *A Week*, and boating back to Concord resumes as
seamlessly as if the intervening off-river days hadn't existed.

We pulled ashore beside a cylindrical culvert through which a small,
unnamed stream trickled beneath railroad tracks hugging the river
on a steep embankment above us. A dank odor, like rotting compost,
poured from the opening.

"Is this it?" Pam asked skeptically.

"Can't be sure," I said, looking into the pipe as if through a giant
gun barrel at swampy greenery on the other side, "but it seems about
right."

"You can't write about it unless you know for sure," she insisted.
"Just because it *seems* right doesn't make it true."

"I guess I could say it was this spot or one very much like it."

She twisted her body toward me from the bow seat, sky-blue eyes
narrowed and scolding. "Guessing isn't good enough. You've got to
write the truth."

"Sometimes writers enhance a moment for literary purposes," I offered somewhat weakly.

"What's that supposed to mean?"

"For example, Thoreau told his story as if it happened in a week, but
the trip actually took two weeks. And I'll bet he didn't have all those
thoughts about Indians, religion, and fishing at exactly the moments
he describes in the book. He added a lot of stuff later. But it was still
true to his heart. He didn't lie about anything."

Pam shook her curly locks and began to paddle. "Whatever," she
said dismissively. "You're going to write about it anyway, so I guess it's
your world."

The river was wide and slow, both shores thick with trees. Hardwoods dominated, especially oaks, but were studded with stately pine clusters. Thoreau found lumbermen rolling timber off the high bank, and as he passed downriver on his return trip, the sound "enhanced the silence and vastness of the noon, and we fancied that only the primeval echoes were awakened."

A telecommunications tower stood high on the horizon, well above hills and greenery, the silvery pylon undoubtedly dispensing all manner of chatter to which we were fortunately deaf. Whole forests of them were springing up throughout the countryside, some disguised as Brobdingnagian trees, many wrapped in the patriotism of flagpoles, and others even preaching from church steeples. Though many people found them an aesthetic anathema and destructive of unique ecosystems when perched on ridgelines and hilltops, they seemed less obtrusive than the poles and wires conceived at the advent of the electrical age, which have grown so familiar as to be beyond complaint.

Perhaps the towers are best looked at as monuments to an epoch of frenetic communication, with twenty-four-hour news cycles, text messaging, e-mails, and wireless voice devices. Ever the optimist, I still hold out hope that our increasing capacity to talk might have the concomitant effect of making us more skilled listeners. It's strange that we have more ways to speak our minds but nothing more substantive to say. That could only come of better listening.

How humbling to see these grand spires with elaborate nests of tubular and wire mesh antennae at their apex. Perhaps I'll be the last person on the planet who doesn't have a personal cell phone, but I'm awaiting something modestly profound to utter. For now, the steel pillar ahead of us only enhanced the silence of the river and left primeval echoes all the more cherished.

Glimpses of railroad tracks on the east bank were matched with dwellings on the west that McPhee labeled "in the trophy range." The houses were busy with multiple windows and elaborate stairways leading to stone and concrete–armored shorelines. Big white fiberglass powerboats tied to well-maintained docks floated in the shallows.

A large hump of tangled sticks lay opposite some of the biggest houses—a beaver lodge well located in a patch of alder, birch, and aspen, fringed by red and silver maple. How odd that the railroad—

which fueled the growth of this area, set the pattern of development, and was once the very symbol of progress—should now provide the more natural shoreline with woodlands and swamps, a place where beavers were comfortable setting up housekeeping provided they remained tolerant of the lawns and seawalls across the river.

Regardless that Pam preferred a more literal accounting, Thoreau clearly needed to fit his adventures into an orderly calendrical structure. The days of the week were not only a travel framework but scaffolding for the philosophical discussions punctuating the journey and filling most of the book. Similarly, his sojourn at Walden Pond was two years and two months, but literary needs dictated a backdrop of four seasons so he condensed the experiences into a single year. When editing an edition of *Walden*, Teale was astounded at how much material originated in journal entries Thoreau made after he had left the pond.

Did it matter that each book lacked a transcript's exactitude? Rather than taking exhaustive minutes of his Walden stay, Thoreau wrote a book about the high points, the "greatest hits" of his life at the pond. If he altered actual occurrences a little to make for better reading and a more coherent story, didn't he therefore make the truth more compelling? Wasn't the tale true as long as it remained essentially factual? "Anything we think of at any time before our book goes in is fair material to include," Teale advised Zwinger.

I found solace in Thoreau's molding of actual experience to create a work of art. After all, I was trying to construct a connected tale out of a diffuse and disjoint series of excursions undertaken with three different companions. At least Thoreau, as well as Mungo and McPhee, took trips in which one day followed the other. Mine were a series of fragments separated by weeks, months, even a year in a couple of cases. The continuity of the rivers in both space and time and the gravitational force of my own imagination were holding the story together, not an accumulation of consecutive days. Could there be more powerful unifying forces? Besides, I was making no attempt to hide the discontinuous voyaging or blend disparate events seamlessly into the narrative. I had approximately a week's worth of traveling days, if not a Sunday-to-Saturday week.

As we approached the towering paired bridges carrying Interstate 93 across the river, houses became more modest. Soon we spied the big boxes of Kohl's, Home Depot, and Target through the trees. A mere scramble up the bank and we could have purchased most any item the world's economy offered. Because they were chain operations with corporate formulas for design, layout, and merchandise, we'd know exactly what aisles to find what we wanted, whether an overcoat, end table, or lawnmower. Though we were hours from home, the same exact stores lay within a twenty-minute drive of where we lived. There was something unnerving in the notion that we could step inside one of them and suddenly all distance from home would disappear.

"Want to run in and get a flat-screen TV?" I asked with a sarcastic grin. "A flyer in this morning's paper had them marked way down."

"You want to sink us?"

"I just thought running into a familiar store might cure any homesickness. Besides, we could catch the Sox game at lunch."

"You *trying* to irritate me?" Pam replied playfully. "I hate going into those places even when I have to. Besides, wise guy, where are you going to plug it in?"

"A currant bush?" I laughed at my own stupid joke.

"Think you're funny, do you?" she said, slapping her paddle sharply on the river and sending a tidal wave of water my way. "Hope that doesn't dampen your sense of humor," she added, looking back at a startled guy in a splash-splotched T-shirt and jeans.

Below the bridge the incessant sound of speeding cars and trucks seemed amplified by the river's slow, quiet pace. Regardless of traffic sounds, big-box stores, or houses crowding the shore, the day couldn't have been more perfect. The hours were filled with sunlit warmth. Ever-shifting cumulus clouds raced across the sky below feathery streaks of high cirrus that grew like frost on a winter window. There was also warmth and comfort in Pam's wide smile as she turned to splash me, her face glowing with an affection that drenched my entire being. I wanted to drown in that smile.

Thoreau may have tweaked his plotline a bit, mythologized the present and used mock heroic language to elevate the gravity of his voyage, but we accept his account as truthful, even more so than a

plain retelling, because it has psychological depth. The trip was un-
remarkable, just a couple of young guys on a boating vacation. But the
book is much more.

Writers increasingly blur the line between fact and fiction. At times,
there is no telling where one begins and the other leaves off. Under
the rubric of "writing what you know," we are, perhaps, more tolerant of having real life inserted into fiction than of accepting fabrica-
tions woven into memoir. But the barriers between genres have been
deteriorating for generations. Hardly the work of charlatans, some of
America's greatest writers have intentionally perforated the boundary. Norman Mailer has written more than one "true life novel," and
Philip Roth's *The Facts: A Novelist's Autobiography* not only tells the
author's life story, but includes one letter addressed to and another
from a fictional character created in other works.

We tend to be skeptical of biographical details and scrutinize them
closely because the differences between fact and fiction in a person's
life are often difficult to discern. However vivid and believable the life
of a individual seems, we demand to know whether particular incidents are true or fanciful. Our understanding of a person's character
depends on it.

We are forgiving when actual places are a blend of reality and fiction, sometimes finding their spell so complete we feel we know
scenes that live only in the writer's mind. Whether it's the Nebraska
prairie of Willa Cather or F. Scott Fitzgerald's Long Island in *The Great
Gatsby*, these real places still ring true despite infusion with fictional
elements such as a house or a hill that doesn't precisely exist. As long
as the portrayal fits the basic context of the place, neither reality nor
fiction is compromised. The landscape is resilient enough to admit
imagination. Thoreau's descriptions of his days on the water in 1839
are of less interest than the creative power he brought to those common moments.

In a playful extreme of make-believe fused to a real place, Michael
Martone wrote *The Blue Guide to Indiana*, a mock travel handbook to
his native state. It reads and is laid out like a classic travel guide, with
notes on weather, currency, and what to wear. Visitors are offered travel tips to the "Site of [1940 Republican presidential candidate] Wendell

Willkie's Ascension into Heaven," the location of "The Trans-Indiana Mayonnaise Pipeline," and the "Annual Baking Powder Festival Commemorating the Great Explosion of 1879." No one could mistake such trumped-up places and events for real. But liberated from Indiana's true topography and history, Martone's *Guide* infuses the actual landscape with an essential essence that speaks to the place's spirit as conveyed through an author's imagination. Especially today, when Chamber of Commerce propaganda extolling even the dullest places are legion, aren't we most interested in seeing behind façades and viewing the world through the prism of a creative mind?

Whether authors are writing fiction, memoir, or an amalgam, readers need to trust their sensibilities. This is only possible when writers are honest about what they are trying to accomplish, regardless of fact or fiction. Thus, we can forgive Hemingway his sleight of geography in placing Michigan's Big Two-Hearted River south and west of where it actually runs in his famous 1925 story that adopts the stream's name as its title. Rather than mislead, the topographical switcheroo reinforces the action of the story, making it all the more compelling.

James Frey breached that trust in *A Million Little Pieces*, his 2005 tale of addiction and recovery, not because he mixed fact and fiction, but because he tried to pass off as actual happenings the clever and well-executed inventions of his own mind. The charade was perpetrated not just through the pages of his work but on national television where he duped talk-show diva Oprah Winfrey and violated the carefully cultivated trust her program has with its audience. Frey not only embellished a few incidents and altered some facts, he created entire characters and fabricated scenes critical to his narrative, including a three-month jail term. Allegedly, he turned what was originally a novel into memoir after seventeen publishers had rejected his manuscript. We may love escaping into a story, but we still crave reality.

"Kind of a schizophrenic shoreline," I said, interrupting about twenty minutes of rhythmic, soporific paddling. "Houses one moment, woods the next. Hard to know what's the real Merrimack."

"Quiet!" Pam said softly, but emphatically. She pointed to the east shore. "Look how close we are."

Only a few canoe lengths away, a great blue heron stood as immobile as a sculpted work of art. It appeared to stare at us from an un-blinking, sharply focused yellow eye, a black plume of feathers swept back on its mostly white head. Standing at the water's edge stretching a long neck, it stood nearly four feet tall.

As we drifted ever closer, the heron was no longer just a tall, slate-hued bird, but a luminously colored avian marvel in shades of white, brown, yellow, and black, its feathers differing in texture, shape, and length, a flossy ruff at the base of its neck. Then without warning, it stretched and double-clutched its wings. We jumped! With a whoosh, the bird was airborne, emitting a deep throaty croak as it flew far downstream and landed on the opposite shore.

We turned toward each other and grinned. "I can't believe you didn't see that," Pam said.

"Guess I was lost in thought."

"Try not to get lost. Knowing you, you'll miss the whole trip. You don't always focus on what's right in front of you," she scolded loving-ly. "You spend too much time in your mind sometimes."

"Check out that cluster of mallards just to our left," I replied. "And I think there're some Canada geese below the bluff where the river bends up ahead."

Mesmerized by bright light, reflective water, and repetitive, rhyth-mic paddling, I gazed at the arched back of my blond, woolly-haired companion, her curls filled with sunlight. I couldn't look at her with-out dreaming of the ring I was having our neighborhood jeweler fash-ion for our engagement. I planned to slip it on her finger in a couple of weeks. I speculated on married life with her, a long future of growing old and going places together. As powerful as Pamela's love was, it was her willingness to be loved that most aroused my ardor and provided comfort. At the moment, even the deepest cynic in me couldn't imag-ine how difficult and hurtful our relationship would become at times in the future. She was the love of my life.

My feelings for Pam enabled me to better comprehend what few people realize about *A Week on the Concord and Merrimack Rivers*— that at its psychological center, it is a love story. Surely, it is a straight-forward river journey by oar and sail that involves camping and canals and encounters with boatmen and local inhabitants. It is also rich with philosophical digressions that implicate Greek philosophers, English poets, the Bhagavad Gita, and American Indians. But Thoreau likely had no plans to write a book and might not have done so without the death of his beloved brother John, his unnamed companion of the narrative.

Scholars maintain that John's death most determines the themes and action of *A Week*, including the elegiac meditation on autumnal phenomena in the last chapter. Thoughts of fall seem odd for a trip concluding in late summer when trees hadn't yet turned color, but its symbolism in remembering the deceased fits perfectly. The book was a species of memorial for Thoreau and a means of working through and healing his loss. Its writing must have dredged up powerfully painful memories, as if he were fussing daily with an open sore. Recalling good times with a lost loved one always hurts the most.

Though my experience lacked the cruel, accidental finality of Thoreau's, in my sometimes broken relationship with Pam, I would feel loss and the harsh self-doubt of faded opportunity by the time I came to write. There was a sweetness in our early times together I was sure I would never taste again.

John Thoreau had "a simple, uncomplicated nature, free from uncertainties and capable of easy happiness," according to Thoreau biographer Henry S. Canby. He was social, deeply religious, and an amateur naturalist with charm unlike any others in his family. Exceedingly thin and always in frail health, he was neat and meticulous compared with his long-haired and unkempt brother. Henry much admired John, looking up to him as his best friend. At the time of their river trip, they had opened a school together.

On New Year's Day of 1842, little more than two years after their voyage, John nicked the end of his left ring finger while stropping his razor. Thinking it just a routine cut, he bandaged it. But eight days later he found the skin had "mortified." He complained of a stiffening jaw on the morning of January ninth, and by evening he had lockjaw, with painful convulsive spasms. A doctor from Boston concluded that nothing could be done. John accepted his fate calmly and was nursed by his brother. Two days later, he died in Henry's arms. He was twenty-seven years old.

Thoreau was in shock; he became passive and kept his feelings to himself. He came down with a psychological case of lockjaw complete with all the symptoms and didn't write in his journal for about six weeks. With John's death, Canby wrote, "a balance wheel was taken from the delicate machinery of Henry's mind." No wonder that the heart of *A Week* is a nine-thousand-word discourse on love and friendship.

After Pam and I passed the trim green meadows of the Intervale Country Club, houses began crowding the shore, becoming increasingly modest as we worked our way downstream against a slight but building headwind. Many looked like they had started as simple summer cottages, growing over the years into an eye-catching mishmash of designs. An unpredictable variety of windows, railings, decks, seawalls, rooflines, and steps created an intricate and eclectic texture that displayed the ingenuity of generations. It reminded me of Rio Vista along the Concord, only more elaborate and scrubbed.

"We should live in that one with all the windows," Pam said, pointing to a place where the porch had been glassed in to extend the living room.

"How about sharing some morning coffee on the deck of that big bungalow up ahead?" I answered. "Imagine me serving you at a small glass café table. I'd put out a vase with a rose in it."

"Only if I could drag you into the bedroom afterward." I gazed longingly at the seductive curve of her back. She turned with an impish grin and arched eyebrow. "That wouldn't be a problem, would it?"

"Not at all."

"Didn't think so," she laughed.

The future seemed to promise such easy domesticity. There would be summer breakfasts on the porch and winter evenings in front of the fireplace.

Perhaps similar dreams entertained Thoreau, for at the time the brothers floated on these same waters, he had a woman on his mind. He was hopelessly in love. Unfortunately, John was in love with the same woman. Ellen Sewall was an attractive, intelligent, and vivacious young lady who had come to Concord for a couple of weeks that summer. Both Thoreau boys were immediately smitten, squiring her about the woods and fields of their hometown. "There is no remedy for love but to love more," was the single-sentence entry in Henry's journal of July 25, 1839.

A month after Ellen's departure, the brothers launched their boat on the Concord. How could their fraternal rivalry for Ellen's affection not have been a strong undercurrent in their relationship as they spent two weeks with hardly a moment out of each other's sight?

The boat was barely out of the water upon their return when John left to see Ellen at her family's home in Scituate, Massachusetts. After Ellen visited Concord the following year, John again went to Scituate in July and romantically proposed to her as they walked on the beach breathing salt air and listening to the pounding surf. At first, she accepted, but later changed her mind under family pressure. Typically more cerebral than romantic, Henry proposed by letter in November. After consulting with her father, an old-line conservative clergyman who scoffed at the wild ideas of Emerson and his acolytes, she rejected him as well. Two years later, she was engaged to a young minister, whom she married in 1844.

By the time Thoreau began writing his book in 1845, his dear brother was dead and the only woman he ever loved was married to another man. How this must have colored his recollections of the voyage and given power and emotional viscosity to the writing. A casual reader would never know. But delving deeply into text and context reveals a man's heart, though it is well hidden in a protective and healing chrysalis of words.

An author's life at the time of writing influences a book as much as the inspiration that gave birth to the idea or the subject about which he or she writes. Only by knowing both can we divine a work's true center of gravity. By the time I wrote these words, Pam and I were, sadly, no longer wearing the engagement rings that had been on our fingers for a year and a half. Our love struggled with circumstances and heartache for several years, but except for brief intervals, the rings stayed off. "I heard that an engagement was entered into," wrote Thoreau in *A Week*, "and then I heard that it was broken off, but I did not know the reason in either case." Neither did I. Perhaps knowing was too painful for Henry. It was for me.

The best books are not merely entertainment, a conduit for information, or escape from daily existence. They contain the very stuff of life. If we travel deeply among their words, we will find unexpected echoes and refractions of our own condition. The most vigorous writing is just well-considered speech.

A Week may be somewhat dull and ungainly, but its unique fusion of inward and outward experience speaks to me. "For books are not absolutely dead things," wrote John Milton in 1644, "but doe contain a potencie of life in them to be as active as that soule was whose progeny they are; nay they do preserve as in a violl the purest efficacie and extraction of that living intellect that bred them." Inasmuch as Thoreau mentions Milton several times in *A Week*, I'm sure he was familiar with those words. I feel the potency of Henry's life in his book. I'm certain he intended it that way.

The river grew straight and broadened, its surface sparkling and rippling with wind gusts. On the west, three tall radio transmitters stood like hypodermic needles injecting blather into the air. We paddled toward the boxy geometric skyline of Manchester floating on the horizon. The wide, water-paved highway seemingly led directly to the city's center.

"Watch out for the wake of that water skier," I warned Pam. "We need to slice it on a diagonal or we could flip."

"We've also got two Sea-Doos coming up on our left which are going to hit us the other way," she shouted over the rumble of an outboard motor.

The river was increasingly busy with speeding powerboats and those whining motorcycles of the water known as "personal watercraft." Anglers in wide, open cockpit vessels trolled the shoreline. Thoreau encountered many canal boats, their sails to the wind on a river that spread "out into a lake reaching a mile or two without a bend." He had neither noise nor wakes to complain about.

The river was on Thoreau's mind when he first retired to Walden Pond. It wasn't just out of some high-minded philosophical resolution that he built his cabin by the wooded shore, but in order to find the hours of solitude to write *A Week*. Like many of us, he needed to get away for a little peace and quiet. Free from distractions, he could give his thoughts and emotions full play. He brooded over the narrative as an experience never to be repeated, wrote Canby. "And as he brooded his inner life attached itself to those memories, enriched them, and set its own memorial next to the record."

The alchemy of the nostalgic boat trip, John's death, and the rapid change brought by railroads and the prodigious growth of industrial cities like Lowell and Manchester fomented a new kind of outdoor writing, one that insinuates a personality into the landscape. The beholder of natural phenomena is no longer a bystander or an observer merely, but a participant. The notion would reach its fruition in *Walden* where Thoreau warns readers at the outset that he is abandoning polite conventions of the past: "In most books, the *I*, or first person, is omitted; in this it will be retained; that, in respect to egotism, is the main difference." It was a difference I felt keenly as my personal life seemed increasingly braided with the landscapes around me.

Today, Thoreau is considered a genius, and *A Week on the Concord and Merrimack Rivers* is continuously printed in multiple editions. But like James Frey and many first-time authors, Thoreau had trouble finding a publisher for his work, spending more than a year shopping the book around and rewriting. At a loss for what else to do, he at last underwrote publication of one thousand volumes in 1849.

Thoreau put everything he had into *A Week*. It is an anthology of his learning and reading. It is chock-full of autobiography, travel adventure, emotional memoir, imaginative philosophizing, and digressive essays on disparate topics that can make difficult reading. Although admired for its organic and original form, the bewilderment expressed by literary critic Brooks Atkinson, who called it "a gloriously elaborated, incoherent chronicle of a boating trip," is commonly felt. Even Emerson, Thoreau's friend and most ardent advocate, called the story line "a very slender thread for such big beads & ingots as are strung on it." Noting that the book is 90 percent digression and 10 percent narrative, McPhee found the writing "commentary, editorial, homiletic—defying generic assignment." It "would be almost pure free association were it not for the river reeling him back in."

After the book suffered mixed reviews and little readership, the publisher returned 706 copies of *A Week* to a deeply disappointed Thoreau in 1853, after much acrimony. "I have now a library of nearly nine hundred volumes," he recorded with dark humor in his journal, "over seven hundred of which I wrote myself."

The headwind stiffened as Pam and I approached the Amoskeag Bridge at the big dam of the same name, and we struggled to make every foot of progress. When at last we took out on the west side of the river at a rough, dirt track near some red-roofed condos built too close to the shore, I had a sun-baked headache and was glad to reach shade where I no longer had to squint. An older Hispanic man was fishing and chatting on a cell phone as we lifted the boat up the rocky, root-tangled path.

"Was this book about the rivers Thoreau's favorite?" Pam asked in gasps of breath as we struggled up the trail with the bulky boat.

"Hard to say. He only published two in his lifetime. *The Maine Woods*, *Cape Cod*, and the other stuff were collected after he died."

"Yeah, but this was about his brother," she insisted as we heaved the canoe onto the pickup's roof. As a girl, Pam had lost an eleven-year-old brother to an aneurysm, so her words had an unbearable poignancy. I caught her face in a fleetingly pensive moment, probably flashing through memories that could be explained in neither a snapshot nor a paragraph.

"On the day Thoreau died of tuberculosis, he lay in bed too weak to even hold a book while his sister, Sophia, read to him from *A Week*. She got to a part where a tailwind is pushing him and his brother down a wide open reach. Out of his half-comatose state, Thoreau said: 'Now comes good sailing.' Then, recalling his Maine adventures, he uttered his last comprehensible words: 'Moose' and 'Indian.' An instant later, he was dead."

"That says it all," Pam replied, slapping the dirt from her hands. "Done deal." After years of hospice work, she understood well what goes on in people's minds as their last moments draw nigh. "And a sister would know."

Walled City

We do not recollect any incident for many years, the occurrence of which,
has caused so general a feeling of deep interest in the community, as the
cause of the Africans captured in the Spanish schooner Amistad. . . .
The crime, for which they are committed, in the technical language
of the law, is called murder or piracy—perhaps both; and
the punishment of either is death. In the language of
humanity they have committed no crime at all.
Boston Courier, September 9, 1839

Police Arrest 11 in Gate City Narcotics Raid
Manchester Union Leader, September 9, 1969

Cost of fighting terrorism: $87B
Lowell Sun, September 8, 2003

Within sight of the squabby Ramada Inn where McPhee and his son-
in-law spent the night a year earlier, Pam and I lifted the canoe off our
pickup as traffic whizzed by on the busy ramp connecting Interstate
293 to the Amoskeag Bridge. Carrying it across a margin of rough lawn,
we slid it down a steep, narrow path of dirt and grass like a bobsled.
We passed through a dense stand of bamboolike Japanese knotweed,
then along a chain-link fence at the edge of a large, boxy hydro plant
of brick and concrete until finally arriving at the muddy edge of the
river almost several stories lower than the water we had paddled the
day before.

Under an increasingly leaden sky we launched from a crescent of
beach into the dark tailrace pool, a back eddy of water escaping the
dam. When the Thoreau boys passed through, a stone dam was under construction, averaging eight feet high in one section and thirty-
four in another. But neither the dam nor the falls forced them to portage. Instead, they used the Amoskeag Canal and locked themselves
through "the successive watery steps of this river's stair-case in the
midst of a crowd of villagers, jumping into the canal to their amuse-

ment, to save our boat from upsetting, and consuming much river water in our service."

The eroded trail served as our canal, and we lacked the cinematic South Pacific–like spectacle of natives diving around our boat. Rather, we put in under the watchful eye of yet another great blue heron, standing stock-still and coldly surveying our activities. As we pushed off with our paddles, the bird took flight. We had seen several the day before, but there was something inspiriting in finding such a wild and untamable creature, almost pterodactyl-like, doing its fishing so close to dams and noisy highways in a city of more than one hundred thousand people.

As we pulled into the current, I glanced upstream at the patched, cracked, and spalled concrete face of the dam. Although it weeped in spots, a craving for electricity ensured that little water escaped. Instead, it was funneled through penstocks to spin turbines. No water cascaded over the spillway save in flood times or during the freshets of April and early May when melting White Mountain snows rushed toward the sea.

Immediately below the masonry wall was a mountainous moonscape of dry, barren rock. Among the jumbled boulders and rough, jagged ledges were pockets of tangled vegetation and a few trickles of water. This was all that remained of the mighty Amoskeag Falls, whose thunder was once heard for miles as it churned the water to a milky froth and sent dense mists heavenward.

"Are you sure we're going to make it through those rocks?" Pam asked, squinting at the river ahead with uncharacteristic hesitancy. "I never did rapids like this before. Those whitecaps are just smiling sharks waiting to bite us."

"I'll rudder around the big obstacles from the stern. Just look out for small stuff I might miss. Push us quickly away with your paddle."

"If we go over, I'll blame you."

"I'm not worried," I said confidently. "Anyway, it wouldn't be the first time I've taken a few gulps of river water."

Dropping more than fifty feet in half a mile, the falls once defined this spot. Without them, there would be no Manchester. Even in their absence, a deep traveler sees their ongoing influence in the relationship of people to this place. Though their water is manipulated through pipes and their position as the area's signal feature has been supplanted by redbrick mills and office towers, the falls are still a seat of power and prosperity. Their force continues to generate electricity, and the remaining rapids attract tourists for their beauty and competitive canoeing and kayaking.

For thousands of years nomadic natives visited the falls, fishing the plenteous runs of salmon, eel, shad, and herring whose upstream progress was stymied by the powerful, swirling water. The name Amoskeag derives from an Indian word meaning "the great fishing place." The Penacooks eventually established a permanent settlement on a bluff above the falls on the river's east side, today occupied by office buildings. During spring fish runs, they feasted, danced, and held councils. They built crude weirs of brush and branches across the river to trap the fish, which they then caught with spears and dip nets.

The falls' awesome appearance and the legendary fishery also drew the first Europeans. At the 1851 Manchester Centennial Celebration, William Stark said, "My father has seen the shad so thick as to crowd each other in their passage up the falls to gain the smooth water above, so that you could not put in your hand without touching some of them, and yet there were more alewives than shad, and more eels than both."

Among early whites was Joseph Seccombe, an itinerant backwoods preacher who styled himself Fluviatulis Piscator, meaning "River Fisher." In 1739, a century before Thoreau, he delivered a sermon at the falls. Subsequently printed as "Business and Diversion Inoffensive to God, and Necessary for the Comfort and Support of Human Society. A Discourse Utter'd in Part at Ammauskeeg-Falls, in the Fishing Season," it can be considered America's first sport-fishing publication.

Migratory fish continue to be seen on the Amoskeag fishway, a fifty-four-step fish ladder where shad, sea lamprey, and herring jump from pool to pool one foot at a time to reach their spawning grounds above the dam. Interactive exhibits and programs at an adjacent interpretive center describe the river, wildlife, fish biology, Native Americans, geology, manufacturing, and hydroelectricity. In less than an hour, the whys and wherefores of the region are revealed. The dam, buildings, highways and streets, rivers, hills, and wild creatures become not only visible, but comprehensible. Order emerges from chaos. Deep travel made easy.

At the dawn of the nineteenth century, the falls were both an obstacle to navigation, overcome by a canal and locks, and a source of power for manufacturing. The boat canal opened in 1807 after fourteen years of difficult work, including two aborted attempts ending in lock failure. The first of two power canals was constructed from the head of the falls in 1837 by the Amoskeag Manufacturing Company. This canal eventually grew to 5,000 feet long and dropped 20 feet to a second canal extending 7,250 feet before falling another 34 feet to the river.

Until 1880, the company ran wholly by means of waterpower. The falling water spun turbines connected to crown gears that turned flywheels with leather belts, transferring energy to horizontal shafts along the ceiling on each story of a mill. Individual machines were driven by smaller belts connected to the overhead driveshaft.

By 1896 electricity was widely used in the mills, and in 1924 the company installed at the dam three seventy-five-hundred-horsepower turbines with associated generators to produce sixteen megawatts of electricity. After the Amoskeag Company dissolved a dozen years later, the facilities were bought by the Public Service Company of New Hampshire, which continues to generate enough electricity from the falls to power, perhaps, twelve hundred to sixteen hundred homes. Amoskeag hydro is renewable energy that cuts dependence on foreign oil. It is also "green" energy that doesn't contribute to air pollution and the implications that would have for global warming. Yet, though it seems almost unpatriotic and antienvironmental, a part of me longs to see the unfettered foaming of the falls, to feel them booming in my chest and watch their thick rising fog obscure the sky.

Only a shadow of its former power, the water nevertheless rapidly pulled our canoe downstream toward a horizon of glass and steel office towers where the shore was defined by massive textile mills. We back-paddled to slow our progress, buying time to navigate past boulders and ledges, finding smooth water chutes in the white, curling rapids.

All senses on high alert, Pam and I moved quickly through rock gardens, among swirls and eddies. We read the water with our eyes, listened for the sound of foaming curlers, and felt with our bodies as the current tugged the boat in zigzags. For long minutes we endured a white-knuckle rollercoaster of a ride that simultaneously terrorized us and made us smile. Traveling in the opposite direction through the same roiling water and enduring the tedium of slow progress, McPhee speculated that "it was easier hauling upstream," poling and lining his canoe rather than fast-forwarding among the rocks.

Manchester seemed a walled city from our tiny vessel. A mile of fortresslike mills with stair and clock towers lined the river's east bank, peering down from tall, divided-light windows high above the water. Dark stone foundations below the redbrick walls revealed arched intake or discharge structures and a few protruding pipes. The west bank had a wild aspect, with thick vegetation, jumbled rocks, and sandbars. Occasionally, we glimpsed I-293, the Everett Turnpike, whose whooshing sound of whizzing traffic was ever present and had fooled McPhee into thinking there were more rapids. Before their demolition for the highway, mills had towered over the west bank as well.

Europeans settled at Amoskeag Falls as early as 1720, and thirty-one years later the town of Derryfield was incorporated. Early residents grasped the falls' industrial potential and changed the town's name to Manchester in 1810 as homage to the great English manufacturing city.

These were among facts we had gleaned a couple of days earlier while walking through the Millyard Museum, which is housed in a renovated factory building a block from the river. It didn't take much historical knowledge, perspicacity, or research to understand where we were. Anyone with six bucks could see the exhibits and get a quick course on settlement, agriculture, waterpower, labor, ethnic groups, urban development, natural history, and other subjects. Again, deep travel made easy.

After our meander through the museum, we'd scouted the rapids from the Riverwalk, a narrow pedestrian passage sandwiched between the Merrimack and the mills. We stared at the turbulent water as the hulking brick buildings cast a long shadow from behind us. After spending time with displays of old factory photos, hydropower illustrations, and explanations of local geology, we felt the connections among people, the ledges, flowing water, factories, and the city with sudden and compelling logic.

On the river it was easy to forget history and science as the canoe bounced and we moved instinctually at a pace that didn't permit contemplation. "What's with all these overhead wires?" Pam shouted above the rapids shortly after we'd passed beneath Bridge Street.

"Let's eddy-turn and stop below that boulder," I suggested, quickly pointing downstream with my paddle as she turned to steal a glance at me.

I angled us toward a big gray rock, and just as the bow reached beyond it, Pam dug her paddle straight into the water. The boat pivoted around, and suddenly we were facing upriver in the calm of an eddy formed behind the huge stone. Just upstream a grid of wires was strung above the water. On the east shore was the only break in the wall of mills, an amphitheater of steps leading from a plaza down to the river.

Pam turned toward me with an unquenchable grin. "That was some bucking bronco ride!"

"Not too scary?"

"I didn't say that," she said, unable to repress her smile.

"Anyway, the wires are . . ."

"I get it now," Pam said, slapping her forehead. "Those steps are at Arms Park along the Riverwalk, and the wires are where they hung the slalom gates for the kayak race we saw yesterday."

"We should've had sunglasses to look at some of those boats. There isn't a florist with such a stock of bright colors."

"Maybe an orchid shop."

"What would some of those old-time mill workers have thought if they could've looked out the windows? People playing in the water where they knew only hard work? A park in the middle of the millyard would've seemed crazy. The river's gone from workhorse to playground. I guess we're part of it."

"The park was nice, but from here it seems strange having a gap in the mills—like a missing front tooth."

"A lady at the museum told me that there was a textile plant there once. In the late 1950s Arms Manufacturing accidentally received anthrax-contaminated goat hides. Nine people got sick."

"Did anyone die?"

"Four or five, I think. For a while workers had to get vaccinated, but someone at a nearby building became infected and died. Eventually they decontaminated the mill, tore it down, burned it, and buried the remains."

"Shades of 9/11."

"Someday that'll just be history, too."

"At least something good came from tearing down that mill. Hundreds of people were in the park yesterday."

Turning the bow of the boat into the current, we were swept out of the eddy and downstream toward the Granite Street Bridge. Like all of Manchester's bridges, it was strictly functional, just a concrete deck supported by steel I-beams. Empty stone piers, now serving as vegetated pillars and roost sites for birds, marked the location of ghost bridges from the past. In the midst of New Hampshire's largest city, the mills created some of the most intriguing and dramatic scenery along Thoreau's route, albeit manmade, and among the best whitewater for canoeists seeking a thrill ride.

When Henry and John Thoreau floated this stretch in 1839, the textile capital of Manchester was under construction and about two thousand people lived there. Although manufacturing had begun thirty years earlier, the Amoskeag Manufacturing Company, incorporated in 1831, was just implementing plans for a cotton complex larger and more intricate than the world had ever seen. Waterpower rights had been purchased for the entire length of the Merrimack; one mill had begun operating, and another was close to completion. The first mile-long power canal had been finished and the second was being built. The sluiced water, Thoreau observed, "falls thirty or forty feet over seven or eight steep and narrow terraces of stone" and "did not seem to be the worse for the wear, but foamed and fumed as purely, and boomed as savagely and impressively as a mountain torrent, and though it came from under a factory, we saw a rainbow here."

Building mills, however impressive, was only part of the plan. Amoskeag had purchased more than fifteen thousand acres of land by 1835 and was erecting a city. Where Thoreau saw woods and meadows, the company envisioned a community of tree-shaded streets, prosperous stores, and comfortable houses.

Wanting to build a classic company town, the corporation was laying out roads and millyards. Six blocks of boarding houses had been constructed. Land for parks, churches, and public buildings was at the larges of the company, and the previous October had seen the first public land sale for house and business sites. By an elaborate set of restrictions and rules, even such private development was controlled down to the type of building materials. Through the company's ownership of virtually all industrial land, no new industry could settle in Manchester for a century save at the company's sufferance. With such autocratic control, Amoskeag brought an enviably coordinated and comprehensive approach to urban design. But this was not what Thoreau had come to see, and he made "haste to get past the village here collected, and out of hearing of the hammer which was laying the foundation of another Lowell on its banks."

The river moved us speedily beneath the Granite Street Bridge near the city's center where the west bank of the river became a featureless concrete wall supporting I-293. A couple of days earlier we'd had lunch at Jillian's, a watering hole in the mill building just above the bridge. The interior was vast, with high ceilings and sunlight pouring through tall windows overlooking the river. Where looms once rumbled among the brick walls and hardwood floors, large-screen televisions, pool tables, and video games were positioned among dining tables and around the bar.

Jillian's was very different from the small, local joint where Pam and I had met, but any place with a bar reminded me of our first meeting. I was sitting on the last available stool that hot August evening and struck up a conversation about gardening, blueberry picking, and jam making with the bespectacled blond next to me. Never before a believer in love at first sight, I was nonetheless hopelessly smitten by eyes the color of faded blue jeans, a whisky voice, and shapely shoulders. Straight talking and affectionate, Pam seemed the perfect anti-dote to the long, loveless marriage I had barely escaped. Every bar we'd walked into since reeled my memory back to that moment, arousing unexpected passion.

Everything we wore that humid night two years ago was made of cotton, and save for rain jackets, the same was true as we paddled past the massive mills—T-shirts, jeans, sweatshirts, even our underwear. At some time during the day, just about everyone on the planet wears something made of cotton, observes Stephen Yafa, author of a cultural history of the fiber.

Amoskeag was among the mills that made this possible. In the 1790s, 4 percent of all clothing was made of cotton; a century later, that percentage was 73. Over these decades the company experienced preternatural growth until it became the world's largest textile man-ufacturer. In 1856, it produced 67,000 yards of cloth daily, enough to stretch 38 miles. By 1912, it wove 471 miles of cloth each day—147,119 miles each year, enough to swaddle the earth's circumference almost six times. At their peak a few years later, the mills encompassed eight million square feet and employed seventeen thousand workers.

But Amoskeag wasn't just making cloth for sheets, trousers, drap-ery, blankets, and the shirts on the nation's backs; it was the great-est exemplar of an economic and social system that transformed the country. Cotton gave birth to the American industrial revolution and established a factory system imitated in the making of other products. It transformed the nature of work from occupations largely dictated by natural rural rhythms to ones of precision time set by the tolling of bells and sound of steam whistles. It brought great wealth to newly established manufacturing cities and to the southern states where slavery spread as demand for cotton increased. "The crop that made America a self-sufficient international power," Yafa writes, "had come close to destroying it from within" as an underlying cause of the Civil War.

Jobs generated from cotton manufacture fostered the melting pot, with diverse immigrants that in Manchester included the Irish, Greeks, Poles, Jews, French Canadians, Swedes, Belgians, Germans, and others. Though Amoskeag has been closed for seventy years, the effect of these groups is still present in the churches, social clubs, eateries, and other businesses that have made Manchester prosperous. It can be seen in telephone listings and faces on the street. Weaving cotton may be long over, but the social fabric the mills created remains a lasting legacy.

Just downstream of the Granite Street Bridge a large pipe was marked with a sign indicating a sewer outfall. Beyond it was a truss bridge supporting only a pipeline, and nearby were big masonry piers from what might have been a railroad crossing. Around it, pieces of old cut stone and rusting metal lay in the river, providing perches for cormorants. Many bird-foot impressions were left in the sand collecting in the lee of the piers, and mussels were scattered in the shallow water. We paused momentarily and gazed upstream at the stolid brick mills that remain Manchester's signature image.

"It's one thing to look at the buildings and know thousands of people were making millions of yards of fabric," Pam said as scattered raindrops created concentric circles in the quiet water behind the old piers, "but if we hadn't been through the museum, I never would've realized how boring the work was. If you ask me, the workers were mostly just babysitting their machines, just emptying and filling them. Can you imagine all that noise and vibration for hours on end?" She paused a moment, mulling over the right words. Her fair complexion reddened slightly, the resentment of an underappreciated and overworked home health-care aide reaching out over decades to other hard workers who never got their due. "These people only wanted a decent wage so they could have homes and get their kids schooled for better jobs. Those fat cats in Boston got rich on their sweat. You tell me how fair that is. And there's nothing historic or quaint about it. The same crap goes on today."

I rubbed my beard and pushed my glasses farther back on the bridge of my nose. "The owners and managers were like feudal lords," I said. "Look at the buildings. They're as big and substantial as castles. They've got walls, towers, and wrought iron gates. The canals probably seemed like moats."

"Forget the fancy architecture stuff for a moment," she shot back. "This company controlled everything. Even when it did good things like provide cheap housing, playgrounds, picnics, and baseball teams, it must have felt like the mills owned you. People need more than being taken care of. So what if the company sponsored visiting nurses? The workers needed dignity as well. I see the same thing in my job. Handicapped and old people who can still do things and make some decisions for themselves have it all taken away like they were imbeciles."

Pam was neither much interested in history nor a connoisseur of architecture, but our deep traveling had somehow connected her to this landscape, had entwined her personal experience with what she saw. Amoskeag was no longer just a big old factory converted to restaurants, shops, and offices. Her heart knew what sociologist Tamara Hareven and architectural historian Randolph Langenbach had described about this "closed and almost self-contained world." Workers had a deep, familylike attachment to Amoskeag but were "painfully aware of its hold over their lives."

Returning to the current, we passed the mouth of the "Piscataquog, or Sparkling Water" as Thoreau called it, a river yielding not a glisten under this day's cloudy sky as it flowed from beneath a bridge carrying I-293. The Queen City Bridge across the Merrimack was directly ahead, marking the south end of Manchester. Turning back to look one last time at the mills, I tried imagining what they were like when cotton was king, the images evoked by our visit to the museum superimposed on the present.

Though the museum's displays were mostly static and compressed into a small space, they had a riverlike flow. On the cascade of history, we floated from four-thousand-year-old stone axes and Indian encampments that sprang up in fishing season, to the rise and fall of Amoskeag and the recent development of Velcro and the Segway Personal Transporter in "the city that would not die" after the mills closed.

In addition to the hundreds of thousands of square feet the company devoted to its looms, Amoskeag was almost self-sufficient in its design, construction, and operations. It acquired brickworks and quarries for building. A foundry with huge furnaces and a giant lathe produced tie-rods and end caps, fences and gates, fire hydrants, lampposts, and decorative ironwork of every kind. The machine shop made both heavy machinery like looms and hand tools like wrenches and axes, items that other companies purchased from suppliers. During the Civil War the shop turned out military rifles and civilian shotguns. A museum display case holds a .58-caliber muzzle-loading rifle, partially complete carbine stocks, and barrel band and lock plate molds. The company also built locomotives, steam fire engines, cannons, and industrial sewing machines. It bought a bobbin factory and had its own print shop.

The Queen City Bridge carried vehicles high above the water, and a pipeline threaded through trusses beneath. Both banks were lined with trees, mostly silver maple. They leaned over the water and cast soft shadows in the gray light. Though the sky brightened and momentarily we caught a few rays of sun through gauzy clouds, the overcast soon thickened and light rain pelted us.

After record profits during the First World War, Amoskeag continued to add spindles to reduce fabric-making costs, discovering too late that the world's productive capacity far outstripped the market, especially in the wake of demobilization following the war. The company curtailed production, laid off workers, and cut wages. When these measures proved insufficient to regain profitability, the machines were sped up.

A damaging nine-month strike in 1922, the first long-term general strike in company history, engendered much bitterness when workers returned on company terms. There were some small-scale sit-down protests in various departments after the unsuccessful three-week national textile strike of 1934, but the company retained the upper hand. Labor unrest, shrinking markets, southern and overseas competition, management's failure to invest in new technologies, the advent of rayon, and the effects of the Great Depression left the company broke. The mills suddenly closed in September 1935, expecting to reopen after reorganization in bankruptcy. Surprisingly, the court ordered liquidation less than a year later, and the company was dissolved, crippling the economy of a city of seventy-five thousand.

Pam and I pulled out and stretched, ate a couple of granola bars and an apple on a sandbar where a small, unnamed watercourse entered

the big river near wooded Baker Island. The bank was steep and severely eroded from highway runoff but must have been a popular fishing spot, judging by the Y-shaped stakes at the water's edge where anglers had rested their rods. Bottles, driftwood, and a brown Christmas
tree were among the washed-up detritus.

As we snacked I caught a slight chill even though the air wasn't particularly cold. My Levi's had gotten a little wet when the tip of some
standing waves washed over the boat. Pam's Levi's also showed dark
patches where she'd caught a little spray in the bow.

"The denim for Levi's was made by Amoskeag," I said apropos of
nothing.

"No kidding."

"Levi Strauss was a Jewish immigrant from Bavaria who ran a San
Francisco dry goods business. He sold some cloth to a Nevada tailor
who hit on the idea of riveting pocket corners and other seams that
tended to rip out when worn by miners and loggers. Short on cash to
pay for the patent, the tailor dropped Strauss a letter asking him to
underwrite the cost. The two went into business together in the 1870s,
and here we are wearing riveted Levi's."

"So we're kind of wearing the descendants of Amoskeag denim."

"I'm told some styles are still made the same way."

Blue jeans would become the most universal and American article
of clothing, Yafa writes. The fabric has an image of being honest, substantial, and tough. People wear them in as they wear them out, developing an affection and intimacy with the pants rivaled by no other
clothing. "Levi's are the single best item of apparel ever designed,"
said fashion maven Bill Blass. But Levi's weren't just a hard-working
pair of trousers. They were John Wayne, James Dean, Elvis Presley, and
Marlon Brando. They were also with Kerouac on the road, along the
beach at Big Sur, and at boozy late-night poetry readings and jazz im-
provisations. A natural and genuine product, they were an emblem to
Mungo and his countercultural colleagues out to remake the world of
the 1960s.

Not far downstream of Baker Island, modest newer homes stood on
the east bank and then on both sides, evidence of improvement in a
river Mungo found smelly and hopelessly polluted. Soon, both banks

were again seemingly wild and densely vegetated. Large trees with
massive limbs overhung the river. A red-tailed hawk perched on a low
horizontal branch, watching us intently as we passed within a couple
of canoe lengths.

Closure of the mills in 1935 was a crisis in the life of Manchester.
Fortunately, public-spirited civic and business leaders formed Amoskeag Industries, which purchased the failed company's buildings,
sold the waterpower and steam plants to the Public Service Company
of New Hampshire, and through much effort managed to rehabilitate
the mills and attract a variety of businesses. A decade later, more than
a hundred concerns in the old mills employed more than eleven thousand people.

Although a shoe manufacturer, knitting mills, machine shops, food
companies, and makers of cloth, rubber, and leather goods used some
of the mill space through the 1960s, most of the buildings were vacant
and rapidly growing derelict by the decade's end. Refusing to paddle
through Manchester on his 1969 trip and driving past instead, Mungo
dubbed it "the worst city on the planet." These were the days when the
mean-spirited and vicious publisher of the Manchester *Union Leader,*
William Loeb, wrote venomously right-wing front-page editorials. He
allegedly shot the office cat, called President Eisenhower a "stinking
hypocrite," and dubbed President Ford a "jerk." No wonder Mungo
would consider Manchester the most reactionary town in New England. On a small Riverwalk plaza just below Jillian's, Pam and I found
Loeb's name inscribed on a brick along with others. It was a pleasure
to put my heel to his memory.

Some of the mills had been vacant for forty years when entrepreneur
Dean Kamen, inventor of the Segway transporter, began buying and
renovating a few of the buildings in the 1980s for use by his own and
other high-tech companies. Then in 1991, a crisis caused by closure of
five of the state's six largest banks on a single day was midwife to the
creation of a Citizens Planning Revitalization Committee, or CPR, in-
volving two hundred community leaders desperate to resuscitate their
city. Building on the work Kamen had done, they developed a plan for
revitalizing Manchester, including getting other private developers
and the city to rehabilitate additional millyard properties.

Since Amoskeag's closing, some buildings have been demolished and the power canals filled, but most of the mills have been renovated. Professional offices, Internet and other technology-driven companies, architects, restaurants, marketing and advertising firms, and the Millyard Museum quietly occupy space once home to rhythmically clanking, dusty looms, and other industrial equipment. The smell of fabric and machine oil has long dissipated. Where canals and railroad tracks once paralleled the mills, there are now broad swaths of pavement. The busy millyard, with goods and raw materials shuttling from one place to another, is but a memory; only an occasional pedestrian or car moves through it today. The impressive buildings are a remembrance of things past, a kind of monumental tombstone. Nevertheless, they remain a vital and busy part of the city.

Housed behind the solid redbrick walls are Reynolds Centre for the Arts, Indoor Climbing Gym, Patriot Healthcare, Advantage Payroll Services, Milly's Tavern, WZID 95.7 FM, Kriss Cosmetics, The Bike Barn, Community Bible Fellowship, Millyard Furniture, and scores of other businesses. Once a company town, Manchester today has a diversified economy with more than two hundred manufacturers. About 85 percent of its workforce is in sales, finance, and service companies. In 1998, *Money* magazine labeled the community the "number one small city in the east." In retrospect, the city of Manchester was Amoskeag's finest and longest lasting product.

"Sometimes you sound like the Chamber of Commerce," Pam had teased as we walked hand-in-hand among the mills after our late lunch at Jillian's. "Give it a rest."

"It's an amazing transformation."

"I think it's kind of yuppie looking."

"At least the buildings still exist. They're Manchester's legacy, what makes it unique."

"None of the old-time mill workers could have afforded to eat or shop here."

"Well, it *is* kind of upscale and scrubbed."

"So what exactly is this legacy you're talking about? It's just a load of crap if you drive working people out for a bunch of bankers and stockbrokers. Read that book of interviews with old-time workers you bought at the museum. Those were the real people who built this place."

Over time, the mills have meant a variety of things to different people. To a young nation flexing its economic muscle, they were a sign of prosperity, independence, and strength, a "supreme expression of the unbounded confidence of the Victorian Age," according to Hareven and Langenbach. To owners, they were a source of wealth. To workers, they were at times a lifeline, allowing them to feed their families and providing order and meaning to their days; at other moments, they were a cruel oppressor, sucking life away with thankless toil. For the city, what was once a sign of dereliction and decay after Amoskeag shut its doors now stands as a proud reminder of the past and a symbol of the creative ingenuity, hard work, and commitment it took to turn Manchester around.

Regardless of their condition or who is looking at them, the mills are the very heart and emblem of Manchester. Just as the health of England under Arthur was reflected in that of the king, the well-being of the city is mirrored in the state of the brick behemoths along the water.

The buildings are so dominant and substantial that even a casual passerby can't help but be affected by them. As a young man traveling past on my way to hike in the White Mountains, they seemed a citadel guarding some fabulous mystery that beckoned me to explore. When Pam and I paddled the river and walked among the mills in a fugue of romance, they seemed more like cathedrals holding forth a kind of redemption we anticipated in a life together. Later, when our bond had frayed, the old brick structures lost their luster, seemed a somber and brooding presence. I imagined the tedious grind of the workers who exhausted their energies in service to Amoskeag. As my relationship with Pam waxed and waned, I realized that my sentiments toward the mills could be as complex as their actual history.

You can't go back in time, but as writer Rebecca Solnit observes, the scenes of experience "become the tangible landscape of memory, the places that made you, and in some way you too become them. They are what you can possess and what in the end possess you."

Our responses to landscapes often have less to do with geography than with our own psychological makeups. Whether it's a distant memory of a like place or the emotions flooding through us at the moment of first sight, we involuntarily invest ourselves in the landscapes we encounter. Our interior lives reflect conditions on the land, and the land renders palpable our inmost interior.

Streaming Relationships

. . . .

THE TREMONT THEATER has been open for a week and
the audiences, we believe, have been satisfied.

Boston Courier, September 9, 1839

Pat Nixon Booed

Manchester Union Leader, September 11, 1969

Murder conviction tossed out

Lowell Sun, September 9, 2003

. . . .

Pam and I approached Carthagina Island with the lofty twin spans
of I-293 looming beyond it. At two thousand feet long, the island was
narrow and thick with trees, especially tall pines and oaks. Thoreau
called it "the fairest which we had met with, with a handsome grove of
elms at its head." Admitting that "an island always pleases my imagination," he would have camped had it been evening. Though the elms
are long gone, it was comforting to see the island little changed since
the brothers passed its "densely wooded" shore. I, too, would have
camped had the hour been right.

On a big rock near the island's tip, McPhee observed a large, imper-
turbable, and satisfied bald eagle that "looked lazy, fat, accomplished,
interested mainly in its investments." Whether his description of "the
icon American bird" as a phlegmatic plutocrat was social commentary
on the decline of a once industrious Merrimack or the nation generally, I couldn't discern. The remark struck me as perversely Thoreauvian, perhaps with a dollop of caustic Mungo thrown in.

Pleased as we were by our conquest of the Amoskeag rapids, the
I-293 bridges were no triumphal arch for us. As we passed beneath
them we worried about Short's Falls just downstream. With boiling
whitewater drowning the sound of the interstate highway above us, we
knew we were in for heavy paddling.

The sky once again threatened rain as we hauled out the boat and
scouted the rapids from the stone outcrops above. Walking slowly

through thick brush on uneven ground, we watched as the noisy water churned and eddied around rocks and ledges in multiple directions before rolling into white, curling manes. McPhee called this drop of seven feet in eleven yards "the whitest water avoided by the Union Canal." Traveling upstream, he and Mark Svenvold lined their boat through quieter water along the shore and then dragged it over the ledges, sometimes wading chest deep as they held onto the gunwales. Thoreau and his brother took the canal.

"Are you sure we can do this?" Pam fretted as we stood on the angled gray rock, surveying the tumbling water.

"No problem," I said, squeezing her hand and projecting more confidence than I felt. Deftly moving in the loud, sudden chaos of tricky rapids was intuitive for an experienced paddler, but even the most cautious novice could easily get confused and make a mistake the river wouldn't forgive. "Don't be so nervous," I smiled. "You asked the same thing at the Amoskeag Dam and did fine." She shook her head in agreement and forced a return smile. Still, I wondered whether she realized how much more difficult it would be running these rips. There were patterns in the flow, ways to sluice among the rocks and avoid the shallows, but it wasn't going to be easy. "Remember, I'll be aiming us where we need to go. Just keep the boat from pinballing off the rocks and help get us into the right chute."

"I guess."

"Just follow the flow. The river will show the way." I pointed out curlers that hid rocks and those that were just standing waves. "We want to hit that big water at the end with our bow on the upswing," I advised. "Otherwise we'll get soaked."

As the sky darkened, I gave her a bear hug and a hard, deep kiss on the mouth that sent a current of warmth through my body. Still, we walked back to the boat more somberly than warranted. I knew she was strong and had reflexes quick enough to get us through. We had no choice but to rely on each other.

"You're sure we don't need to portage this?" Pam asked, turning toward me, her voice tense and her face a little drawn as we pushed off from shore.

"Too late now," I replied with a wide grin, turning us into the current.

We avoided the worst turbulence by running hard by the western shore. Sucked downstream by the water, the canoe moved quickly, buffeted by waves and unseen rocks in a rushing, hurricane-sounding maelstrom. I worked reflexively, steering in a zigzag from one glassy V of water to another, sliding over ledges and grazing the gunwales on a boulder. Pam leaned over hard at one point with a fast cross-draw stroke to avoid a submerged rock. A couple of quick twists, and we rolled into the big standing waves at the bottom.

Unfortunately, the bow bounced down just as we hit the first curler. The tip of the wave exploded in front of Pam, soaking her as the boat took on about three inches of water. Suddenly cold and wet, she turned to me with a grin usually seen on children getting off amusement park rides.

"That was fun!" she said, gesturing with two fists over her head. "Let's do it again!"

"Don't worry. We're headed for more."

Bailing water as Pam changed her wet T-shirt, I stole glances at the lithe arch of her back, the slight bumps of her backbone interrupting the smooth expanse of soft skin. Something in the way she moved, however quick and functional, captivated me. Though we loved lustily, this wasn't just some sexually charged voyeuristic glimpse, but a tantalizing glimmer of the deep affection, warmth, and comfort she had brought into my life.

Heading downstream on the dark and waxy river, we easily fell into a rhythm of sticking our paddles in the water just forward of where we sat, pulling them alongside the canoe to just behind us, and lifting them into the air before dipping them back where we had begun. She paddled on the right while I leaned along the left gunwale, our motions soon becoming complementary, almost choreographed, her strength leveraging mine and moving the boat swiftly along. Every mile drew us closer, seemed to reinforce our life together. The rapids especially had pushed us to a crisis of trust and coordination.

Highway sounds faded and the east shore became wilder, more

densely forested. Swallows dipped and dove as they chased insects, and several mallards cruised through reedy shallows. In contrast, the west shore was dominated by the functional geometry—rectangles and cylinders of masonry—of what looked like a sewage treatment plant and by other low and boxy modern industrial buildings. Whatever stood on the bank, we slipped slowly and silently past, no different from any other species of wildlife on the river.

Sometimes the mode by which we travel is more important than where we are going. Above any other means of transportation, a canoe demands a partnership, enforces a relationship. Companions may switch drivers or trade navigation duties on a car trip, work together aboard a motorboat or sailing vessel, or be copilots in the air, but only one person is at the wheel, the tiller, or joy stick at any given moment. A canoe insists on the coordinated effort of two people, and failure to work together can cause frustration and undermine a friendship. Partners not in synch, who don't appreciate each other's strengths and weaknesses, can induce disaster, causing injury or death, even on a fairly mild-mannered stream like the Merrimack. "For a companion, I require one who will make an equal demand on me with my own genius," Thoreau wrote. A canoe requires such equality, makes such demands.

At its best, a canoe creates a single organism from two people. Likening paddling with his partner to dancing, writer Alan S. Kesselheim observed that "the boat is something we wear, a thing the two of us put on like clothing. You create a kind of luminosity by your movements together." But in spite of such delightfully synchronous efforts, paddling partners can, nevertheless, be distinctly focused. Ever Thoreau's heir, Teale emphasized the canoe's "silken silence" enabling him to slip through the landscape undisturbed, while boat-mate Zwinger noticed "the seductive sound of water perking beneath the bow."

In less than a mile Pam and I spied an old railroad bridge crossing the water where a "handsome green islet" divided the river. It was a rusting fretwork of triangular metal trusses. The sound of Goffs Falls, like a furious wind, came from just downstream and captured our attention as we approached.

We beached on the island's rocky shore, walking carefully on slippery ledges where crevices cupped small pools of water. First we scouted the rock-studded west side. It required quick left and right turns in places where the current would want to take the canoe forward, sucking it down into deep souse holes and hurling it toward barely avoidable ledges. But the east side was worse. High, swift rollers would be unforgiving to the slightest mistake and could easily swamp us and wrap the boat around half-submerged boulders. The river boiled with power, roaring loudly and full of foam. We felt its thunder in our chests.

With some debate while snacking on a bag of peanuts, we charted a course among the west side rocks. Manchester's rapids had sharpened Pam's hydraulic acuity, and she no longer relied solely on my judgment. She was a quick and eager learner, and we read the river together.

Tightening our life jackets and ensuring the gear was secure, we pushed into the current with some trepidation. Backpaddling a few moments for a better view of the drop below, I reflexively drew a deep breath and let the river take us. We moved deftly among several rocks in the accelerating flow, scraped a ledge, and sluiced through a narrow opening between boulders. Suddenly we were hurtling through a maze of rocks and seething water.

Veils of spray erupted around us, the booming flood drowning out my heart's pounding. We made a sharp left turn as Pam deftly avoided a submerged stone shelf. But with my glasses dotted by mist, I briefly lost focus and headed toward the wrong glassy V of water. I hurriedly ruddered the boat back into position, and we bumped over a series of hidden rocks. I turned the canoe hard to the right and Pam lost her balance, hesitated, and we ran broadside onto a ledge whose top barely broke the surface.

"Push off with your paddle," I shouted. Pam grimaced with frustration at getting stuck, and my drill sergeant order, which suggested blame, made things worse. Pitched at an upstream angle and gradually taking on water, we had to act swiftly or find the boat inexorably folding around a rock. Still, even with both of us pushing hard on our paddles, the canoe didn't budge. "Forget the paddles," I yelled in exasperation. "Let's try rocking the boat back and forth with our bodies." When that too failed to move us, Pam looked at me in alarm, her lips quivering.

"I'm getting out to lighten the stern," I bellowed over the noisy rapids. "You push to the side with your paddle. Then I'll give a shove and hop back on."

"Are you sure that's a good idea? You could slip and fall."

"We can't stay here," I said, punctuating my words with a tense laugh. "When I get back in, we're going to move quickly over the next drop. You'll need to stabilize us till I get to my seat."

"You sure you're going to be okay?" she asked nervously, her curly locks flattened with water and plastered to her cheeks. "Don't let me float away without you."

"I love you," I smiled.

"Be careful," she said, her barely audible words trailing away in the rapids.

I leapt into the river, desperately trying to balance on slippery cobbles while keeping both hands tightly on the stern. The water rumbled and boomed around me, filling my ears and isolating me in the moment. I threw my weight against the canoe. It didn't budge. I pushed again. My leg muscles grew tight and my back stiffened. I might as well have tried to roll a boulder upstream. Suddenly, on the third shove, the boat gave a little. One more push and we slid free.

Jumping back in the canoe, I grabbed my paddle and targeted us over the last ledge. We slid smoothly, then bumped and splashed in small standing waves at the rapids' end.

"Sorry about missing that rock," Pam said sheepishly as we looked up the staircase of frothing water.

"Don't worry about it. I lost my bearings in a pretty tough spot." I looked into her liquid blue eyes. She smiled weakly, cueing me that some further explanation was needed. "And I'm sorry for yelling. We had to do something fast and I just wanted to make sure I was heard."

"It's okay," she said with a sigh. Though at a loss for what to do, I knew at the moment it wasn't okay. She chafed sometimes at my control from the stern, an issue resonating elsewhere in our relationship. In the long run, however, I sensed that we would probably work things out.

Despite separation of only a few feet, where we sat in the canoe framed our understanding. In the bow, Pam was perched at the very brink of our experience. The world came up fast there, where a strong stroke and quick reflexes were at a premium. Navigating from the stern, I was saddled with more responsibility for picking our way around obstacles and through big water. Experience had dictated our relative spots, as it had for Teale and Zwinger. He liked the authority of the stern and couldn't abide the bow, while she felt "confined in a supervisory world of steering" and liked "being at the edge of a world that ends two feet in front of me." But Pam and I had a personal, not professional union, and switching positions, however briefly, might have benefited both our relationship and canoeing prowess. I had to let go a little, and she needed to better appreciate the difficulty of finding a course.

Below Goffs Falls the steady current threaded through a rock garden, and just out of sight of the railroad bridge we pulled up on a huge ledge jutting into the water. The sun struggled through gauzy clouds, enabling us to see shadows for the first time all day. Stepping out of the boat in exhaustion, we removed our life jackets, threw them onto the rock, and plopped down. We gazed at each other for a few moments, knowing we'd been through something special. "My friend looks me in the face and sees me, that is all," Thoreau wrote the first day he and John were on the Merrimack.

The canoe not only demanded teamwork to transport us, I thought, as we stretched on the ledge and unwrapped sandwiches we'd bought that morning. Despite differing functions and responsibilities between bow and stern, it ensured we saw everything in tandem and with a shared perspective. There was no distinction like that between driver and passenger, where one concentrates on the road while the other daydreams, reads, or fusses with some ancillary task. We weren't hurtling at an engineering design speed of sixty-five miles per hour where the countryside flashes by the windshield in a cinematic flicker. The tempo of the river and its life was ours.

Though we'd traveled little over a dozen river miles and spent only a day and a half on the water, the rhythm of paddling and its languid pace, enabling us to see in luscious detail, had had the effect of time and circumstance, and it felt as if we'd already enjoyed a long and eventful trip. The canoe's openness heightened experience as it allowed us to see, hear, smell, and sometimes even touch the world, a sensory feast unmatched on ordinary days.

This immediate shared experience the boat demanded seemed to bind the two of us more tightly together. It confirmed my sense that what we see depends not just on *where* we are, but *with whom* we are traveling. What you hold in view on a trip to Niagara Falls with your parents, for example, is likely to be vastly different from that which you see on your honeymoon with your beloved, even if you patronize the same attractions. We develop an affection or distaste for places not just because of their inherent characteristics, but because we share them with certain people, experience them at particular seasons of our lives. Though it sounded corny, I knew that somehow, by the alchemy of my feelings for Pam, this ordinary river had been transformed into a stream of deep, personal meaning and wonder. For the rest of my life, its surface would reflect not just the clouds and sky others would see, but like a fairytale looking glass, a spectrum of memories and feelings revealed to my heart only.

As I daydreamed, Pam took a mouthful of the humus, tomato, and onion sandwich I held in my hand. "Hey, you just have to ask, if you want some!" I cried out.

"It was more fun stealing a bite," she said playfully. "Serves you right for being off in never-never land again."

"I was just wondering if Thoreau might have seen things differently along this stretch of river."

"Amazingly enough, I'll bet it was pretty much the same—just woods like this."

"I was thinking less of how things *looked*, and more of how *he* looked at things—his perspective. Except for going to college, which was less than twenty miles away, he'd really never been gone from home before. Everything must've seemed new, his life at a turning point, his experiences exotic even though he hadn't traveled far. Maybe that's why the book mentions so many romantic heroes and places like Robin Hood, Achilles and Hector, Hercules, Robinson Crusoe, Mount Olympus, Arabia, and Camelot."

Pam slid closer to me on the ledge. "And this trip is a real break with the past for us," she uttered softly in my ear. "It's magical almost. Something we'll always remember and have together."

Magic is what it seemed. Her presence gave everything a future, shot brightness onto the horizon, and lent an aura to the most common objects. The longer we floated, the farther I traveled from an empty marriage and its cruel impossibility of affection and intimacy. Wedged between memories and hopes for the future, I wanted desperately to build a new life. I felt a glossy and glorious optimism. I leaned my head on her shoulder. A whispered and elongated "Yes," was all I said.

Relationships affect our sense of place more than we typically recognize. As a result, deep travelers rarely venture alone. They require the foil of another viewpoint to sharpen their acuity and test their perspective. They need companions to challenge their assumptions, people whose friendship gives experiences greater resonance. One set of eyes misses too much.

Shared experience has always been critical on the Concord and Merrimack rivers. The more we know about Thoreau's relationship with John, the more insight we have into his journey, book, and life. Likewise, fully appreciating Mungo's writings and outlook requires at least a passing familiarity with his paddling partners, especially poet Verandah Porche. The same holds for McPhee and his companions, me and mine. The inner and outer landscapes are more tightly braided than we commonly acknowledge. A story always lurks behind a story.

With Henry and John in love with the same woman, it's hard not to imagine their feelings vacillating between fraternal tension and a giddy optimism as they each quietly speculated about love and life with Ellen. After the voyage, issues with Ellen may have cooled relations between them. Canby notes that they never took another trip and appear not to have spent much time together. This likely made John's sudden death tougher on Henry, and left a residue of longing for the happier days before Ellen. He never had time to right any wrongs, real or imagined, with his brother, no opportunity to forgive or be forgiven.

Camping beside the brook in Hooksett where they stowed their canoe while traveling to the White Mountains, the brothers fell asleep listening to its murmur. To the soothing sound, Thoreau dreams of an event that had occurred long before: "It was a difference with a Friend, which had not ceased to give me pain, though I had no cause to blame myself. But in my dream ideal justice was at length done me for his suspicions, and I received that compensation which I had never obtained in my waking hours. I was unspeakably soothed and rejoiced, even after I awoke, because in dreams we never deceive ourselves, nor are deceived, and this seemed to have the authority of a final judgment."

This passage is easy to read past, especially if you don't know the story of John and Ellen. But if you understand the background, Thoreau's pain clearly resounds down the years though clothed in high-toned language. Reading carefully, it is hard not to feel a tear.

Healing from this earliest and most painful adult emotional wound involved a number of therapies for Thoreau, the most lasting of which was a lifelong bachelorhood devoted to nature. The most mundane was the sale of his handcrafted boat to Nathaniel Hawthorne for seven dollars in the year of his brother's death on the third anniversary to the day that the voyage began. Most of all, he wrote about his dreams and visions in *A Week* and imbued the landscape with emotion, giving his words uncommon power. The pivotal essay on friendship is an intellectualized outpouring of feeling for John and is more intensely personal than his digressions on fishing, religion, and Hindu philosophy. Shortly before he died two decades later, Thoreau gave his dear friend Edmund Hosmer a signed copy of *A Week* that included a lock of John's hair.

Pam and I finished our sandwiches and lounged on the rock, enjoying the river's soft rippling and what little warmth we could get from the sun as it vainly tried burning through the clouds. Friends "cherish each other's hopes. They are kind to each other's dreams," Thoreau declared. But writing at a distance of a few years from this moment, I found it was sometimes increasingly hard to live this advice, to recapture more than a fugitive twinkling of the hopeful optimism and pure delight for each other's company Pam and I once shared. Our relationship had become tempestuous; periods of deep passion and warm affection unpredictably exploded in bruising anguish and despondency. The centrifugal spinning would have torn asunder any bond between less devoted people, but we persisted, if unhappily at times.

Even the river's roughest whitewater proved not nearly as arduous as winding our way through the difficulties of blending two lives together with all the stresses of growing children, ex-spouses, and aging parents. At middle age, even the best intentions become loaded down with more baggage than will leave safe and adequate freeboard in a canoe. We bring more than an accumulation of furniture, dishes, and knickknacks to a relationship.

Older lovers can never be alone, even when they are by themselves. The disingenuous ghosts of former liaisons linger and take revenge on the present. Like a canoe that can be flipped, or worse, by the submerged remains of dams and other hidden obstructions, our relationship was prey to past hurts and deep emotional wounds that could be ripped open even by the most innocent remark or well-meaning gesture. Dealing with the incessant demands of children and their ever-changing needs was like navigating difficult rapids in dense fog where unforeseeable danger required quick action that could only be poorly coordinated between bow and stern.

At the worst moments, when our love seemed to have devolved into a catalog of my character flaws and her language became so venomous I couldn't recognize myself, I would often drift back to our days on the river. Somehow, I remembered them all as sunny ones and drew strength from memories that tantalized me with the possibilities for love if we could only make our way through life's mundane but vicious rapids. "The constant abrasion and decay of our lives makes the soil of our future growth," Thoreau noted in *A Week*.

After we rode through the bumps and twists of Goffs Falls, smooth water made the river seem lackadaisical. Nevertheless, the current remained strong, and whenever we stopped paddling, we were still carried steadily and quietly downstream. The banks were steep and wooded on the west, where the railroad hugged the shore, and were dotted with a neighborhood of modest homes on the east. Flush with a confidence birthed in fast water, our paddling continued in a regular and unconscious rhythm, seemingly as natural and necessary as breathing.

"Forget about Thoreau for a minute," Pam said, breaking the silent cadence. "I know he's great, but what's the story with this Mungo guy? He seems pissed off at the whole world. And then you talk about McPhee. I know you think he's a super writer, but isn't he a little chichi for the river? This isn't a luxury cruise or anything."

"You're partly right with both of them."

"So what's the real deal? I mean, who actually are these people and why do they care about this river? Don't get mad at me, but sometimes I think you like the river mostly because it means something for your writing. Thoreau and those other guys are just as guilty."

"Mungo's anger was almost his job. He was a thin guy with dark hair and thick glasses who edited Boston University's school newspaper in the mid-sixties just as protests against the Vietnam War were gaining steam. With his canoeing partner Verandah Porche and their friend Marshall Bloom, they founded an organization that collected articles and photos for radical newspapers. Bloom's suicide just after the canoe trip left Mungo increasingly cynical and isolated. Like Thoreau, writing helped him mourn. At the time they paddled the river in 1969, Porche and Mungo were living in a big old farmhouse on a Vermont commune."

"They were hippies. That explains it," Pam scoffed.

"Well, sort of. But they weren't just growing their hair long and doing drugs. They tried making the country better."

"By running away to a commune out in the woods?"

"They wanted to get back to the land and grow their own food, sort of like Thoreau at Walden. Pesticides and chemical fertilizers were poisoning everything, and they tried farming without them. And also like Thoreau, they hated a culture that put the almighty dollar ahead of people."

Pam paused momentarily in thought and then nodded approvingly. Nothing got her going with juicy, four-letter invective like people flaunting expensive clothes and fancy cars or getting their jollies shopping. She was more interested in people's characters than their jewelry, in relationships than houses. She liked gardening and cooking with fresh, natural ingredients. Though her job as a home health-care aide paid poorly, she liked it because it was all about getting to know people. In some ways, Mungo's anger at an increasingly dehumanized, materialistic, and poisoned society gave voice to her own feelings.

"Did they go organic?" she wanted to know.

"Don't know for sure, but they were headed there."

I wished I could convey not just Mungo's outrage at an America that turned people and nature into commodities, but his frustration with the counterculture as well. Mungo and Porche had become disillusioned with a peace movement whose politics had begun to undermine its ideals. Pam was right, the farm *was* an escape. But after their bout with politics, they had gone to Vermont not so much to hide as to perfect their vision and make amends. "We till the soil to atone for our fathers' destruction of it," Mungo wrote. They were also licking their wounds. Mungo's experience trying to improve the country had left him cynical. "Outrage leads to action, and action leads . . . where? Usually into a morass." Or, as Porche later put it:

> Once I did what was needed hammered and canned.
> Took my medicine from that land.
> Swallowed what it told me like a bitter pill:
> You'll never get it together on that backwards hill.
> Move out or make your will.

The landscape became increasingly verdant. We passed a couple of small islands. At a third, larger island not much farther downstream, a light rapid known as Coos Falls bounced us gently over a few waves and sped us on our way. Thoreau ascended by means of a canal whose locks were under repair by two stone masons interested in the brothers' adventures. One of the workmen helped them through, and "it was plain that he would like to go with us, and as he looked up the river, many a distant cape and wooded shore were reflected in his eye."

"When Mungo and Porche paddled the Merrimack," I continued, "it smelled of chemicals, raw sewage floated on the water, and there were fewer trees along the banks. At the same time, America's cities were decaying and the textile industry that had employed thousands was collapsing. The country seemed to be breaking down."

"But they pick apart everything," Pam complained. "Something good must've been happening."

"That's what radical journalists do," I said, shaking my head. "Being critical is their stock-in-trade." In the end though, even the cynical Mungo was tainted by a twisted optimism. "We'll try to stay alive," he wrote, "for what else can we do?"

"So, what's with them now?"

"Mungo wrote a bunch of books. Some were read and others he admits were 'complete stinkos.' He wrote a lot of articles and ran a bookstore. Now he's a social worker in southern California tending mostly to AIDS patients and people who are severely mentally ill."

"A good place for his social conscience," she said approvingly. "Imagine all the crap he went through, and he winds up making his living a lot like I do."

"Porche kept writing poetry, published some books and developed something called 'Told Poetry' where she helps elders, schoolchildren, and others turn their own words into poems."

"At least it's not some uppity fancy stuff just for a library shelf. She's actually trying to help people. Old folks have such great stories. Letting them disappear is a crime. You wouldn't believe what I hear toward the end of a hospice job. Stuff not even family knows. Dying people don't want to take certain stories with them, but they don't want anyone else to know either."

"I guess when Mungo and Porche realized they couldn't change the system, they found small ways to make a difference with ordinary people. Maybe, in the end, that's the best outlet for the anger and frustration left over from the sixties."

"It's always about people. Just everyday people. Always," Pam concluded.

As the day wore on, the breeze freshened until again we were fighting a fairly strong headwind that tried to push us upstream. Fortunately, we were helped by a strong current. We encountered a few rock gardens where the river flowed swiftly over cobbled shallows, but the riffles were easy to navigate.

Crossing beneath a couple of sets of power lines, we found ourselves working through long rapids known as Moore's Falls. It was shallow and loud, with many rocks that thumped on the canoe's underside, but there was no single drop that could be called a falls. Ever the urbanite, McPhee likened the rapids to Manhattan's "Lexington Avenue in a heavy rain."

Pam and I picked our way through the obstacles, quickly twisting and turning with the flow of water, banging the side of the boat, pushing with paddles in shallow spots. We began more than ever to move easily among the rocks, working well in tandem, the canoe heading downstream like a squirming organism. Looking up as we bobbed in the eddy at the bottom, we found that Moore's Falls appeared like an aquatic version of the stoniest Yankee pasture. Thoreau used a two-thousand-foot canal with two locks to climb these rapids, and McPhee portaged with his boat atop his wife's minivan.

"So this McPhee guy is like Mr. Yuppie, isn't he?" Pam asked.

"I wouldn't go that far, but he writes for the *New Yorker*," I said, turning the boat back downstream. "It's a moneyed audience heavy into highbrow culture."

"Well, he sure has a highfalutin way of seeing things."

"For sure. But when he talks about famous golfers, the glass column of books at Yale's Beinecke Library, or a 1945 Margaux wine that costs thirty-six hundred dollars, I think it somehow helps his readers understand the canoeing at the same time he's drawing a contrast between our times and Thoreau's."

"Well, go figure. It's sure a different world. Thoreau wouldn't stand for it and you know it. Same for that radical guy and the poet named for a car."

"On the other hand, he's paddling the river with people he cares about. We have that in common, at least."

"I suppose," Pam said, unconvinced.

McPhee paddled the Concord with college buddy Dick Kazmaier, whom he affectionately calls "Kaz." A gifted athlete who is among only a few Heisman Trophy winners declining to play professional football, he went on to become a well-connected and successful businessman in marketing and financial services. For the rugged voyage up the Merrimack, McPhee engaged his son-in-law, Mark Svenvold, a creative writing professor. McPhee describes him as "six feet three, in his early forties, athletic," with "the high fluency and ironic humor of someone else who went up this river, long ago." Three years after paddling with his father-in-law, Svenvold published *Big Weather: Chasing Tornadoes in the Heart of America*. Equal parts memoir, natural history, and folklore, the book is very much in the McPhee mold. These canoeing partners come from the antipodes of McPhee's experience—a close friend from before his fabulous writing career, and a relation whom he can mentor and to whom he can pass on his mantle. Though McPhee's sentences sparkle with crystalline brilliance, his writing can strike one as cold. His choice of companions ensures a strong emotional undercurrent.

Pam and I slipped our paddles in the water simultaneously and started pulling hard against a headwind that had begun whipping up whitecaps. The shore was now wooded, and only the sporadic grinding of truck gears on a local road broke the sense of wildness. An occasional house or rope swing attached to a sturdy tree limb reminded us that people weren't far away. Clouds raced across the sky, reminding me of a Svenvold poem:

> Hello . . . flanneled
> blanket of clouds, clouds
> fueled by more clouds . . .

McPhee may have glimpsed a bit of Thoreau in Svenvold, but there is likely some of the Concord naturalist in all who ply these waters. Mungo's sharp, albeit comparatively clumsy social criticism echoes Thoreau, as does McPhee's intense power of observation. Without some Thoreau legacy, why would they be here?

Something Thoreauvian lit the lives of each of my companions as well. Pam's defiantly independent and indomitable spirit would have been simpatico with the denizen of Walden Pond, and her virulently disdainful attitude for formalities, fashions, and fancy trifles would have given them much to chat about. Like Thoreau, she dresses plainly and leans to simple foods. For years she wore a jacket with a prominent rip in the back. When I offered to buy her a new one, she refused. It was a badge of honor, an anti-fashion statement that Henry would have understood.

Alan has Thoreau's wry humor and adroit playfulness with words. They share a talent for quick-witted social criticism that skewers the high and mighty. Neither suffers fools lightly. Both of them bachelors, they have passion and respect for the landscape and persistently pursue their vision.

Josh possesses Thoreau's knack for simple questions and his sheer wonder at the world. Clouds and ants remain a miracle to him. He wants to know how the Indians lived and what farmers grew in times past. He's impatient with pat answers. Eleven years old when he and I paddled together, he was closest in age to Thoreau and shared Henry's adolescent defiance.

Relationships have a streaming quality that makes it hard to say precisely how particular companions affect the way we see the world. Nevertheless, their presence has an emotional timbre evoking subtle but distinct differences, just as our own age and experience affect how we see places. Heraclitus' maxim that we can't step into the same river twice is less a commentary on flowing water than on the flow of our lives.

Paddling with Pam kept me attuned to the humanity of the landscape. She didn't care so much for the grand play of economic and social forces but rather wondered how families made their living, educated their children, and cared for their elderly. The daily realities of a garden, wash hung on a line, or the proximity of the bus stop meant more to her than the studies of planners and promises of politicians.

Through the lens of our love, I more readily imagined myself in each landscape we encountered. The world seemed refreshed, reflecting my emotional healing after years in the cold. Sharing places and events with Pam became as important as the places and events themselves. Our relationship projected a more empathetic outlook on everything I saw, and deep travel became a means to deepen our relationship.

Perhaps our canoeing partnership made the possibility of life together seem too simple, as if it were just a matter of shared effort and the power of pure joy brought to ordinary moments. Wasn't that the essence of love? Maybe we were wrong thinking love would be enough. Still, people neither regret nor forget the intensity of a bond that makes them feel so unbearably light, however painful the aftermath. "Ignorance and bungling with love," Thoreau wrote in *A Week*, "are better than wisdom and skill without." And so our relationship remains a work in progress, ever growing richer, more complete. Maybe as time accumulates, our ongoing survival as a couple is owing to an increasing ability to deep travel into each other's lives, appreciating that our emotions, physical abilities and frailties, and past experiences create their own landscape as complexly layered as any geography we encounter together.

Friends for more than two decades, Alan and I share a vast treasure of common experiences defining our lives and aspirations. We are the old married couple finishing each other's sentences. A phrase can evoke days of past adventures or ordeals. A single word can cause laughter from the remnants of an old joke, reminiscence, or personality from our past. As neighbors a five-minute walk apart, we spontaneously get together for home maintenance projects, meals, concerts, or movies. I may pass a week or ten days without seeing him, but I know he's there for me. Alan is the brother I never had. Thoreau would have understood: "My Friend is not of some other race or family of men, but flesh of my flesh, bone of my bone. He is my real brother. I see his nature groping yonder so like mine. We do not live far apart."

Through Alan's eyes I more readily envision the political geography of a landscape. Having been a land-use planner in a rural town, suburb, and small city, he not only sees patterns in the typical hodgepodge of development, he senses the social forces conspiring to create a place. He knows that the location of roads, shopping centers, or schools isn't just a function of topography or need, but the result of compromise among politicians, bureaucrats, bankers, and developers seeking myriad opportunities. He understands that both sunlight and money are sources of energy giving rise to places.

Josh allows me to relive my childhood. I crave his uninhibited and unprogrammed energy. Bringing renewal and awareness to simple pleasures, he injects playfulness into the most mundane day. I am more likely to contemplate the shapes of clouds, notice the way sunlight filters through overhanging trees, and be startled by the color of flowers with him beside me. He keeps my perceptions honed and opens the flow of raw, unfiltered information that adults sometimes lose in a cacophony of conflicting demands. "Any child is a reminder that the rivers of our senses once ran clear," author Scott Russell Sanders observes.

Josh vaults me out of the past and beyond the present. I contemplate what this landscape will be like when he grows up, when he reaches my age. I worry about homogeneous sprawling subdivisions and commercial strips devouring the countryside, global warming, and species extinction. I wonder whether any farms and forests will be left for him to show his children. Kids force us to contemplate the future. They chasten us to be good stewards. They are our conscience.

Pam and I took out in Reeds Ferry, at a small and neatly manicured parklike area where massive stone steps led to the water. A cool spot overhung with trees, its existence isn't a modern civic improvement but appears to be the remnants of some historical use long faded from existence. As we carried the boat up a walkway and through a tunnel beneath railroad tracks, my deep traveler's mind filled with questions about the site. But answers would have to await another day. We passed out of the tunnel into the cloud-filtered light of afternoon.

Crosscurrents

Brown University. Commencement at this
institution was held yesterday.
Boston Courier, September 6, 1839

Getty Makes Record High Bid for Alaskan Oil
Manchester Union Leader, September 11, 1969

Municipal officials: Cuts hurting homeland security
Lowell Sun, September 9, 2003

Not long after Pam and I had pulled our canoe out of the river and passed through the short masonry tunnel penetrating the railroad embankment at Reeds Ferry, I returned with Alan. Shouldering the boat from a rough dirt parking area at the edge of an old residential neighborhood, we entered the arched portal and found ourselves in the well-tended park. Isolated from the workaday world by the berm on which the tracks were laid, and sandwiched between the river and railroad with impenetrable woods on either side, the space felt like a small outdoor room. Pam had been taken by the quiet, Zenlike beauty; Alan admired the engineering—the broad, druidical stone steps leading to the water, and the culvert providing passage not just for people, but for a small stream that flowed beneath grates fitted into the concrete tunnel floor.

Before the railroad's coming, this hidden spot had not only been a focal point of the settlement here, but its very reason for being. Today, the ferry landing was merely a reminder that before the day of reliable bridges, the river was not just a north-south highway, but an obstacle to people heading east or west. Now only a cluster of tired houses and small businesses strung along the Daniel Webster Highway, Reeds Ferry had once been a bustling transportation link.

With our deep traveling interest piqued, Alan and I speculated about the enigmatic launch site while we paddled. Our curiosity wouldn't be satisfied until we got off the water and returned, stepping into a barn just up the street from the forgotten landing. Here we found Charles H. Mower, the unofficial "mayor," who crafts Windsor chairs just as they did when Reeds Ferry was a busy freight and passenger terminal two hundred years ago.

Mower is a bearded, burly man with a genial manner and an impassioned voice. Born in the old brick house with granite lintels standing next to the barn, he doesn't just know local history, he feels and breathes it. Alan and I spent two hours in his small workshop littered with wood shavings and filled with the rich, pungent odor of red oak as he spun tales about the life of Reeds Ferry. With a deep breath he began by telling us about ancient Narragansett land grants, the split of New Hampshire from Massachusetts, and the town of Merrimack's original charters, one of which complained of land that was "mean and ordinary." Though he had traveled widely, including a tour of duty in Vietnam, he was the deepest of travelers on his home turf.

Engaged in making a spindle for the back of a chair, Mower axed a kindling-sized piece from an oak log. In the 1700s, he said as he worked, Reeds Ferry was an important crossing enabling people to attend church in Londonderry on the far side of the river. It also allowed those living east of the Merrimack to shop at the store established in McGaw's Tavern, which once stood next to Mower's barn. Today, a Getty Station occupies the spot, pumping gas for motorists on the Daniel Webster Highway, called "The Great River Road" in Mc-Gaw's heyday. Reed, he noted, as he shaped the angular stick of wood with a draw knife, lived on the opposite shore and operated the ferry from there.

"Fine silica and alumina filtered out of glacial Lake Merrimack, and the town was built on this ancient lakebed of clay," he related. "Adam was made of clay, the most humble and pedestrian of materials, and the basic stuff of the earth. In this town they made the bricks that built the factories of Lowell. In one day one hundred thousand bricks were shipped from that little landing on the river. Like plain clay, it's ordinary people working in concert that build cities, entire civilizations even."

Planing the slender piece of wood with a spokeshave, Mower needed less than ten minutes to transform the rough stick into a delicate spindle. "It doesn't have to be perfectly rounded," he said, "only enough so as to tease the eye with the illusion that it is."

Mower looked us each in the face and rubbed his beard thoughtfully. "Our predecessors didn't just come and go without consequence," he opined. "Even if they didn't shine individually, we can't dismiss their collective effort. The legacy they left is our tapestry, the fabric that binds us together knot by knot."

Mower's magnetic enthusiasm and empathy for people's relationship to a place remained with us. After our conversation, I couldn't see or remember the Merrimack Valley without hearing the rich humanity of his voice. Pines along the river reminded me of his chair seats and oaks of spindles. In his mind's eye, Reeds Ferry was both an irrelevant cosmic smudge and a microcosm of the universe. Deep travelers understand far-flung places because they are rooted in their own place.

"What in the world are you trying to hum?" Alan asked, as we shoved the boat into the water and began our downstream float.

"Just an old Civil War tune," I replied, thinking of my redheaded imp of a son. After his reenacting passion had been stirred by the soldiers at the Old Manse the day we camped along the Concord, I had hummed an equally poor rendition of the song around our campfire. Josh had been embarrassed even though we were alone.

"Either I've never heard of it, or your humming is way off. Given your musical talent," he quipped, "it's probably the latter."

I smiled weakly, knowing he was right. "It's pretty obscure today, but 'Tenting on the Old Camp Ground' was an emotional number soldiers often sang in the evening at encampments on both sides." Regardless of its provenance, the music recalled the bond Josh and I had formed visiting battlefields in Virginia, Maryland, and Pennsylvania.

"Am I missing something? We're not camping. We're not doing the Civil War thing. What's the deal?"

"Surfing the Web for stuff about the river, I stumbled on a reference to a self-taught musician from Reeds Ferry. Walter Kittredge wrote 'Tenting' and hundreds of other songs."

Knowing that this tune had been written nearby, I felt a connection to this place, however tentative, one that made me feel Josh's presence and transformed Reeds Ferry from a dot on the map into personal emotional territory. Such serendipitous links between ourselves and places we visit are more common than we realize. Deep travel uncovers such relationships.

"What's really eerie," I added, "is how the lyrics still resonate. They're as fresh as the headlines about Iraq we saw in today's paper."

> Many are the hearts that are weary tonight,
> Wishing for the war to cease.
> Many are the hearts looking for the light,
> To see the dawn of Peace.

We pulled away from the shaded shore. Brilliant sunlight reflected on the water even as we felt the cool breath of a light wind blowing upstream. The banks were steep and dominated by silver maple, but also thick with oak, sugar maple, and some pine.

Approaching a pair of large islands, we came upon a pair of bass fishermen in a Boston Whaler. They sheepishly shrugged their shoulders, acknowledging that the fishing was slow. "But, hell," said the one wearing a camouflage T-shirt, "sure beats even a good day at work."

The islands were heavily wooded and sometimes had sharply eroded banks. Around them the river grew shallow with a silent but visible current where grassy vegetation floated just below the surface. Minnehaha and Minnewawa islands had been granted to the great Indian sachem Passaconaway by a 1662 treaty. Legend had it that he summered here. Leader of all Merrimack Valley natives, Passaconaway is said to have possessed magical powers enabling him to burn water and transform sticks into snakes.

"Thoreau and his brother took a long rest on the big island," I told Alan. "I guess the woods weren't so thick because cattle were pasturing. They landed for lunch and shot and cooked a pigeon."

Alan stopped paddling and turned toward me in disgust. "A pigeon?"

"It isn't what you're thinking," I replied, shaking my head. "Not the type that shit all over statues of famous dead guys in city parks, not . . ."

"Rats with wings," he said, completing Woody Allen's quip.

As Henry and John boiled rice over an open fire, Henry waxed rhap-
sodic over a flock of birds congregating in the trees. He listened to "the
slight wiry winnowing sound of their wings" and "their gentle and
tremulous cooing." Before long, the brothers "obtained one of these
handsome birds, which lingered too long upon its perch, and plucked
and broiled it." In somewhat arch reflection, Henry observed that "it is
true, it did not seem to be putting this bird to its right use, to pluck off
its feathers, and extract its entrails, and broil its carcass on the coals;
but we heroically persevered, nevertheless, waiting for further information." Unfortunately, by the time further information was received,
tuberculosis had silenced Thoreau's eloquence.

"It was a passenger pigeon. They were like mourning doves only
larger, with slate blue heads, gray backs, and red breasts."

"Aren't they an endangered species?"

"Worse. They've been extinct since about the beginning of World
War I when the last one died in a Cincinnati zoo. In Thoreau's time
there were millions, maybe billions of them."

Passenger pigeons were once probably the most common bird in
North America. By some estimates, there were as many as five billion
of them. A social creature, they lived in huge flocks, the largest reported being a mile wide and three hundred miles long. It could take
several days for these massive flocks to pass over, darkening the skies
as they went. Within little more than a century, however, they were
hunted to extinction for food, hog feed, as live trap-shooting targets,
and sometimes for fertilizer. They were common fare in most eastern
restaurants, and in 1830 Audubon observed them "so abundant in the
markets of New York that piles of them met the eye in every direction."
In 1878 fifty thousand birds a day were killed at Petoskey, Michigan,
for almost five months. The pigeons were shot and netted, smoked out
of their roosts, and trapped with bait and decoys.

Dependent on forests for breeding and food such as acorns and
beechnuts, their demise was also hastened by widespread tree cutting for agriculture and fuel. Their numbers began to drop noticeably
by the time *A Week* was published in 1849, a decade after the Thoreau
brothers enjoyed their repast. Two years later, Thoreau was startled to
stumble on a pigeon trap while walking in the woods near his home.

Grain was spread on the ground and a blind established where a hidden man could pull a string, dropping a net on the feeding birds. The last substantial wild flock of 250,000 pigeons was killed by hunters in a single day in 1896. Four years later, a fourteen-year-old boy shot the last wild bird in Ohio.

"Look," Alan said, pointing to a crude shelter built of sticks and vegetation on the downstream tip of the larger island, "some kids built a fort."

"That's a duck blind."

"I guess Thoreau wasn't the last hunter here."

"I don't know that Thoreau was much of a hunter. He sold his gun in his twenties. Still, he both appreciated the beauty of creation and realized that people weren't just observers, but part of nature's cycles. Sometimes that included killing and eating abundant wild animals. He was poetic, not sentimental."

"It's not what your Audubon Society types usually think."

"Hell, Audubon sometimes shot hundreds of songbirds in a day so he could pose them for paintings," I said, remembering that Teale called the artist "the most terrifying sight a bird could see." I paused in mid–paddle stroke. "People forget that hunters and fishers started the conservation movement after seeing what was happening to the passenger pigeon and other critters. Hook and bullet types, like Theodore Roosevelt, pushed for regulations to protect fish and wildlife, fought for strict enforcement, and championed parks, national forests, and refuges. Then they accepted taxes on everything from fishing rods to ammunition to make it happen."

"Need a soapbox to preach from?" Alan asked with a wry smile. "Sounds like a canned speech from work."

"I get frustrated with both the fin-and-feather hunting types and granola-chewing birdwatchers mistrusting each other while around them development devours wildlife habitat. If they'd remember where they came from and just get together . . ."

"Exactly," Alan interrupted. "I see it occasionally even at the local level. Nature center folks and the fish-and-game clubs both do great conservation work, but they're separate countries."

At first, it seemed a peculiar contradiction. Thoreau couldn't have more lovingly described the graceful beauty of those birds, and still, he ate one. Yet, by each act, he understood a wholly different aspect of the animal. It sustained both his spirit and his body. Hard as it might be to accept at first blush, such contrariety was, perhaps, as close to the truth as you could get.

Not far below the islands, power lines sagged over the river. Modest houses appeared behind trees on the right while the opposite shore sported docks tethering small powerboats. Nearby, canoes had been beached onshore. As we paddled past these markers of settlement, turkey vultures wheeled overhead, their black bodies silhouetted against a deep sky of purest azure, their fingerlike wingtip feathers stretching for the horizon. An osprey flew low over the water, its harsh shriek echoing down the river.

After passing some abandoned concrete tubes scattered at the water's edge like the forgotten toys of distracted children, we came to a large irrigation structure with pipes running up the bank. Behind a band of trees were the carefully manicured fairways and bright, close-cropped greens of a golf course. We heard a *whoosh* and the loud *thwack* of a club striking a ball.

"The Passaconaway Country Club," I said, unfolding a map.

"The old sachem must have been a founding member," Alan wisecracked. "Didn't know he played. It makes sense, seeing how he summered on those islands. Could've floated down with his woods and irons neatly tucked into his birch bark canoe."

"A stylized version of the Scottish Highlands is an odd memorial to a native leader," I observed, shaking my head.

"Maybe he looked good in a kilt."

"I'm sure the club thought it was an honor."

"They couldn't have named a wildlife refuge after him?"

The river became shallow, its sandy bottom imprinted with wind-driven riffle patterns. Several pointy-billed mergansers, their cinnamon heads glistening, floated close to shore near a cluster of bright red cardinal flowers. Willows and silver maples overhung the water with dappled shadows while oaks and pines stood at attention on higher ground and aspens fluttered nervously in the breeze.

As we passed the Souhegan River, several metallic blue kayaks floated out from between the concrete piers of the railroad bridge at its mouth. Especially in spring high water, the Souhegan is a popular paddling destination with more than twenty-five miles of quickwater and rapids surging over rocks and ledges. But like many rivers in the Merrimack Valley, its image as a recreational paddling destination is barely a couple of generations old. In Thoreau's time, free-flowing whitewater was considered a wasted industrial opportunity rather than a natural wonder. Even the Concord naturalist was caught up in waterpower boosterism, noting as he passed the Souhegan that a nearby tributary, Baboosic Brook, was said to have "some of the finest water privileges in the country still unimproved."

Sometimes we forget that Thoreau's seemingly pastoral trip occurred at the cusp of rapid change when the Merrimack emerged as the most renowned industrial river in America. By the time *A Week* was published a decade later, the river had been transformed from a slow-paced artery of transportation carrying goods and passengers to an industrial machine serving the power needs of textile mills and other factories. Four significant industrial cities—Manchester, Nashua, Lowell, and Lawrence—were rapidly expanding along its banks.

"The amount of manufacturing along this stream is not equaled by any other river in the world," wrote Meader in 1869. By then, the river had five substantial dams, was crossed by twenty-five rail and highway bridges, and supported more than one hundred textile mills. In addition to cloth, riverside factories produced hats, wagons, cigars, buttons, railway cars, spools, pails, chairs, pianos, leather, paper, metal tools, matchboxes, combs, staves, carriages, and doors. Merrimack water was the lifeblood of industrial America.

Under a pale thumbnail slice of moon and a few ragged clouds, the high banks lining both sides of the river leveled out as we headed downstream. Within a mile we passed Naticook Brook, whose water Thoreau sampled. Nearby, he saw the "small village" of Thorntons Ferry. Given that a pond just upstream was ringed with houses, we declined to imbibe at the brook as Thoreau had. We also failed to see the village, which must have grown away from the river when the railroad came about a year after the Thoreau brothers floated past. Thorntons Ferry nevertheless survives as a place within the Town of Merrimack, though there have been neither any namesake Thorntons nor a ferry for well over a century.

The area was named for Matthew Thornton, who signed the Declaration of Independence though he was sent to Congress too late for the debates. A native of Ireland who became a revered physician, judge, statesman, and elected official, he retired to Merrimack around age seventy to run a farm and the local ferry. Today, the "village" is a car-choked commercial strip on the Daniel Webster Highway. Traffic speeds past a historic marker dedicated to Thornton beside the small, dignified cemetery in which he is buried. Dunkin' Donuts is across the street.

It takes a deep traveler to find Thorntons Ferry because it is little more than a node of fast food restaurants, filling stations, motels, and stores just beyond the toll booths of the Everett Turnpike. Still, the place name is important if for nothing else than to commemorate a patriot who, though too old to take up arms, did his part to secure American independence even as citizen soldiers were risking their lives far down the watershed at Concord's North Bridge.

We passed beneath a cat's cradle of power lines carried on three sets of massive standards. With the river smooth and quiet, their crackle seemed particularly loud, like an amplified pan of frying bacon. It was the third set we had encountered that morning.

"Those things give me the creeps," Alan said, peering warily overhead. "I know there's a lot of scientific brouhaha and I'm no expert on cancer clusters, but it's hard to believe electromagnetic fields don't cause problems for people living or working nearby. That humming and sizzle sounds so malignant."

"Sure are ugly. Sometimes I imagine those humongous stanchions are like the Martian invaders out of H. G. Wells's *War of the Worlds*, tromping in giant steps across the landscape and bent on destruction."

"Humongous? Martians? Destruction?" From the bow he turned toward me with an arched eyebrow. "You've been spending too much time with Josh and his video game imagination. The only destruction is the treeless swaths cut through thousands of miles of woods."

"Unless we turn the lights out, I guess we're stuck with them until there's a better way of transmitting electricity."

"Highways of electrons, rivers of electrons," he sing-songed.

"You're more right than you know. Everyone talks about how televisions, computers, and other machines connect the world, but out here wires and poles literally knit one end of the horizon to the other."

"That's a stretch," he said, with a touch of brotherly ridicule. "Do I feel a speech coming on?"

"If we've got to have them, we can at least make them more useful, if not beautiful. Ornithologists claim the shrubby rights-of-way are good for certain sparrows and birds like towhees and indigo buntings. Apparently, most shrublands are disappearing. The corridors also have miles of edge habitat that deer and other animals like. Maybe we can even make better use of them for hiking and snowmobile trails."

"Seems a bit over the top."

I shrugged. "Realizing the ugly telegraph poles along the railroad at Walden were there to stay, Thoreau thought the vibration of wind on the wires sounded like an Aeolian harp."

Alan turned toward me again, this time rolling his eyes. "Proves he was as nutty as you are," he laughed

William Ellery Channing, with whom Thoreau wandered around Conantum, felt that his friend's ability to transform a barked chestnut pole into an instrument of celestial music evidenced profound "poetic insight." In *A Week*, Thoreau wrote about "the telegraph harp singing its message through the country, a message sent not by men but by gods." I dared not suggest to Alan that the crackling wires making him uncomfortable could include a divine message. "So have all things their higher and their lower uses," Thoreau reasoned.

A little downstream of today's power lines, Thoreau climbed the bank that then, as now, was skirted by trees rising on terraces before reaching open country. At a quarter to half a mile, he spotted the "river-road," the incipient Daniel Webster Highway, where the stagecoach passed in a cloud of dust. In the absence of fast food restaurants, motels, and gas stations, he gazed across fields that may have grown corn, rye, and hay.

The farmhouses were usually sheltered in a copse of trees "with every house its well, as we sometimes proved." Today, Thoreau would have found many places to quench his thirst, including the Anheuser-Busch brewery, which produces more than ninety-six million gallons of beer annually. We could see its boxy yellow buildings, replete with towers and stacks, like a golden city from the top of the bank, but they were hidden while we were on the water.

No doubt Henry and John could have used a few thirst-satisfying pulls on a Bud longneck during those hot, sunny days of early September. Many years ago I went on a brewery tour here that started in a welcome center and gift shop. With a red roof, pseudo half-timbering, and fieldstone walls, the center was a Disneylike rendition of a Bavarian beer hall. All I remember of the tour is a series of big rooms with pipes and tanks and the rattling sound of the bottling plant. It isn't so much the lapse of years that blurs my memory as the time spent afterward sipping the fruit of all the labor I'd witnessed. I wobbled out in the bracing fresh air toward the palatial stucco stables where the company's huge Clydesdale draft horses are kept. They seemed the size of dinosaurs.

The river widened and moved swiftly with patches of boisterous whitewater. We worked our way through a series of small islands and rock gardens, carefully picking a route among the obstacles where sufficient water kept us from getting hung up. Some of the islands were merely mounds of sand where killdeer skittered nervously. Swallows dove and darted, and geese and a few mallards swam among the rocks.

A low stone wall, or at least the remains of one, angled from the shore toward midstream. It looked like something teenagers might build to enhance a swimming hole, only it was long and almost parallel to the current. This ruin was once the guide wall that in Thoreau's time channeled commercial vessels to a canal around the rapids. We had arrived at Cromwell's Falls, which drops about six feet in half a mile.

We followed the wall to a lock, a narrow passage lined with stones between the steep shore and a riverward earthen berm also reinforced with stone. Roping the canoe to an oak sapling, we climbed the grassy berm, which has a large seven-trunk silver maple growing in the middle of it. This lock is said to be the best-preserved remains of canal days on the river, but the wooden lock doors had long succumbed to rot and the spot was overgrown with vegetation. The large stones made the lock look like a tiny Mayan ruin.

Though this was once the site of sweat and toil, Alan and I stretched out and relaxed at the water's edge. A pipe clenched between my teeth, I blew smoke rings and listened as the river's riffles found harmony with a zephyr fluttering the leaves above.

Built in 1815 for nine thousand dollars, the lock was a traffic bottleneck where the Thoreau brothers found themselves "now fairly in the stream of this week's commerce" as they waited for other vessels to pass through. The canal boats were poled upstream with fifteen-foot, iron-tipped poles. Going down, they employed an oar at each end. A sail was used in favorable winds. On their long, open decks, they could carry fifteen tons of material, except in dry times. Freight may have included lumber, cords of wood, potash, and bricks downstream, while upstream cargos consisted of cotton, textile machinery, and machine parts.

Thoreau romanticized and envied the vigorous outdoor work of boatmen, imagining it "an easy and contented life," with opportunity for observation of nature. No doubt it could be hard labor and tedious, especially poling upstream and being exposed to cold, wind, and rain. But recalling the trip from the cozy confines of his hut at Walden, Thoreau can be forgiven a bit of nostalgia. By the time he wrote, the world of boatmen was rapidly fading. "The locks are fast wearing out," he noted, "and will soon be impassable, since the tolls will not pay the expense of repairing them, and so in a few years there will be an end of boating on this river." Thoreau was right about commercial traffic, but recreational boating such as he pioneered would endure.

Perhaps I was intoxicated with Albert Einstein's notion "that pipe smoking contributes to a somewhat calm and objective judgement in all human affairs." My puffing as we lolled on the grass induced yet another fit of philosophical reflection, contemplation being as much a danger of pipe smoking as throat cancer and lung dysfunction. "Isn't it interesting," I suggested enthusiastically, "the way the railroad, D. W. Highway, and Everett Turnpike all parallel the river?" I felt as if struck by revelation, my voice loud enough to disturb Alan as he lay on his back, cap over his face, soaking up sunshine like a reptile.

"And your point is?" he replied with the pique of the awakened.

"Just that even when you're cruising on pavement at sixty-five miles per hour with the river invisible and out of mind, it still influences where you're going. Furthermore, the Merrimack determines how the whole built environment lays out. The river doesn't change much, but human relationships with it do."

"I suppose," he said sleepily, sitting up and flipping the cap back on his head. "Of course, this lock was critical to that relationship. It's hard evidence that people once relied on the river for commercial shipping, a concept as obscure today as buggy whips." Alan took a deep breath and sighed. "It's kind of obvious, though."

"Maybe to a professional planner. Don't you think most people see the landscape as just a stage for human events? I'm saying it's an active partner. Waterpower and the big-time clay deposits to make bricks for factories vastly affected how people lived here."

"I'm not sure how *active* the landscape is, but it's a textbook cliché that people are altered by the land even as they transform it," Alan reflected. "Call it an ecological conscience if you want something fancy sounding, but today we may have more in common with the Indians and early settlers than with the textile era. Fishing and traveling by canoe, even canals, kept people tuned to natural cycles. Power production controlled the river almost in defiance of nature. Now maybe we're in what you might call a stewardship phase, trying to work *with* the river."

Using water for industrial power radically altered people's relationship with the Merrimack. Even though some human order had been imposed with canals and locks, fish weirs, and portage trails, there was a synergy between human needs and natural phenomena. But in serving the textile mills, the water came under absolute control. The river became merely a commodity, another industrial input. Its role was not merely to facilitate commerce; it became the very stuff of commerce.

Money, time, and intelligence were brought to bear in subduing the river, to squeezing out each Btu, horsepower, or kilowatt of value until the Merrimack resembled just another well-ordered machine. Its flow was regulated from its source, dammed, dewatered in stretches, funneled into penstocks, spun in turbines, and expectorated. Perhaps no natural system has ever been so manipulated as the late-nineteenth-century Merrimack River. Conquering water "was a driving ambition of an industrial culture desperate for progress," wrote Theodore Steinberg. "The unquestioned attitude of dominance is among the most powerful legacies of industrialization."

When waterpower declined with the advent of fossil fuels, factories were freed from narrow river valleys and migrated south and then offshore. But we still suffer a hangover from the arrogant triumph of that first flowering of industrial power. Whether the issue is building on barrier beaches, disposing of nuclear fuels, or meeting the challenge of global warming, faith abides that money and engineering prowess can solve all problems arising with natural systems. We remain rapt believers in technology even as the ecological and social legacies of the mills tell us something different.

Shaking off our lethargy, Alan and I returned to the canoe and paddled through the narrow, stone passage that had floated Thoreau and uncounted tons of freight during its days as a lock. Daylight dimmed between the walls, and overhanging trees cast darkly mirrored reflections. I felt almost as if we were passing through a tunnel.

Odd-shaped and ever morphing cumulus clouds gathered in the once clear sky. At some distance we heard the annoying drone of an irrigation pump, whose volume and timbre varied with the wind's direction. The high banks revealed clayey soil with oozing springs that wept in discolored streaks. Occasionally we saw a house, a path to the river, a rope swing, or an overgrown driveway. Two great blue herons flew low above us. Clumps of loosestrife grew in the shallows like magenta navigation markers.

Big industrial buildings appeared through the trees just before we reached Pennichuck Brook. Thoreau called this tributary "a wild salmon stream," though he passed it unseen in fog. We might have been better off with fog as well, since the brook, which forms the jagged boundary between Merrimack and Nashua, has a mouth straddled by railroad tracks and choked with debris.

An upscale housing subdivision appeared on the left, and the low bank opposite was reinforced with metal sheet piling, behind which was a narrow strip of neatly mown lawn. Curious about this carefully groomed area, we pulled as close as we could float. Alan stepped out and sank into black mayonnaise-like goo. Spotting a manhole on the lawn, he climbed a wide trail that slabbed the bank and led to a sewage pump station. Quickly returning, he clambered back into the boat after a modestly successful attempt at rinsing the muck from his shoes.

As we got under way, a couple of fishing boats passed. One was a fair-sized center console bass boat, the other a small skiff with an outboard. From downriver we heard the high-pitched hum of personal watercraft.

This river reach had much to gossip about in its relationship with humans in the post-textile era. It watered crops, diluted sewage, offered handsome home sites, provided habitat for plants and animals, and, if rope swings were any evidence, attracted young swimmers. It still lured fishers, and although commercial traffic was long gone as Thoreau had reported, there were plenty of opportunities for boating.

With growling stomachs eager for lunch, we landed on the macadam boat ramp in Nashua's Greeley Park just before one o'clock. McPhee and Svenvold had begun paddling to Manchester from here in a light rain a year earlier. We weren't far from where Henry and John camped on their third night "by a deep ravine, under the skirts of a pine wood, where the dead pine leaves were our carpet, and their tawny boughs stretched overhead." As I hopped out on rubbery legs and pulled the boat clear of the water, a pair of Sea-Doos were preparing to take off, their engines rumbling and spewing grayish-blue smoke.

The boat launch was in an area of winding, eroded trails and ad hoc parking beneath a thick tree canopy. We climbed a bluff overlooking the river and ramp, sat on our life jackets, and leaned against a stout pine as we dined on sandwiches purchased at a chain grocery store. Powerboats came and went at the launch, their loud, deep vibrato carrying on the water and through the woods. The sound did nothing to aid our digestion but wasn't any worse than the time Thoreau tried to sleep while an amateur drummer practiced for a country muster. The river was busy with every manner of vessel, from rowboats to small sloops. Several bright plastic kayaks played in the wake of a powerboat with huge twin outboards. The perfume of exhaust mingled with the scent of pines.

For about ten minutes we were entertained by a band of twenty-somethings spouting a cascade of curses when their ancient Evenrude failed to start. Two guys stood chest deep in the water steadying the boat, one directed traffic around the disabled vessel, and three removed the engine cover and tinkered. Their vocabulary long exhausted, they at last got the beast started. With our afternoon's entertainment concluded, we returned to the canoe and were soon under way.

Below the launch the river became ever busier with fishing vessels, small speedboats, and Sea-Doos. Power lines crossed the water and houses lined both banks, many with docks or swimming floats. Still, the river corridor retained an overall wooded appearance.

The parallel spans of the Taylor Falls Bridge, carrying busy Route 111 into the heart of Nashua, were visible at a distance, with thick concrete piers and heavy blue I-beams. A nearby steeple poked above the trees, a quaint remembrance of village days juxtaposed with the modern crossing. We paddled below yet another set of power lines and then passed the wide, gaping mouth of the Nashua River where it quietly met the Merrimack just before we slipped into the shadows and vehicular rumble beneath the bridge. As had often been the case, just beyond were the stone piers of some long-ago demolished predecessor, now thick with greenery.

We encountered an old couch, a door, and vehicle axles washed up onshore. A large, rust-colored pipe crossed a small brook on the right not far from a rope swing where kids were giving Tarzan yells as they jumped into the water while companions screeched and squealed around them. It was only about a dozen kids, but they sounded like fifty.

Alan turned toward me, hands to his ears. "I prefer traffic noise."

"Reminds me of home," I replied, thinking of the neighborhood kids and the riot of friends they brought around.

Modest dwellings appeared on the left where the shore was littered with old household items, food wrappers, and beer cans. A few trees leaned over and strained the water with their lower branches. A pipe armored with riprap was ominously labeled "storm sewer overflow."

"Imagine what gushes out of that in a hard rain," Alan said, shaking his head.

"I think the polite term is 'floatables.'"

Just downstream a geyser shot white, foamy water about two feet above the dark, placid Merrimack. Here the cloaca of Nashua's wastewater treatment facility discharged the city's drains and flushings into the river, punctuating the old adage that "the solution to pollution is dilution." Mallards and black ducks cruised nearby without interest in the hydraulic display. The eruption had a faintly sour, soapy odor, with the slight scent of chlorine. A grayish plume floated downstream, slowly fanned out, and then dissipated.

Though we paddled between thickly wooded banks, it began to feel as if we were on a drag strip. Racing motorboats zoomed by us, their bows angled upward and slapping the water, unmuffled engines echoing along the river. One boatload of bikinied girls and boys with bulging biceps didn't even seem to see us, buzzing so closely we took on about a gallon of water and almost tipped into their wake. After baking in the river's reflected sunlight all day, and infuriated by fumes and noise, I exploded. I felt color rise in my face and shouted a string of epithets so vehemently I seemed to frighten Alan.

"Take it easy," he urged. "They're just a bunch of young punk assholes. No sense having a heart attack. Good they didn't hear you over the engine. Their boat is bigger, and so are they."

I took a deep breath. "I suppose I should be grateful they're here at all," I said, my muscles relaxing as exasperation leaked out of me like gas from a punctured aerosol can.

"Grateful? Sun's really fried your brain now."

"I mean, at least the water is clean enough for boating. Remember, it wasn't that long ago when Mungo found it disgusting, with people flushing their toilets directly into the river. The idea of camping near Nashua was so gross that he and his friends hopped in the car and headed north to Bow Junction, New Hampshire." There, they paddled into what looked like a substantial forest, but Mungo felt "cruelly tricked." The woods were merely a remnant patch into which lights shined from suburban houses. The spot echoed all night with traffic.

The next day Mungo continued north, alternating between the car and canoe, paddling until "sections of the river gave out underneath us, became too foul to navigate, turned into a bed of high sharp rocks, and trickled weakly through dams and obstructions." Eventually he found a small tributary with a majestic stand of pine. Constitutionally pessimistic, Mungo imagined the trees wouldn't grow unmolested much longer. Nevertheless, he assuaged deep disappointment at having "so badly botched up Thoreau's itinerary" by hugging a tree so big he could hardly get his arms around it.

A hundred years before Mungo's ill-fated adventure, Meader described the Merrimack as "a continual succession of silver cascades, sparkling ripples, broad, calm, mirror-like waters, or romantic, majestic, and useful waterfalls." But even in 1869 it was hard to imagine that the river downstream of the great manufacturing cities was "naturally incomparably pure and transparent."

At first the river purified itself of human wastes and organic by-products of textile manufacturing such as plant dyes, animal oils, and soaps. But as city populations along the Merrimack grew from hundreds to tens of thousands in a few decades, the river became overwhelmed. In addition, inorganic wastes such as chemical dyes, acids, bleaches, petroleum, and alkalis were increasingly discharged, not only fouling the water, but destroying the microbial life necessary for the river to break down organic pollutants. The problem became increasingly vexing as some of these growing cities sought to slake the thirst of burgeoning populations with river water.

Ultimately, the river would turn color with dyes, shimmer with greasy and oily films, float human waste, be poisoned with harsh chemicals, smell of rotting garbage and excrement, and carry away everything from cotton and wool wastes to sawdust and tannery sludge. "The temptation to cast into the moving water every form of portable refuse and filth, to be borne out of sight, is too great to be resisted," investigators for the Massachusetts State Board of Health wrote in 1873. Despite such warnings and bouts of typhoid in some cities, pollution grew worse. Just downstream of Lowell in Lawrence, Massachusetts, the *Evening Tribune* called the Merrimack "a gigantic sewer." By the 1960s, the river had the dubious distinction of being one of the ten most polluted in the country.

"Mungo must've seen the river at its absolute worst," Alan said, digging his paddle deep into the water and pulling hard.

"The first Earth Day was six months away. It was warm and sunny, April at its most perfect. Hardly anyone today gives it a thought, but back in 1970 more than twenty million people were involved in Earth Day. Congress adjourned so members could participate. Everyone agreed that we'd pushed the planet too far and something had to be done."

"Protests, teach-ins, speeches, marches. It was a grassroots movement that worked," Alan chimed in. "Somehow it all seems so quaint and dated now."

"Two years later Congress enacted the Clean Water Act," I said, recalling part of a speech I had recently given. Finally there was money for sewage treatment plants, and city wastes became increasingly harmless geysers like the one we had just passed. New standards for industrial discharges were developed, with penalties for violations. "Mungo was kind of cranky, but it was people like him who drew attention to pollution, built the momentum for Earth Day, and got ordinary people involved. Maybe disgusting rivers were necessary before anything got done."

"So the cradle of industry becomes the poster child for cleaning rivers," Alan added.

"Maybe if Thoreau hadn't made the river so famous and idyllic, people might not have gotten so hot over it. The real scandal of pollution wasn't chemicals and sewage, but how long it took to do anything significant."

A bass boat came at us full throttle and we braced for another wake. On drawing near, it slowed and we were only gently rocked. "Any luck?" I shouted. The two sunburned men with long beards looked like they had posed for the Smith Brothers cough drop box.

"A pair of keepers," the pilot replied while adjusting his cap. Once past us, they gunned the engines.

"I don't remember Mungo mentioning fishermen on the Merrimack," I said to Alan.

"You'd have to have been crazy. I can't imagine there were many fish back then, but only a person with a suicide wish would've eaten one."

Fishing epitomizes people's ongoing relationship with the river. Fish not only provided sustenance for Native Americans, they were at the heart of seasonal migrations and festivals. Runs of shad, salmon, and herring later made a life-or-death difference for colonists, who ate their catch fresh and preserved even more by smoking or salting. But fishing became degraded as more English settlers arrived. "If the savages gathered at this spot for the annual fishing festival, to secure the food on which they mainly depended," Meader wrote of Lowell's Pawtucket Falls, "the palefaces subsequently flocked here with no less eagerness, and scenes enacted by them would do no discredit to the barbaric orgies of a prior date."

Fish eventually became an article of commerce, and by 1820 Pawtucket Falls alone annually produced more than twenty-five hundred barrels. As the eighteenth century drew to a close, overharvesting left fish stocks in precipitous decline, and both New Hampshire and Massachusetts legislated fishing days, gear types, and other matters.

Early in the nineteenth century, dams built for canals around Cromwell's Falls and other rapids impeded movement of anadromous fish and confused migratory instincts. Power dams for textile mills exacerbated the situation, and with completion of the thirty-two-foot-high Lawrence Dam as the nineteenth century reached its midpoint, anadromous fish runs in the Merrimack Valley had all but ended.

"Perchance," Thoreau speculated, "after a few thousands of years, if the fishes will be patient, and pass their summers elsewhere, meanwhile, nature will have leveled the Billerica Dam, and the Lowell factories, and the Grass-ground River run clear again." Luckily, the fish did not have to wait so long. Shortly after the Civil War, New Hampshire and Massachusetts established multiyear moratoria on taking migratory species, and the Bay State made fishways mandatory. During the same period, experiments with hatchery-raised fish and restocking efforts were under way and meeting with some success. By the late 1880s, salmon were returning to the upper part of the river in numbers unseen for fifty years. Unfortunately, overfishing, pollution, and poor fishway operation left the revival short-lived. It was a political, social, and technical failure.

A renewed cooperative effort among states and the federal government to restore salmon runs began in the mid-1960s. With completion of fish passage facilities in 1986 at Lowell's Pawtucket Dam, migratory fish could swim upstream to Manchester for the first time in a century. But restoring fish, including capturing them for spawning and releasing them back into the river, has proved more difficult and complex than originally contemplated. Success has been elusive, though the work of healing continues.

Between high banks our progress grew slow and tedious in a stiffening wind. Whitecaps rippled the water. Occasionally we detected the railroad on the west bank, and beyond it the backside of megastores fronting on the broad, commerce-choked D. W. Highway.

"Maybe the more fishermen we see, the healthier the river is," I said. "A kind of litmus test?"

"They wouldn't be here unless there were fish. Since fish breathe in the water, I'd say they're a fairly good indicator. Even trout are stocked now, and they're pretty finicky."

Although the river is cleaner now than it has been since Thoreau's time, elevated bacteria levels continue to be the most intractable cause of pollution. Combined storm and sanitary sewers could take twenty years and a billion dollars to separate. Other sources of pollution well illustrate the range of human activity in the Merrimack Valley, including industrial discharges, urban and agricultural runoff of everything from oils to pesticides, septic system effluent, pet waste, storm drains, and underground leachate plumes from hazardous waste sites and landfills.

Despite these ongoing issues, the river is increasingly treasured for its natural character, and the segment from Merrimack to the Massachusetts line was recognized in 1990 under New Hampshire's river program. The corridor is a key migratory route for waterfowl and songbirds, and its large trees are roost sites for wintering bald eagles that fish the open water. Unusual species like hognose snake are present, as are wild lupine and several other rare plants.

Cleanup and healing initiated a revolution of interest in close contact with the river that we had witnessed on this warm, summer day. It wasn't merely a matter of aesthetics or frivolous play, but a significant business for those who rent hotel rooms, sell fishing tackle and boats, serve meals, and pump gas to deep travelers and others. As early as a half century ago, Raymond Holden, who wrote *The Merrimack* for the Rivers of America series, observed "the emergence of the idea of making an industry out of the task of giving to men, women and children in search of pleasure and relaxation exactly what they want and, if possible, more than they might ordinarily hope to get." Today, this once emerging idea is a way of life.

As new homes and commercial developments encroach on the river, boat launches become congested, and fishing pressure increases, the Merrimack no longer suffers from indifference. Rather, it is in danger of being loved to death. But at least with so broad a constituency from businesspeople to anglers, boaters to birdwatchers, municipal officials to developers, it is unlikely that the river will ever again be hijacked for a single purpose that so gravely compromises all other values.

Even as it flourishes as a magnet for recreation, contemplation, and aesthetic enjoyment and as a reservoir of natural values, the Merrimack continues to be used in relative unsung and underappreciated ways. More than three hundred thousand people consume its water, making it New England's second largest drinking source. Six hydroelectric dams supply power. Twenty-six sewage treatment plants in the New Hampshire portion of the watershed alone have a design capacity of almost ninety-seven million gallons per day. These and other elements of the increasingly complex relationship of people to the Merrimack may bring it closer to fulfilling Meader's 1869 portrayal of a river with "that rare combination of use and attractiveness along its whole course which renders it, *par excellence*, the most magnificent stream in the world."

Alan and I were exhausted as we pulled out just past the Hampshire Chemical plant, whose stacks and vents poked above the trees. A maker of organic chemicals for shampoos and other health-care products, the company was about to close. More than a year later, it would pay a thirty-two-thousand-dollar federal penalty for improperly treating hazardous waste.

Sweating in the late afternoon humidity, we hoisted the boat past an uneven cluster of riprap protecting a concrete culvert. Yanking it up a steep, narrow, and eroded embankment lined with poison ivy, we crossed the railroad tracks and reached the pickup parked at the terminus of Spit Brook Road. Just a stone's throw down the street, we could see the busy retail mecca along the Daniel Webster Highway.

Flow

Its seventy-two pounds conspiring with gravity, the canoe sluiced
quickly down the steep, overgrown path to the water and landed with
a splash. Seemingly as eager as a puppy for a swim, it almost took us
with it. Where the day before Alan and I had worked tediously to haul
the boat up the bank, it now yanked us down on a white-knuckled rollercoaster ride ending in laughter.

The morning was cool and misty, the sky low with a modulating
brightness that shifted in shades of gray swirling slowly around us.
Not quite thick enough to be fog, it was a gauzy, translucent atmosphere softening the overhanging trees, hills, and nearby buildings.
Within fifteen minutes though, the sun had melted through, and almost instantly the world was bright with hard surfaces, the mist disappearing as suddenly as if we had awakened from a dream.

Without a breath of wind, the water was at first a flat calm. Dark, but
reflective, it had the quality of an old, faded mirror. As the mist evapo-
rated, a slight and fickle tailwind arose, rippling the surface, which
erupted in sparkles of fractured sunshine.

The banks were not quite as steep as they had been upstream, but
still we paddled below the level of the surrounding countryside. The
east shore was thickly wooded with large trees, evoking storybook images of English royal forests. Many of the bigger trunks were prominently posted with "No Trespassing" signs. BAE Systems of Nashua,

an international maker of avionics, navigation, combat, and electronic warfare products, sternly threatened prosecution for violations.

"Imagine walking around up there," I suggested.

"Like Lilliputians among huge trees."

"Who cares about trees? All those No Trespassing signs are a dare," I said, suddenly flush with a bit of adolescent defiance. Maybe tooling around in a boat after a long winter and spring confined behind a desk brought out a quixotic juvenile streak in me.

Had we been younger, we might have taken up the challenge laid down by the signs. But we were two meek, middle-aged guys, and to us the placards might as well have been pit bulls or armed guards. Kids walking or camping on the land might have been seen as a lark. But two grown men violating the perimeter of a high-tech defense contractor gave me cold war shivers of prosecution for industrial espionage.

In this area Thoreau found a fifteen-acre sandy desert several feet deep "which was interesting even refreshing to our eyes in the midst of the almost universal greenness." Stopping to chat with an old man working in a field on the opposite shore, he learned that the "impressive and beautiful" patch of sand had been a cultivated field of grain and corn. But fishermen had pulled up riparian bushes so as to more easily haul their seines. With the bank exposed, windblown sand created a miniature Sahara. Along the riverbank where the grit was blown off, Thoreau found fire rings of burnt stones in which charcoal and small animal bones were mixed. He also spied ancient wigwam foundations, flakes of stone, and one perfect arrowhead.

In a glance, Thoreau saw a landscape changing as its relationship with humans evolved. A forest and Indian encampment had become a cultivated field and commercial fishery. With careless treatment, the property had succumbed to desertification.

A century and a half later, our observations picked up where his left off. Fishing was now almost solely from boats and for sport, and the land had healed and reverted back to forest, though it was forbidden ground with ominous signs threatening severe penalties. Paradoxically, the need for twenty-first-century militarylike secrecy now kept loggers and developers at bay, leaving the land as close to its primeval state as it had been in four hundred years.

The opposite bank presented a contrasting environment, with large buildings and vast stretches of macadam parking visible beyond the thinnest veneer of trees. Sandwiched between the Merrimack and the D. W. Highway were a series of shopping malls and big-box retailers. Among them was the massive one-million-square-foot Pheasant Lane Mall, a Xanadu of retailing.

Much of the development, fortunately, remained beyond our line of sight from the canoe. Nevertheless, from our drive the previous afternoon we knew that in little more than half a mile we had passed huge department stores such as Filene's, J. C. Penney, Sears, and Target; chain restaurants like McDonald's, Starbucks, and Chili's; and the big-box retailers Office Depot, Staples, Toys R Us, Costco, Petco, and Home Depot. There were national and regional bookstores, furniture dealers, housewares discounters, and sporting goods outlets—a retail opportunity for every occasion. You could, I imagined, buy just about any item necessary for daily existence and some for which there was yet any definable need. Inside, with the bright light, soothing air conditioning, and enticing glitz, it was easy to confuse the good life with the goods of life.

Especially when standing up, Alan and I could see loading docks, dumpsters, and idling refrigerator trucks; barrels, piles of pallets, and scraps of lumber. Ours was a more novel and interesting view than the storefronts we commonly saw, with their illuminated logo signs and orderly plate glass doorways. What the proprietor would never suffer to be seen from the road was visible from the river whose banks were occasionally strewn with the detritus of retailing, including foam cups, crushed and weathered corrugated boxes, winter's sloughed-off accumulation of sand, and lemminglike shopping carts that had committed suicide by leaping into the water.

Apparently, people on the river were so few or marginal to the developers that what they saw didn't matter. Once a highway of commerce and communication and the economic lifeblood of the region, the river was now not even an afterthought. No one, it seemed, even imagined that it might attract trade with a scenic walkway or bird blind. We were mesmerized by an odd voyeurism, like being backstage at the theater or in a small room at a political party caucus. Mostly, we reveled in a certain schadenfreude at seeing, in a state of undress, places that so depended on image.

I must admit to finding visual interest in the variety of geometric shapes and contrasting building sizes populating this landscape. The burst of shimmering light that exploded from the expansive parking lots not yet filled with the balloonlike colors of cars was, like Thoreau's desert, a stimulating counterpoint to the deep green woods opposite. After many changes, the fields of his time had been transformed into what seemed like a final harvest of concrete block, brick, and bituminous paving.

These temples to consumerism appeared to be the final act in the landscape, but like the imposing mills and dams of the industrial era, they too would change. Perhaps river travelers in the next century might find a plastic pill bottle, a mannequin's leg, or the silvery shard of a compact disc, just as Thoreau found an arrowhead and charred stones. Like us, they may marvel less over what exists or what used to be than over the raw power and inexorable process of change.

"The landscape is indeed something real, and solid, and sincere, and I have not put my foot through it yet," Thoreau wrote in *A Week*. Still, there is a constant evanescence to the landscape as it gradually fades into something else. Forests, for example, have returned because coal and oil supplanted cordwood for heating, agriculture declined in the face of cheap imports, and automobiles replaced horses needing hayfields. With these lands no longer producing fuel and crops, they not only grew trees, but ripened for commercial and residential development.

Much of the transformation to houses and stores was made possible by improved transportation in the form of limited-access highways that enabled people to live in New Hampshire and commute to jobs in greater Boston. Transportation also drove development in Thoreau's day, with industrial growth facilitated by increasingly efficient movement of raw materials and finished products via canals and later railroads.

It would be easy to telescope this change into a linear progression from natural to increasingly more artificial surroundings, but the transformation has been neither direct nor simple. In the mid-1850s

Thoreau lamented an impoverished countryside without the bears, moose, deer, porcupines, beavers, and turkeys of yore. Today, with woodlands regenerated, all have returned to even the most suburban environments, some in nuisance proportions. It would be comforting to think of these creatures as emblematic of a landscape healed from the ravages of human exploitation, but with the loss of open fields, some animals common to Thoreau, such as bobolinks and meadow-larks, have become increasingly rare. The abundant frogs and sala-manders he encountered are under continuous assault from pollution and habitat destruction. Other animals, like the passenger pigeon, are extinct. The clock has not been turned back to an earlier era; we are merely transitioning to the next phase. The landscape is our col-lective biography, and like the story of our own lives, it is fraught with complexity and contradictions.

"The east bank may look enticing with all those big trees, but at least we could get out on the other side and wander around the stores with-out being prosecuted," I said, trying to think of something redeeming about a mall with its backside to the river.

"Sure," Alan said with his trademark wry smile, "if your wallet is full. Otherwise, you're a vagrant. And remember, it may seem like a main street shopping district, but don't hand out a political leaflet. This is as much private property as the posted woods on the other shore. You're only invited to spend money."

"Need to buy anything?" I asked facetiously.

"How about a snow blower?" We both laughed aloud at the image of the ungainly and unseasonable machine perched between the gun-wales. Your mode of transportation often determined your purpose, was your destiny.

"With all these malls and highways, you've got to wonder whether eagles and beavers on the river, trees, and cleaner water are almost a kind of deception," I said after a few quiet moments had passed.

"I don't get it. Yesterday you were raving that all the fishermen and boats on the water signified things were getting better."

"The landscape may be healing, but only from threats a century old. It doesn't seem like much is happening about problems we can see from here—paving over the watershed and polluted runoff like pesticides and oil, grease, and salt from parking lots. Seems like we're always fixing yesterday's problem."

"At least when pipes were spewing chemicals or raw shit you could see the problem and knew who the enemy was. Everyone's guilty now. That goes for us driving around."

"What was the name of that comic strip possum?"

"Pogo? The one that said 'We have met the enemy and he is us.'"

"Something like that."

Suddenly the huge stores and acres of parking disappeared. "We're in Massachusetts," Alan announced, though there wasn't a welcome sign emblazoned with the governor's name such as greets highway travelers.

"How do you know?"

"The malls are gone."

"People from Massachusetts don't buy things?"

"Sure they do—in New Hampshire, where there isn't any sales tax."

It was the clearest political boundary I had ever crossed. How strange that the manner in which states levied taxes would become an artifact as visible on the landscape as a border fence or mountain range.

McPhee found this stretch of river "peaceful, mostly silent, [and] secluded" despite the occasional "surf of highways" he could not see. Though we, too, saw the kingfishers, geese, great blue herons, Styrofoam cups, truck mufflers, and shopping carts he catalogs, our eyes couldn't avoid the retail temples surrounded by acres of parking. Perhaps McPhee was caught in the fugue of a pastoral moment. Sometimes the river, isolated behind its high banks, can weave a green illusion.

Unfortunately, cursed by our professional training, Alan and I couldn't just paddle blithely in linear seclusion. Issues of planning, development, and place had become instinctual with years of education and experience.

A deep traveler is never a tourist merely. Whether a carpenter, plumber, chemist, landscaper, machinist, social worker, doctor, lawyer, or Indian chief, deep travelers apply their working experience to what they see on a journey, allowing them to perceive diverse places more fully. Professional background is far from omniscience, but it enables us to employ our own peculiar sensibility and not just rely on the judgment of guidebooks, tourism officials, and other authorities. Whether we're truckers, teachers, or dental hygienists, truck routes, school locations, or the condition of people's teeth helps us understand the places we visit and see some things invisible to most other people.

Our working backgrounds had led to a lively discussion about traffic, urban development, and land-use patterns the previous evening after we had gotten off the Merrimack and camped at the Red Roof Inn on Spit Brook Road less than half a mile from the river. After we had showered, consulted the weather channel, and drunk a cup of weak and burnt, but free, coffee from the lobby, there was still plenty of daylight in the late afternoon. Staring out the window overlooking the Everett Turnpike, I became restless watching the endless stream of traffic. Listening to the whoosh of speeding cars and the rumble of trucks was a call to get out and go somewhere. Having been confined to the river for the morning and most of the afternoon, we decided to leave the motel and scout the downstream reach by car even though there were no rapids, any quickwater having been drowned by the Pawtucket Dam at Lowell about ten miles south. At least we'd get out and exercise my roaming urge and see some of the area not visible from the water.

What we discovered could hardly be called a discovery. It was all both reassuringly familiar and disconcertingly the same. The short stretch of Spit Brook Road leading to the Daniel Webster Highway was a confusion of traffic lights; bright and garish commercial signs in a mishmash of shapes, sizes, and heights; and turning strips across multiple lanes of oncoming vehicles. It wasn't a trip for the impatient.

The procession of cars and trucks moved slowly and tediously with regular flashes of red brake lights as we crept past parking lots and large stores, including Shaw's Supermarket, Marshall's, Sports Authority, Barnes & Noble Booksellers, and Blockbuster Video. Drivers suddenly decided to make left-hand turns and then just as quickly changed their minds. Tailgaters stopped with little warning. Some people seemed to putter along aimlessly while munching a burger or chatting on a cell phone.

"We might as well be home," Alan said, while we fretfully waited three light cycles to make a turn. "Same stores, same traffic."

"It's like a Kafka story where you wake up and everything is like home but it's clearly not home. You might be in California, Detroit, Atlanta, or Houston and not be able to tell the difference. How weird is that?"

"Like that guy who gets out of bed one morning and finds he's a bug or something, but otherwise everything is the same."

"What's his name? . . . Gregor . . ."

"Samsa."

"I wouldn't mind the same stores so much if they at least made some effort to look a little different. You could sell the same products and still not confuse New York with Los Angeles."

"It's architecture as trademark. It's a form of advertising. Each store is a giant billboard. Unless you push these national retailers hard, they won't make the slightest design change. I've heard it time and again at zoning commission meetings. They know their marketing strategy, and don't see any town as unique. Communities are as interchangeable as their product lines."

The sluggish traffic only grew worse when we turned south on the Daniel Webster Highway. We were in an immense, sprawling retail city of bright boxy buildings surrounded by macadam moats and a chaotic forest of cheerfully beckoning signs. It was like being inside a pinball machine, with lights and glimmering objects, cartoonish colors, and intricate passages for cars playing the part of silver balls. Total Fitness, Honey Baked Ham Company, Linens N Things, Bob's Discount Furniture, Tweeter, U-Haul, David's Bridal, and a myriad other retailers called to us with their logos and storefronts like street corner hookers. Store after store stretched to the Massachusetts line like a giant net fishing for the dollars of Bay State consumers.

Navigating our way through the clogged lanes of the parking lot of Filene's, we came upon a back entrance at the far end of the store, the only door for customers facing the water in more than a mile of malls and shopping centers. The entry fronted on a small patch of parking beyond which the Merrimack flowed like a grayish ribbon obscured by fencing and vegetation, barely visible even to the most observant.

Driving past Filene's we cruised along the stores' backsides, going by dumpsters and stacks of flattened corrugated boxes. We found ourselves behind a Target store and then a parking garage. The only evidence of the river lay in the interest of swallows, gulls, and other birds that were drawn to the water beyond a berm covered with ragged vegetation.

The next cluster of stores was set on a bluff high above the river and included Bed Bath & Beyond, Famous Footwear, Eastern Mountain Sports, and Modell's Sporting Goods. The passage behind them was narrow, with unexpected jogs as we passed loading docks and metal stairwells built into featureless block walls punctuated by utility structures and steel doorways. Though the river was visible in places, the stores treated it as if it didn't exist, showing off only the cheapest and least maintained part of the buildings where litter caught in weeds at the pavement's edge and water stains and peeling paint gave the only character to faceless façades.

"What in the world . . . is that a grave?" Alan asked, pointing to a grassy knoll overlooking the river.

"A pink granite bench, I think."

We pulled over, nonplussed by a tiny memorial with overgrown plantings crying out for weeding. Between two small arborvitaes was a bench that offered a better view of a blank block wall than of the river. Alan bent over and read an inscription carved in the stone: "In loving Memory of Dana L. Clark who, at this past site of Blue Line Express, brought his family happiness by the truckload."

"I guess there was a trucking company here once," I said.

"You'd never know just looking. Everything's been obliterated by pavement and stores. I wonder if this bench was a sales condition. I've reviewed commercial development plans for almost three decades and never seen anything like this."

Like the arrowheads and fire-blackened stones Thoreau had found, we had discovered evidence of past occupation obscured by later development. A quick online search a week later revealed that the company had gone under in 1989.

"It's sort of touching in a way," I said, surprised at a slight lump in my throat. "It's not just a marker for an old building or long past event.

It's about a man and his family, a reminder that a business is also a livelihood for people."

Despite the warmth of the day, I felt a chill. An eerie discomfort overtook me, like you might feel at a gravesite still too fresh to be grass-covered. This humble, obscure monument momentarily stamped a wasteland behind a big-box store with something distinctive and gave it character, made it more real.

"It's also a little pathetic. Think of the thousands of people who come here every day to shop. How many see this or stop to read what it says?"

"Just deep travelers and people who get lost."

"Same thing."

As we headed north toward downtown Nashua for dinner, Alan couldn't help but be reminded of planning issues he faced on returning to the office. Frequent curb cuts bled cars onto the D. W. Highway, drive-up windows twisted traffic in knots, signs blocked sightlines, and despite all the driving lanes and driveways, places were hard to get to in the confusion of clamoring signs, traffic lights, and entrances. With all the cars flowing down the road, there was mobility aplenty, yet one couldn't reach the stores and restaurants easily. It was a delicious paradox in a country where "places are about access and absence," as journalist Howard Mansfield put it. "Getting in and getting out. Flow." Of course, the river was also about flow. That was why we were here.

Despite our growling stomachs as afternoon faded into evening and sunlight turned vermillion and butterscotch, an oasis of green caught my eye soon after passing an Exxon station, Old Navy and Pier One stores, and a Burger King. Reflexively, I hung a left and turned in. We found ourselves parked beside a tiny gable-roofed brick building with granite lintels. Next to it we saw a rusted hand pump, and beyond that the ancient Old South Cemetery rose up a hillside. Shaded with large trees, the burial ground was immaculately groomed though the stones were cocked at odd angles from years of settling and frost. It was a quiet place that by rights belonged beside a white-steepled church at a rural crossroads lined with hoary maples. Instead, it was in view of a Best Buy and Comp USA, a CVS pharmacy, an oil change joint, and a real estate office.

"Where the hell are we?" Alan asked.

"I think we fell into a time warp," I replied, getting out of the truck.

"This brick building was a one-room schoolhouse," Alan said, scrutinizing a plaque. "I think it's been protected by the dead. The one thing developers can't pave over with impunity is a cemetery."

"How appropriate. The dead are left to be guardians of their own history. Without them, no one would think twice about this place ever having had a past."

"I doubt anyone would think even once, anyway."

The endless rumble of traffic and smell of exhaust fumes faded as we strolled through this shard of a faded era and read the biography of a long-gone time and place in headstones. Finely carved death angels and descriptive inscriptions were dated to the dawn of the eighteenth century. Here lay young children who died of disease, mothers lost in childbirth, and people who had had their full threescore and ten. Miniature British flags stood beside the stones of the King's soldiers, like Josiah Willard, who died in 1750. Many of the dead were killed in Indian raids, including the 1724 death of Thomas Lund, whose stone informed us that

> this man with Seven
> more, that lies in this
> Grave; was Slew, All in
> A day, by the Indiens.

By a startling incongruity with its surroundings, the cemetery bore powerful witness to a past of Spartan scarcity, disease, and threat of deadly attacks. But the big, garish commercial buildings nearby this quiet patch of yore provided, perhaps, less contrast than we satisfied twenty-first-century consumers did with our long-dead compatriots. The bloody frontier history of struggle with the Indians in this area is forgotten and buried more deeply than the interred bodies. Does anyone stop here when running out for groceries, buying a couch, or looking for a high-definition television?

Our collective amnesia is not only a modern phenomenon. After describing the brutal encounters of colonists with natives, Thoreau admits that "these battles sound incredible to us. I think that posterity will doubt if such things ever were; if our bold ancestors who settled this land were not struggling rather with the forest shadows, and not with a copper colored race of men."

There were plenty of places to eat among the malls fronting the D. W. Highway, from Pizza Hut and Bickford's to Wendy's and Applebee's. Since we could enjoy all of them within a short drive of home, they underscored our determination to cruise past car dealerships and apartment complexes toward downtown in search of something authentically Nashua.

The only city in the country twice named *Money* magazine's "Best Place to Live in America," Nashua is an exemplar of sprawling, low-density growth fueled by improved highways, its forty-mile proximity to Boston, and a relatively laissez-faire attitude toward land use in a state where license plates proclaim "Live Free or Die." Yet even as Nashua sprawls, its center remains a vibrant and active place filled with interesting architecture, shops, and happenings that give it an idiosyncratic personality. Despite the city's rapid change—it grew from nearly fifty-six thousand people in 1970 to almost eighty-eight thousand in 2004—Nashua's official website nevertheless touts history as its greatest amenity because "it imbues the City with authenticity, character and strength."

Nashua began as a business enterprise with the founding of a fur trading post on the Nashua River in 1656 but grew slowly, owing partly to Indian hostilities. By 1790 it had more than six hundred residents, and a post office was established a dozen years later. Soon the sleepy village changed rapidly as the result of a significant transportation improvement. With the opening of the Middlesex Canal in 1804, Nashua became the head of navigation on the Merrimack, and its importance as a commercial and industrial center was launched. By the time Thoreau paddled past, it was home to about six thousand people and had two textile companies operating five mills. Before the Civil War, six railroads crossed through the city, with fifty-six trains departing and arriving daily. By the 1860s, Nashua was "one extensive workshop," according to Meader, "a beautiful city" with three newspapers.

Textiles remained the city's employment backbone until firms started closing and moving south during the Great Depression, the last shutting its doors not long after World War II. A civic-minded community whose boosters wouldn't let it die, Nashua reshaped itself with high-tech companies, including computers, software, specialty papers, Internet training, and optics manufacture.

Far from the malls and fast food joints surrounding Old South Cemetery, we walked into Pub Grainery, a long, two-story clapboard building tucked behind parking lots and big, chunky hospital buildings at the southern outskirts of downtown. Built in the late 1800s, it had been a foundry, feed store, and plumbing warehouse and showroom. The inside felt like an old-time roadhouse, with stout wooden columns and joists exposing post-and-beam construction that gave the dining room a cozy, informal atmosphere. We sat in a wooden booth and gazed into the bar as laughter, whistles, easy chatter, and cigarette smoke wafted freely toward us from the joyfully rowdy locals blowing off steam at the end of a long workweek.

"How's the steak?" I asked Alan, leaning back and taking a couple pulls on my Guinness.

"Super tender. I think they used some kind of garlic marinade. Want a bite?" He handed me a forkful. "The fish good?"

"It'd still be wiggling if it was any fresher."

"Sure beats Chili's or Pizza Hut. At least we can say we've actually been in Nashua and not some place that could just as easily have been Cleveland, Little Rock, or a short drive from home."

Despite loss of its principal industry, and an ever sprawling edge that began with construction of the Everett Turnpike in the late 1950s, downtown Nashua has managed to survive and thrive. Bounded on one end by a regal city hall with classic pillars and at the other by a stolid Civil War obelisk, Main Street is a broad and handsome avenue of masonry buildings enlivened with architectural details that intrigue the eye.

The street is a marriage of varying uses and designs that illustrate the city's growth over time. A prominent bell tower and rough-cut stone at the Church of the Good Shepherd contrasts with the suburban brick storefront of Alec's Shoes. TD Banknorth is housed in a classic, early-twentieth-century urban financial building with tall, fluted columns, while the white brick of Jordan's Luggage is reminiscent of the 1960s. This is not merely a tourists' street with gift shops and ice cream vendors. Aubuchon Hardware, Chuck's Barber Shop, Jackie's Diner, and Wingate's Pharmacy and Compounding meet the needs of people working and living nearby.

My first time downtown had been a romantic sidewalk dinner with Pam at Martha's Exchange on a warm evening before our second day paddling the Merrimack. We were full of speculation about rapids, old mill dams, and birdlife as we held hands and watched a cavalcade of cars pass by. The sidewalk was busy with middle-aged couples in well-pressed clothes and twenty-somethings in sleeveless shirts revealing tattoos and muscles. Storefronts were bright and lively, and people paused to peer at displays.

As we sipped beer and nibbled calamari, light from the setting sun moved across the buildings on the other side of the street. The fading and shifting illumination revealed and almost set into motion elaborate pilasters and floral masonry medallions. There were carved cornices and decorative brackets, windows that were round, rectangular, arched, square, and pointed.

Next to the Pompanoosuc Mills store opposite us was a tobacco shop called Castro's Back Room. Its cigar store Indian was in the bearded Cuban leader's image. With its politically incorrect product and signature name, the store may not have been the darling of downtown boosters, but to me it epitomized what made this late-nineteenth-century downtown worth a stay at the dawn of the twenty-first. A unique establishment with a quirky, edgy image, it captured our curiosity without a huge sign or garish lights. It was the kind of place that could draw regulars from a distance and invite newcomers to the street. Nearby were other idiosyncratic businesses such as Blackbird Books, Bilancia Gallery, and Renaissance Glassworks, but Castro's led the way.

Deep travelers unable to resist, Pam and I entered this exotic den of dark woodwork with its long counter and cigar-filled cabinets. The walls were busy with nostalgic memorabilia, and a large television played softly before an eclectic semicircle of old barber chairs. In front of the chairs, a table that had once been a cart for hauling cloth in a local textile mill displayed a range of sport and men's magazines. We felt as if we'd been invited into the proprietor's home.

Pam bought clove cigarettes and I purchased an Excalibur cigar. We sat and blew smoke, chatting with the owner and customers who came and went, learning more than we wanted to know about one man's divorce and another's history of Chevy repairs. It took only moments to become part of the scene and to know we had been to Nashua and nowhere else.

"Nashua's got lots of distinctive, quality buildings," Alan was saying as our Grainery dinner wound down and we noshed on the few French fries remaining on my plate, "but the kind of vibrancy you see here doesn't just happen. Someone's working at it."

I nodded. "You've got to wonder what's different from the typical small city downtown. Plenty of them have old factories and a river, but usually, soaped-up storefronts look out on quiet sidewalks."

Later we learned that a local revitalization organization called Nashua Downtown put dollars and energy into making the area attractive. It had staff and a board of directors that included key players like the mayor and representatives of large and small businesses. They distributed promotional brochures, sponsored television commercials, and got retailers and others to work together on marketing strategies. They organized streetscape improvements and maintenance activities such as litter cleanups. Nashua had a history of such civic commitment.

"So many cities think they're going to save themselves with a stadium or a convention center," Alan opined with professional authority, "but community revitalization is a process, not a project. Projects build egos for politicians who cut ribbons and have their names engraved on plaques. They don't build cities."

We rode back to our motel room past all the symbols of sprawling retail and residential development. Such places may waste energy, recklessly gobble up land, pollute air and water, and squander time for people who endure long waits in traffic, but their unrelenting and numbing sameness bothered me most. Tourists have nothing unique and refreshing to see, and residents lack anything to take pride in. It was all the same.

Perhaps civic-minded people need a deep traveler's test to determine what constitutes an engaging landscape that gives a place interest and texture. A deep traveler's gaze allows us to see anew what we look at with a tired and jaundiced eye at home. Worse than contempt, familiarity can breed indifference; it can blind us.

Maybe not all sprawl is bad, I thought, as we whizzed past signs glowing with bright colors otherwise reserved for plastic children's toys. Who hasn't taken advantage of a nearby strip mall to avoid a trip into town? Some products can be purchased only at such locations, and the buying power of super-sized stores helps keep products affordable. Furthermore, backyards in cookie-cutter subdivisions are perfect for vegetable gardens, throwing a baseball, and family barbecues regardless of their political geography.

The real problem is a pattern of using land that increasingly leaves little choice in a nation where choosing among alternatives is a birthright. Maybe sprawl is a bit like what Ogden Nash quipped about progress: "Progress may have been all right once, but it went on too long." When development devours whatever else we value in our landscape, it has indeed gone on too long. Even freewheeling Nashua has its limits. In 2006 Wal-Mart's attempt to build a 140,000-square-foot store on a busy commercial artery was rejected after a bitter fight and close vote of the city planning board.

Perhaps we can't or don't want to put an end to this seemingly endless flow of tract houses and garish commercial strips. Can we find and create unique islands that are attractive and engaging? Can we bring meaning and a bit of beauty to such places even if we can't make them coherent and efficient? Can we, like Robert Frost's ovenbird, learn "what to make of a diminished thing"? And is there anything that could make us feel more diminished and disheartened than thinking we live in a place that is no different from any other? Such places are petri dishes of apathy. We need to find, build, and flaunt the uniqueness of the places we live if for nothing more than to sustain our democratic institutions.

A distinctive place integrates open lands into the developed landscape not just to protect ecosystems on which life's web depends, but because healing fragmented landscapes offers us healing and wholeness as well. It's no surprise that in the awful wake of September 11, 2001, people sought solace and refuge in parks and other natural areas where they might spot a soaring hawk or a secretive fox.

A singular place values forests and farms not just as the picture in the picture window, but because they yield clean water, wood products, food, and fiber that put us in touch with the origin of some of life's basic necessities. The wood in our houses and eggs on the breakfast plate are more than shelter and sustenance, they are about our relationship to the land.

A unique community protects historic structures not as a frivolous aesthetic luxury, but because they deepen awareness, provide a sense of continuity, and inspire commitment to improving the here and now. The past in such a place is never over. It's always about the present.

The issues are complex, intractable even. Walkable communities with a few shops and a bank, perhaps a tavern clustered near homes, save energy, create community, prevent pollution, and promote good health. Yet with the easiest buck and complicit regulations fueling development, these values are readily bulldozed. Perhaps paddling is the right rhythm for such ruminations and offers the clearest landscape view. As Thoreau observed, "he who hears the rippling of rivers in these degenerate days will not utterly despair." After all, nothing teaches a landscape's contours like a river.

I mulled over all these musings of the previous evening, mesmerized by a few high cirrus clouds and hearing water rippling against the canoe. We passed beneath twin power lines, and traffic echoed between the banks though the road remained invisible to us. Fresh beaver-peeled sticks littered the eastern shore. Alan spotted the dark silhouette of a cormorant, its long, sinuous neck stretched to one side as if listening to a message carried on the wind.

Although the landscape along the road above us had changed radically during the years since Thoreau, we could see little difference from the river. But deep travel wasn't about blocking out what was beyond the riverbanks or enjoying a fairytale past. It wasn't merely about relaxation or an escape from life's challenges, but a means of confronting them. We had gladly fled the doldrums of our regularly paced days, but inasmuch as the concerns motivating our everyday lives had true meaning, they never went on vacation without us.

Even while deep traveling we can't expect to gain more than a surficial understanding of issues like sprawl, urban revitalization, and open space protection in distant regions. But looking beyond landmarks and pretty and prominent spots to take a true pulse of the places we visit can energize us to learn more and open our eyes to similar situations and vistas close to home. If Nashua gave me a clearer understanding of Hartford's environs and some renewed motivation, I'd deem the trip successful. Such is a deep traveler's most highly prized souvenir. Sometimes the depth in deep travel comes only after we have returned home. At its best, travel deepens our experience of the place we live.

As I watched the low hills go by and felt the current draw us like a leaf, log, or piece of waterborne detritus, I was intrigued that the river was the only constantly moving feature of the landscape even as it was also among the least changing. It appeared linear in its relentless slide to the sea, and yet the hydrologic cycle made the water part of a planetary circulatory system. Like the United States, it was all about flow, all about movement; yet unlike the built environment, no one would mistake mere flow for progress. While cities, roads, and subdivisions often produced a disjointed mishmash, the river and its tributaries lent coherence to the landscape, embodied the logic of nature. It wasn't a very profound thought or an original idea, but after a day ruminating with Alan over sprawling development and the dynamics of downtown Nashua, the notion had emotional resonance.

"We'd be a lot better off," I ventured aloud after an interlude of silence, "if we thought more ecologically." Alan cocked an ear and grunted. It seemed a modest encouragement. "We should forget town boundaries and zip codes when planning and building and just consider where the rain flows after it falls." There was a heavy silence.

"Have you raised this with the post office?" he at last asked laconically.

"Well, I . . ."

"Good thought, but it's not going anywhere. These design-with-nature concepts or bioregionalism approaches or whatever you call them always run into practical difficulties—like laws that recognize political, not natural boundaries."

He was right, of course. But still, the logic was backwards. Political boundaries were about separation while rivers united places. Rivers were real and tangible while political boundaries were the fancy of politicians.

"Maybe we need to teach the logic of rivers in schools."

"Organic food for thought, I suppose."

We approached a long-dead and sun-bleached oak leaning over the water, its leafless branches straining the current and capturing pieces of plastic, driftwood, and other junk. An osprey perched atop the horizontal trunk, surveying the scene with a cold eye. Massachusetts and New Hampshire meant nothing to him.

What Floats Your Boat

At a meeting of the Mayor and Aldermen yesterday: Petitions of
Nathaniel Greene, postmaster, for the use of the whole of the lower
floor of the building he now occupies for the Post Office, that the
public may be better accommodated; referred to the committee
on public buildings, to be joined by the City Council.

Boston Courier, September 10, 1839

Chou and Kosygin Confer

Manchester Union Leader, September 12, 1969

Mentally ill overwhelm hospital ERs

Lowell Sun, September 2, 2003

As the sun gained its zenith, it transformed dark water into a highway
of polished silver, sparkling sporadically whenever the wind riffing
through overhanging trees touched down on the river's surface. The
banks were often eroded, illustrating where the current rubbed up
against the shore in high water.

A large oak worthy of Druid worship stretched its thick, muscular
limbs and seemingly pushed all other trees away as it reached for the
sky and created its own clearing along the bank. A rope swing hung
from a branch leaning over the water. A few shirts, some trousers, and
the underwear of intrepid swimmers were sprinkled beneath it in
daubs of blue, yellow, and red on the leafy forest floor.

Modest houses appeared occasionally on both banks. Piles of lumber, children's bicycles, a tree fort, a small boat pulled up on the grass,
barbecue grills, and other objects around them hinted at the lives of
people within. The river was broad, slow, and pondlike, the power of
its current visible in small, swirling thumbprints of motion welling up
from below the surface, and in the tree trunks, barrels, broken-off pieces of buildings, and other flotsam tossed onshore by spring freshets.

Before long, the breeze became a steady headwind strong enough
to balance out the slight downstream tug of the river and hold us in

stasis when we stopped paddling. Neither driven back by strong wind nor pulled along by the river, we fell into a steady, hypnotic tempo with our paddles. Transforming us into a single entity, the canoe became an extension of our bodies, supplely responding to our will as readily as arms and legs. Not merely a leaf on the current, we passed through the landscape strictly by the effort we put into each stroke.

Following in Thoreau's wake on the Sudbury, almost literally, Teale felt more alive in a canoe, which signaled adventure and projected him back to the days of Indians and French Voyageurs. He felt suffused with buoyancy, freedom, and grace, enjoying the duality of the vessel's instability, which repelled some people and lured others through a sense of controlled danger. With the wind and sun against my cheek, I at last understood that galvanizing mélange of liberation, fluidity, and vulnerability.

Though our arms and shoulders grew tired and our backs began to cramp, Alan and I pressed on, sharing an almost musical synchronicity, a giddy endorphin rush urging us forward. The contours of the river became our own, and I felt as if the moods of the sky, the banks, and the water were my moods. I felt as deep into the scene as the Cooper's hawk glaring at us from a dead willow branch, or the fish rising in the shallows for a mayfly that had fallen into the river. I had fallen, too.

I fell into the time machine of my own childhood, the wind in the hawk's willow recalling the adventures of Ratty and Mole that were read to me as my head lay securely on a pillow in the far safety of youth. Forty years later, at last my heart was full with Kenneth Grahame's dictum that "there is *nothing*—absolutely nothing—half so much worth doing as simply messing around in boats."

We passed a tidy little cornfield, a reminder of the farms that one of the Thoreau brothers would run to for a sip of water or milk while the other handled the boat. I wasn't sure whether this productive little slice of agriculture, which enjoyed the rich, alluvial silt gifted by regular flooding, was a sign of hope that rural living still survived in this suburbanized landscape or was a sad, remnant reminder of what once was. Regardless, the neat rows were welcome relief to the eye, standing in stark contrast to nature's own unkempt and tangled garden of trees and vines typically lining the banks.

Almost immediately our gaze shifted to another manmade plant-ing along the river. Just ahead was a small, well-kept trailer park at a big bend Thoreau called the Horseshoe Interval. Although a bit quea-sy about development up to the water's edge, I was also pleased that people of modest means could live along the waterfront. Weary of the speculations and judgments we had made about Nashua's sprawl, I was almost gladdened by this mild visual dissonance, which added in-terest and made this stretch of river lively to look at, for even unrelent-ing beauty can be dull.

Mungo would have railed against such defilement, and sometimes I envied his righteous anger. Perhaps we'd become anesthetized to such insults to the earth as they grew ubiquitous. Although I was paddling, maybe in Mungo's lexicon I was "missing the boat" by my complacen-cy at being an observer merely. "Missing the boat," the sixties radical wrote, "is just about the worst thing that can happen to a young man in America today, for where is he if he is still on the other side?" His was a world of polar opposites in which you had to take sides. Perhaps our current reluctance to do so is allowing the countryside to be par-celed and paved and chewed up beyond recognition. In a democratic society, the legal right to remain silent on public issues may be mor-ally wrong.

Though we often fail to notice, we make moral and political deci-sions with most every action we take. It happens every time we choose between a glass of milk produced on a local farm and a can of cola made by a distant multinational company, or when we shop at a big-box store for something we can purchase at a nearby hardware. The choices that influence our landscape are more often the product of daily decisions than of a ballot cast on a chilly November election day. We vote daily, early, and often.

Even when we don't "miss the boat," the crafts we pilot speak more about us and our world than we realize. Since our vessels are objects of leisure-time choice, we vote with our boats as much as we do with anything. Though muscle power and river current were as much our primary means of locomotion as they were Thoreau's, the difference between our canoe and his rowboat struck me the moment Josh and I began paddling on that first dank morning along the Concord. I realized then that the distance between us and our predecessors wasn't just in time, but in technology and in the pace and manner with which we lived our lives. Any inability to duplicate Thoreau's journey had less to do with changes in the river and how we traveled than with who we were before getting on the water and who we would be after getting off.

Thoreau's flat-bottomed skiff was fifteen feet long, with a dory's sharp prow, painted blue and green and outfitted with oars and a sail. He built it near the water, perhaps with the trip down the Concord and up the Merrimack in mind, and invested it with a unique design, provenance, and personality. Getting into the boat must have felt as natural as slipping into a pair of trousers. A few years after the trip, Nathaniel Hawthorne observed that Thoreau "managed the boat so perfectly . . . that it seemed instinct with his own will, and to require no physical effort to guide it."

Mungo's canoe was an eighteen-footer painted orange. Fabricated of aluminum, it was most likely constructed by Grumman, an aircraft manufacturer and full-fledged member of the military-industrial complex. Given Mungo's political bent, the boat was loaded with more irony than supplies. At the time, aluminum was the latest advance over birch bark, canvas, and fiberglass. It was nearly indestructible but sounded like a dropped tin can with every movement on board or obstruction it met on a watercourse. The metal boats also tended to grab on rocks and become stuck. Such qualities made them feel intrusive in nature. As a means of advertising the 1969 antiwar march on Washington called the Moratorium, one of Mungo's colleagues painted the date "October 15" in big, black letters on one of their two vessels "even if the Moratorium showed signs of being a schmucky liberal thing."

McPhee and I paddled canoes of high-tech plastic laminate that made them almost unbreakable, enabling them to rub against boulders and slide over submerged rocks with little consequence, as if they were creatures born to the river. Modern plastic miracles with ancient Indian lines, his was an Old Town Penobscot 16, made by the venerable Maine canoe company; mine a Mad River Explorer, a versatile V-bottomed boat built by a small Vermont outfit only decades old. Perhaps they were the perfect boats for the dawn of the new century, using materials created through chemistry that nevertheless could be fabricated by small, decentralized designers and builders.

Although they are close to indestructible from impacts, high-tech boats do wear out after hard use. Neither endlessly repairable like wood and canvas, nor recyclable like aluminum, the boats eventually find their way to a landfill. Perhaps my paddles of handmade laminated wood in alternating light and dark strips assuaged my guilt at using a plastic boat that would one day be just another piece of garbage.

The plastic's forgiving durability also makes for sloppy paddlers who no longer have to worry as much about hitting rocks. On the other hand, it has democratized whitewater boating in true twenty-first-century fashion, requiring that people invest little time either in maintenance or in developing paddling skills.

Coming around the river's big elbow at the Horseshoe Interval, we spied a lone white goose, fat and floating, without forward motion, like a buoy. Its hoarse, plaintive honk echoed between the banks, a monotonously recurrent sound like a foghorn warning of shoals in thick marine murkiness.

"What's with the goose?" Alan asked me in my role as the poor-man's trip naturalist.

"Got me. Probably an escapee from a farm or estate pond somewhere."

Was it calling for a mate, sounding an alarm to other waterfowl, or warning us to stay clear of its territory? Whatever the reason, I was alerted that despite our attempt to deep travel, we were merely transients and didn't really grasp much about what was going on along the river.

I felt in a quagmire in which the more I learned, the less I seemed to know. In lieu of real information, was I just seeing my own longings and preferences reflected on the water? Had I overlaid my private matrix of expectations on the landscape like so many pieces of collage paper? However desperately I wanted to understand this place, I would remain a visitor, always with a surfeit of questions and a paucity of answers. Only superficial snapshot tourism leaves us satisfied that we have adequately seen our destination.

The lines and curves of the countryside were slowly becoming imprinted on my consciousness, altering my personal geometry. By deep traveling, the pattern of this seemingly simple but inscrutable landscape became engraved on me, and I would soon feel the shadowy residue of its pattern wherever I went. The full measure of deep travel lies not in what is revealed during the journey, but how it alters the way we see whatever else we encounter. The mind becomes a species of landscape. Geography and identity merge imperceptibly and unexpectedly.

The goose was still faintly sounding downriver when the graceful green arch of the Tyngsborough Bridge appeared on the horizon. A white steeple poked at the sky just beyond it. After a brief absence the railroad again ran hard by the west shore, and funky, cottagelike houses dotted the east. Despite the human infrastructure, we encountered a flotilla of fifteen black ducks, with golden eyes and puffy green-glossed heads, and two great blue herons. One of the herons flew so low overhead we could hear its wing beats and watched its shadow move across the water within a canoe length. The other worked the shallows, dipping its sinuous neck so quickly that I wondered whether I'd seen it move until noticing a fish wriggling in its dagger beak.

No bridge framed Thoreau's horizon. Rather, he encountered a ferry established thirty years earlier by Henry Farwell, whose big center-chimney house still sits on a knoll above the west bank. The classic colonial is set among a cluster of eighteenth- and nineteenth-century buildings, including the white clapboard old town hall, which has a handsome fan window in the gable. Although the real action in Tyngsborough is now at the highway interchanges, along the roads leading out of town, and at a new municipal government campus, enough is left of the tiny old village center for Thoreau to recognize it were he paddling the river today. The comforts of Farwell's house can now be enjoyed by all, it having been reborn as the 1727 Day Spa Salon, with the Bittersweet Bake Shoppe in a small wing of the grand old structure.

Although he was on the water early, with the river yet indistinct in fog, Thoreau found the ferry "as busy as a beaver dam and all the world seemed anxious to get across the Merrimack River at this particular point." Among those crossing were children "with their two cents done up in paper, jail birds broke loose and constables with warrant, travelers from distant lands to distant lands, men and women to whom the Merrimack river was a bar." They waited impatiently as the ferry moved from shore to shore.

We watched a constant flow of traffic cross the bridge, testimony that while the facilities had changed since Thoreau's day, people remained just as eager to cross the river. Drivers slowed as they moved over the narrow span, perhaps getting a glimpse of the wind-whipped water floating a lone canoe. Did any of them wonder what it was like to experience the river as a highway rather than as just a barrier and choke point for travel?

Rounding the river bend we felt the full brunt of a headwind now strong enough to turn the ever broadening Merrimack into a choppy sea. It forced us to work harder for our progress, and there was no just floating anymore, lest we lose ground. Erratic gusts stirred intermittent whitecaps. With our arms growing weary and our shoulders knotted, we decided to rest near the bridge. As we made slow progress downstream, the green arch became our Emerald City of the moment, a goal, and a place to relax and recuperate.

Though nothing particularly recommends it as an oasis, Tyngsborough is a place of convergence where all parties seem inclined to stop for a respite. The Thoreaus camped on the east shore just below the ferry. Beneath an oak and near a cornfield, they hung a lantern on a tent pole and spread their buffalo hides on the grass. Here they cooked over a lively fire, had dinner, read their gazetteer, and jotted journal notes. Though they didn't have to contend with the sound of today's traffic, their slumber was interrupted by "the boisterous sport of some Irish laborers on the railroad . . . who would not have done with whirling up and down the track with ever increasing velocity and still reviving shouts, till late in the night."

When McPhee passed through, he climbed the bank a little farther downstream to the upscale Stonehedge Inn. Its wine list, he said, was "only a little shorter than the Boston Area telephone directory, and might have appealed to a British banker." Perhaps in deference to his urbane *New Yorker* audience for whom such benchmarks would have meaning, he recites the year, estate, and price of half a dozen wines, some of which cost more than Thoreau's Walden house even after accounting for inflation.

Set back from busy Route 113, the shingle-style inn is sumptuous and sprawling, with large brick chimneys. A brochure describes it as "designed after a luxurious European country manor" overlooking "acres of landscaped gardens, pastures and scenic woodlands." A sign at the door warned, "Proper Dress Required." The dining room where McPhee ordered "Herb Crusted Cod with an Organic Baby Vegetable and Wild Rice Casserole Maple Smoked Bacon Reduction" ("sans punctuation," he points out) was hushed and posh.

Mungo's Tyngsborough interlude lay at the other end of the spectrum but was no more Thoreauvian for its simplicity. Out of cigarettes and carrying no money, he and his companions found several old two- and five-cent soda bottles embedded in the silt near a half-rotted sunfish washed up on shore. They "cashed them in for a pack of smokes at the variety store conveniently located on top of the bank."

The need to cross the Merrimack observed by Thoreau continues unabated and is only increasing as evidenced by a new bridge that was being erected downstream of the existing one. Concrete piers rose from the water, encased by wood forms and sporting rebar spikes. Workers with hardhats and tool belts clambered up and down the structures with simian agility. They eyed us with curiosity and perhaps envy that we were off from work on this warm summer day to do nothing more than hang out in a boat and enjoy the whim of wind and current.

I admired their raw physicality, which seemed a cross between an acrobat's grace and a boxer's power. Like Thoreau watching the canal boatmen, I longed for a workday that would take me outdoors with such a fine perch above the river and with the sun and breeze in my face. Unlike the continuous stream of paperwork and meetings that define an executive desk job, here was a project with an end from which the workers could step back and see the results of labor that would last generations. They could show their children and grandchildren that they were part of a grand enterprise.

Tired and hungry, Alan and I landed the canoe on a small spit of dirt and grass just below the new construction where the rumble of bridge traffic mixed with the productive pounding of hammers and the whine of saws. A crane on a barge floated near the west shore. Beyond it was a massive stone wall armoring another big bend in the river, above which the railroad and the Middlesex Road held close to the water's edge. Conditions being what they were, we made quick work of a few hunks of bread and some Swiss cheese sliced with a pocketknife and washed down with water.

Below the bridge the river's girth grew to more than three football fields long, and the shoreline flattened out. The banks were mostly wooded, with occasional structures sandwiched between the river and the roads that ran close on both sides. After days on the Merrimack, we noted that macadam and rails clinging to the course of the river seemed routine, reinforcing the notion that we were on the original and natural highway revealing the land's true cast.

"Other roads do some violence to Nature, and bring the traveler to stare at her," Thoreau muses in A Week, "but the river steals into the scenery it traverses without intrusion." Lacking directional signs, traffic lights, or double yellow lines, we were on our own, needing to be observant of our surroundings, making calculations about hazards, and divining where we were and how far we had to go. Roads and railroads merely drained their flow of traffic in accordance with the drainage of waters.

The river had become the road less traveled, an alternative highway, almost a parallel universe. What was commonplace to even the longest-lived resident or most frequent visitor was magically transformed by the view from the boat. Here we traveled almost privately, without the hustle and hurry of tailgaters, passing vehicles, and merging traffic. We were free to tarry and observe, and because a river valley concentrates and focuses life, there was much to see. "The river is by far the most attractive highway," Thoreau advises, with "a much fairer, more wild and memorable experience than the dusty and jarring one . . . on the roads which run parallel with the stream." The river was simultaneously a conduit of travel and a destination. Rather than riding over the landscape, we flowed with it.

By paddling slowly, with each foot of progress made under the power of our own muscles, we gained a certain possession of the countryside regardless of deeds and mortgages filed in dusty vaults. The canoe's pace made us more aware of people, houses, factories, and fields. Its quiet and simplicity stimulated awareness and deepened memory with sounds and smells unavailable at the rumbling and enclosed sixty-five or even forty-five miles per hour at which we commonly traveled. We didn't need to break our stride and stop for snapshots of famous buildings, sunsets, mountains, and other wonders because the pace of paddling was tied to the wind and current, which gave us lavish allowances for taking in the sights around us. "An author who has to stop and take notes," Teale wrote, "gets many a rest from paddling."

River time therapeutically loses some precision. We become more concerned with daylight rather than the exact hour, how hungry we are rather than where the hands of the clock point. Unlike train and plane travel, we are interested more in *where* we are than *when* we get there. During an automobile trip, everything is either past and tucked into memory or is waiting to happen as we tick off mileposts, but a canoe forces us to live in the moment. "One of the sweet and expectable aspects of life afloat," writes William Least Heat-Moon, who has chronicled travels cross-country by both road and river, "is the perpetual present moment one lives in and a perception that time is nothing more than current." What we see is inversely proportional to our speed.

Our means of travel determines what we see as much as where we go. Certainly you can see the U.S.A. in your Chevrolet, but a canoe can transform even a short trip in the most familiar of surroundings into an exotic adventure. The canoe breaks the daily familiarity of vehicle and pavement. We may be close to home, but everything enjoys a fresh perspective. An ordinary voyage assumes mythic proportions as we scrape away the shiny lacquer of programmed expectations and recover some childhood spontaneity. Because no mode of transportation is so naturally suited to its medium as a canoe, a paddling trip brings us to the apex of intimacy with the landscape.

Though slow going enables us to see more, it also forces us to confront how difficult achieving such intimacy can be. We feel more of a need to understand surficial and bedrock geology, hydrology, land-use patterns, the synergies of plants and animals, and the politics and economics of human migration and settlement. Thus, the character of the journey depends on a traveler's resourcefulness. Rivers, observes Terry Osborne, help teach us to think as "we unknowingly replicate the process, mimic the river's eroding course with our own thinking, with ideas that spring undetected from remote ground inside us and ride tendril trails toward awareness." Reflections we see on the water are figurative as well as literal. We are reborn with such thoughts and in the passage of events that achieve the patina of time.

Ahead of us loomed Tyngs Island, at sixty-five acres the Merrimack's largest. To the east it is separated from the mainland by a channel about 150 feet wide that was once a canal with a lock. The rapids it bypassed were flooded by the dam at Lowell before Thoreau's voyage. On the west the river remains so broad that we wouldn't have realized we were approaching an island were it not for the palatial yet handsomely understated home of the Vesper Country Club, whose golf course occupies the entire island (as well as a piece of the mainland) to which golfers cross on a bridge. With the wind picking up and whitecaps multiplying, Alan and I looked forward to the channel's shelter.

The Indians called the island Wickasuck, and it belonged to Passaconaway's family. The site of an important cornfield, it was the sometime residence of his son Wonalancet, who sold the island to free his brother, who had been imprisoned for a debt to a white man around 1663. Thoreau notes that the colonial legislature restored the island to Wonalancet in 1665, and Indians lived and farmed there for a number of years. Ultimately, according to Meader, Wonalancet moved away after "the uncalled-for and inhuman slaughter of his defenceless people at Chelmsford" and "having been crowded out of possession by the grasping and constantly encroaching English." Ironically, the island was then granted to Indian fighter Jonathan Tyng as payment for garrisoning soldiers at his house.

Sitting at the north tip of the island, the white clubhouse stands out against a broad green lawn lined with flowerbeds sloping gently to the river. With its long roof, gables, and multiple chimneys, it looks like the country estate of a wealthy industrialist.

"Fancy place," Alan said. "Don't think they want our kind."

"I read on some golf website that denim is banned and collared shirts are required. Only Bèrmuda shorts are permitted."

"Time for a quick change?"

"I'd rather wear a Bermuda onion."

Only the five hundred club members and their guests can play the course, which is known for its wide fairways and large, undulating greens. However, for a price, anyone can rent the banquet facilities for weddings, bar mitzvahs, retirement parties, and business retreats.

Vesper was founded in 1875, and *Golf* magazine recognizes it as one of the first one hundred clubs in the United States. It started as a boating group that held regattas with sculls and canoes, and the clubhouse was used for dinner dances and bowling. In 1894 a cycling oval was laid out and baseball diamonds constructed. Soon afterward, golf was introduced. It rapidly swept the club, and early in the twentieth century the current course was built, the work of Scot émigré Donald Ross, perhaps golf's most famous designer.

The wind quickly died as we entered the narrow channel. Momentarily it felt like a bayou, with murky water and a shoreline of unkempt and tangled brush. We paddled past a huge white oak, below a narrow metal vehicular bridge, and then by a small white building with irrigation intake structures. Soon a fairway came into view, and we pulled onto shore beneath tall trees.

We clambered awkwardly out of the boat, having sat with our muscles clenched from working against the wind and whitecaps, and then stretched and settled down with our backs against a tree to snack on pretzels, peanuts, and water. Under the thick tree canopy, the grass was thin and large roots protruded above the ground like frozen snakes.

Just beyond some tall pines and spruce, a young, willowy blond in a tight-fitting blouse and short skirt stood at the edge of a green instructing several children in the art of putting. She glanced our way several times, looking at us malevolently as if we were criminal commandos establishing a beachhead from which to pillage the club.

"I'm going to stretch my legs," I said, looking up from a map as I popped a last pretzel nugget in my mouth. "Coming?"

Alan shook his head with an emphatic "no." He shot a glance at the blond. "That girl looks like she's ready to have us arrested. I feel like we're stealing just by enjoying the view."

"All the better for adventure."

"Sure," he said with the skepticism a father might reserve for a hare-brained notion of an eleven-year-old. "At least take off the yellow life jacket."

For five minutes I strolled along the edge of the fairway in forbidden denims that marked me as a crasher as easily as old-time jailbird stripes. The grass was as neat and uniform as a carpet, and not so much as a candy wrapper or cigarette butt was to be seen. I walked to where I could glimpse the baronial clubhouse through well-pruned trees. I passed an elderly foursome at their game, two waiting in a golf cart, and then a cluster of neatly attired teens beneath a large tree along the clubhouse driveway. Far from screaming and running in fright at the sight of an obvious intruder, they acted as if I didn't exist, as if I were invisible. Since I wasn't a member of the club, they probably couldn't even see me.

When I returned to the canoe, Alan was pacing nervously. "Look what's coming," he said softly, pointing downriver at a large, boxy vessel piloted by a sour-looking, jowly faced man. "Let's get going."

Cruising close to the island's shore, the white boat moved slowly as the man at the wheel searched for golf balls, which he retrieved with a device at the end of a long telescoping pole. I couldn't tell whether he had seen us trespassing, but he eyed us with malignant suspicion, his bulldog face knotted.

"Did you see the look on that guy?" Alan asked after we'd passed.

"He's either mad or suffering really bad hemorrhoids—maybe both."

"It's just a golf course."

"They don't want the great unwashed like us."

"At least it's green. If this were one of those high-end yuppie housing developments, we'd've probably been chased to the water by some woman in tennis whites swinging a racquet."

Mungo had also experienced hostility at the golf course, lamenting that Vesper left the island without a place to camp. He encountered "three lady golfers, the kind with jewel-encrusted sunglasses roped to their necks on aluminum chains." One of them saw the canoeists and chirped, "Well, isn't that adorable," a patronizing remark that must have set Mungo's teeth on edge.

McPhee, on the other hand, has no complaint with the place. Instead, he extols its history and lore. After speculating what Thoreau would make of "men riding in little carts and seeming to kill things on the ground," he drops the names of famous golfers who had played at Vesper: Walter Hagen, Joe Kirkwood, Harry Vardon. Although I shot a few rounds as a teen, I had never heard of these men and assumed that many of McPhee's readers were more schooled in the sport's history. Vardon, McPhee points out, who would win six British Opens, was here in 1900, slept in a tent, and awoke to set the course record.

The contrasting portrayals of the golf course emphasized again that much of what we see in a landscape depends on what we bring to it. Vesper is beautiful and club members clearly care about the place. Knowing little of golf, I was incompetent to judge its merits, whereas a player and student of the game might see meaning in the species of grasses grown, the position of sand traps, the contour of greens, and the placement of trees. There was a whole world of meaning to which I was blind. Knowing more might transform this sculpted recreational pasture into a place of intrigue and wonder.

Having a golf course on the river emphasized the Merrimack's value for recreation. Perhaps the course's existence and the political clout of members helped ensure that the river would never again revert to the fetid, polluted state it was in when golf balls first began flying on the island.

Though its form has changed, recreation has been evident at Tyngs Island at least since Thoreau spied "a pleasure boat containing a youth and a maiden" on his way downriver. The notion that someone might, like he and John, be out in a boat for enjoyment was a relief to him "since it proved that there were some hereabouts to whom our excursion would not be wholly strange." Inasmuch as Alan and I were on a recreational jaunt, perhaps, I hoped, we would enjoy some similar empathy from our own fellow recreationalists, the golfers.

Maybe like Thoreau we should have been grateful to see these other recreationalists enjoying the river, however different they might be.

Although Alan and I were concerned about the volume of fertilizers and pesticides that must be poured onto the ground to achieve such deep green vegetative perfection, the course was nevertheless a work of art. Any ugliness here came from an apparent snooty exclusivity. Of course, in our own casual way, we were a bit snooty ourselves. Perhaps, like Teale, we should have been comforted by the notion that golf courses retain the openness of farmland.

The channel felt very canal-like as we slipped beneath the footbridge leading to the fourth hole, which, McPhee notes, plays over the channel and is a par three. The manicured grounds faded away as we approached the island's tip, and it became remote and wild looking, as if nothing had changed in three hundred years save the addition of a few invasive plants like the thorny Japanese barberry, a shrub escaped from garden plantings and highway landscaping. We pulled off to obey a call of nature, enjoying the guilty pleasure of "watering" Vesper-owned ground. Cardinal flower, the brightest thing in sight and a wholesome and refreshing symbol of wildness, grew at the edge of the bank. But clumps of purple loosestrife—that beautiful magenta invader that seemed to be taking hold in so much of the watershed— were also thriving.

Suddenly the trees parted and we entered the river's main channel. An inspiriting eruption of air and space invested us with renewed energy. We eagerly dug our paddles into the river and made our way back onto the wide, wind-whipped surface toward Lowell. Despite straining to fight rough water, I felt the river exerting a tug that had little to do with wind or current. "We were responding, in some vague way," as Teale put it, "to the attraction of the flowing stream as the stream responds to the pull of gravity on its water."

Confluence

Over and over again I have said that the commonplace aspects of the
contemporary landscape, the streets and houses and fields and
places of work, could teach us a great deal not only about
American history and American society but about
ourselves and how we relate to the world.

John Brinckerhoff Jackson,
Discovering the Vernacular Landscape

You may paddle all day long; but it is when you come back at nightfall,
and look in at the familiar room, that you find Love or Death
awaiting you beside the stove; and the most beautiful
adventures are not those we go to seek.

Robert Louis Stevenson, *An Inland Voyage*

The Miracle of Lowell

Though the Concord River flows to the Merrimack at Lowell, Thoreau never came to their confluence. Instead, he avoided the shining City of Spindles and took a shortcut along the Middlesex Canal. He probably did so for practical reasons. The famously tranquil Concord becomes a raging torrent of whitewater in its final two miles, frothing through rocky rapids and roaring over falls. Today the passage is even more difficult. Old dams appear without warning, and other manmade obstructions can slice the skin of a canoe as easily as that of a banana.

This river reach is where Mungo's canoe "became trapped between and on top of rocks which shared the water now with old tires, a refrigerator, a washing machine, wrecked cars and trucks, metal hoops, and bobbing clumps of feces." With the water much cleaner today and modern technology able to produce vessels with flotation capabilities unheard of in Thoreau's time, the Lowell Parks & Conservation Trust offers whitewater rafting trips during high water in April and May for seventy-nine dollars. Wearing life jackets and helmets, participants pass old mill sites and arched bridges through the heart of the city as they negotiate rapids with monikers like Twisted Sister, Three Beauties, and Middlesex Dam.

Even had rafting existed in Thoreau's time, low water would have made the river impassable during his September voyage. How paradoxical that his passage to the Merrimack on what now is viewed as a bucolic journey would be with the flow of commerce along the canal, the interstate highway of its day. Yet it seems typical of the ironical Thoreau, who would spend much of the voyage rowing upstream against both the river and social currents.

Avoiding Lowell, he bypassed the emerging future of America and missed, perhaps, the ultimate expression of humanity's arrogant command and control over the waters he extolled. No doubt the city would have made a worthy whetstone against which he could have sharpened his rapier social criticism to the amusement of posterity. Even so, Lowell was never far from his mind, whether he was contemplating the inability of fish to overcome dams or observing boats loaded with bricks made of New Hampshire clay headed downstream to build factories. He mentions the city almost twenty times in the course of the book. He could not escape its influence even as he rowed away on the impoundment-fattened Merrimack, the dam at Pawtucket Falls making the river like a lake for the first eighteen miles.

A sounding horn startled me out of Thoreauvian thoughts induced by a brief interlude of white-line fever as I drove the pickup on I-495. I grasped the steering wheel tightly. Around me was a forest of signs giving direction, offering place names, advising me of the speed limit and turning lanes.

"Don't miss the exit!" Alan shouted. "It's here," he pointed.

"Got it," I replied, giving him a thumbs up as I moved across several lanes and wove in and out of traffic like a stockcar driver jockeying for position.

The logical flow of navigable waters dictated that Thoreau skirt Lowell, but caught in an even more powerful current, Alan and I couldn't help being drawn to the mill city. We rocketed off the highway and headed at sixty-five miles per hour down the Lowell Connector toward the heart of the redbrick metropolis. The current of America's destiny drew us. It may sound a little melodramatic and pretentious, silly even, but there is hardly a better way to describe what impelled us to Lowell.

Since its creation as the nation's first major planned city, Lowell has been a lens through which America can be seen. Even for citizens who have never heard of the city, the arc of its life is embedded in the way they think of their country. Lowell is the epitome of the rapid rise of industry that made the United States wealthy and powerful. In the middle of the twentieth century, it was a symbol of urban decline, its vacant and deteriorating mills an effigy of failed capitalism and rotting social relations. Now Lowell reflects the deindustrialization of the country. But it is also an avatar for urban revival based on an architectural and cultural heritage beckoning to visitors like us.

The future that was Lowell in Thoreau's time became the past generations ago. Now it seemed, strangely enough, as if the future of Thoreau's time had converged with our past in a tectonic collision. Fragments of what was the future in 1839 had become lodged in our present with the creation of heritage parks.

It didn't matter that Thoreau had been a no-show more than 150 years ago. Lowell was a destination for us. We were marching to a different drummer, paddling to a different current, driving to a different tune on the radio. Such was the mantra throughout my journey on the Concord and Merrimack. I had paddled where he had sailed, had put in where he had taken out, had gone downstream where he had gone up.

"You got the city map?" I asked, as we got off the connector and began navigating our way through Lowell's dense street network. We quickly passed the large, turreted stone building housing Keith Academy next to an old factory with a towering square chimney that is now the Comfort Furniture Showroom. Concentrating on traffic was hard amidst the distractions of peopled sidewalks and quirky buildings.

"Hold on. It's in this pile somewhere," Alan said, shuffling through a bunch of papers and a couple of guidebooks. "We need to be on Bridge Street. Go slowly because there are weird angles near the canals and some of the names change. First we have to find Gorham Street." He laid the map on his lap, glancing down one moment and out the window the next. "This isn't as easy as canoeing," he said with annoyance. "At least on the river the current tells you where to go."

"I think we're on Gorham," I said, hoping for a sign in an area where some intersections were unmarked.

"Watch out for that guy trying to cross between those cars!" Alan shouted. Reflexively I stepped hard on the brake and we bolted forward. "Easy does it," he said.

Having rested from strenuous paddling against the wind with a night in a suburban motel, we were psyched to explore Lowell. Not wholly in the dark about the city, we had eagerly devoured many tourist brochures, and a quick Internet search yielded reams of information. Furthermore, Alan and I had been to Lowell briefly in the past for professional meetings.

Lowell was a boomtown of twenty thousand in 1839 when Henry and John Thoreau were on the Merrimack. Its twenty-eight mills employed eight thousand people. Within memory of the Thoreau brothers, however, the area had been a remote farming settlement in the far northeastern part of Chelmsford. People had supported themselves by making home handicrafts, fishing at Pawtucket Falls, and working at a few small mills engaged in sawing lumber, manufacturing glass, and producing cloth.

In the mile before its confluence with the Concord, the Merrimack fell more than thirty feet. Though the falls were an essential fishery for Indians, it was an obstacle for floating timber to shipbuilders in Newburyport at the Merrimack's mouth. In 1796, eight years before the Middlesex Canal opened, downriver merchants dug a one-and-a-half-mile canal around the falls for passage of logs, attracting some small mills at the outset of the nineteenth century.

Like North Billerica, the area might have remained a small industrial enclave at the edge of town had it not been for an audacious case of industrial espionage by a wealthy and chronically ill Boston merchant with a prominent lineage. Francis Cabot Lowell sailed for England with his family in 1810 to recover his health. An importer of British cloth, he took the opportunity to tour Manchester, then the world's textile manufacturing capital. When English cotton barons refused to license construction of similar mills in the United States, or even let Lowell make a single drawing, he committed the design of complex power looms and spinning machines to his photographic memory.

On his return, Lowell reconstructed the machines in Massachusetts with the assistance of a creative engineer. Along with other blue-blood investors, who became known as the Boston Associates, he devised the country's first integrated cotton mill in Waltham just up the Charles River from Boston. For the first time, a single mill would take raw cotton bales and do the picking, carding, spinning, warping, and weaving and produce a bolt of finished cloth.

With waterpower on the Charles exhausted within a few years, a handful of Lowell's colleagues visited the area around Pawtucket Falls on a gray and snowy November day in 1821 when the river ran full and loudly. Where Indians had seen food and shipbuilders an obstacle, they saw power enough to produce millions of yards of cloth. Within a few years, a great industrial city would arise on the spot, a city named for a man who died without ever having heard of it, a city whose prosperity would grow from a plagiarized idea and purloined designs.

Alan and I walked into tiny Arthur's Paradise Diner, which squats hard by the Eastern Canal in the shadow of the massive Boott Mill. Beside the brick colossus, the barrel-vaulted shoebox of an eatery seemed like a toy. We sat at one of the battered wooden booths that had seen generations of carving. Ceiling fans moved slowly overhead. The place was packed and only one stool was empty at the marble counter. I was reminded of the diner Kerouac described at the outset of *Visions of Cody*, "with that oldfashioned railroad car ceiling and . . . full of lovely pans of eggs, butter pats, piles of bacon" and "stools with smooth slickwood tops . . . wooden drawers for where you find the long loaves of sandwich bread" and "coffee served in white porcelain mugs" on a counter that "is ancient, cracked, marked, carved."

In no small measure I judge a city by its diners. With three that have been serving plain comfort foods since before World War II, Lowell passes the test. Though the Paradise Diner's slice of culinary paradise is the humblest among them, it is unsurpassed for raw energy and rough blue-collar ambiance.

"You see any menus?" Alan asked.

"I guess that's it," I replied, pointing to a sign over the grill.

The Paradise was a simple operation. Food was served on paper plates, plastic utensils were available from a container on the counter, and paper towels acted as napkins. A burly bear of a man, Paul, whom everyone seemed to know, took orders, cooked the food, and ran the register. Tips weren't left on the table but tossed into a jar on the counter.

Above the din of sizzling bacon and conversation, we shouted our order. "You got it, guys," Paul replied in a booming voice as he flipped something on the grill.

"What's a Famous Boott Mill Sandwich?" Alan wanted to know.

"Got me. Named for that big cotton mill behind us."

"Boott? Sure it wasn't a footwear factory?"

"Real funny," I chided, with a fake laugh. "A brochure I picked up said it was among the first big mills in the city and one of the last to close in the 1950s."

"I think I remember reading about a guy named Boott. Wasn't he the no-nonsense former British army officer charged with building the city?"

With a surveying and engineering background from military school, the stern-visaged and clever Kirk Boott was the first agent of the Merrimack Company. He had responsibility for developing mills and worker housing, canals, and locks. He laid out streets and designed buildings. He acted as construction boss, architect, and planner. A hands-on type, Boott even did some of his own engineering drawings. Under Boott's aegis and that of his successors, Lowell became a planned city, a machine for the production of cloth.

Boott wasn't involved just in bricks and mortar. A rigorous disciplinarian, he determined strict rules for workers. Supervising establishment of the first church on company land, the imperious Boott decided it would mirror his own Episcopalian faith even though the majority of company directors were Unitarian and most workers belonged to other sects.

By 1850 Lowell's population stood at more than thirty-three thousand. Almost six miles of canal had been constructed, powering ten massive mill complexes that employed more than ten thousand people. About a million yards of cloth were produced in a week, amounting to sixty-five thousand miles of fabric a year, enough to circle the planet more than twice. This growth reflected a high rate of return for the Boston Associates, whose profits averaged a robust 24 percent between 1824 and 1845.

From mill construction flowed the development of houses, stores, hotels, restaurants, and institutions of every stripe. By 1868, Lowell's population was roughly forty thousand, and the city boasted twenty-two churches, eleven banks, and fifty-seven schools with seven thousand students. Within memory of middle-aged residents, Lowell had sprung from obscurity to a world-renowned industrial power.

"Two eggs up, home fries, wheat no butter," Paul bellowed as if calling my name.

The yolks were just slightly runny, the home fries peppery with a hint of bacon fat, and the toast warm and crisp. Though the wooden bench was hard and the entire place from tile floor to Formica table had a worn, tired look, it was as comfortable as a faded pair of jeans.

"What amazes me," Alan said while scooping a piece of scrambled egg onto his fork, "is that despite brutal working conditions, Lowell was considered a kind of industrial utopia."

"It almost seems like there were two cities. Maybe the one you saw depended on whether you were on the outside looking in or the inside looking out."

Lowell's founders were determined to avoid the industrial slums of England. They hired young farm women and established strict rules of conduct, creating a well-ordered existence that simultaneously assuaged their moral concerns and ensured a productive workforce. Their approach also projected an image acceptable to an American public suspicious of urban life. Unless they stayed with family, the women lived in company boarding houses overseen by older women. There was a ten o'clock curfew, no drinking on company property, and sometimes compulsory church attendance. Typically, the workers stayed one to three years before leaving to get married or move elsewhere—or because they were fed up with mill life.

Viewed from the outside, Lowell was a nation's economic dream. It proved that the American entrepreneurial spirit could produce both profits and moral and social improvement. All manner of dignitaries flocked to the city, from President Andrew Jackson to British novelist Charles Dickens. Each was mesmerized, Dickens observing how "the very river that moves the machinery in the mills . . . seems to acquire a new character from the fresh buildings of bright red brick and painted wood among which it takes its course."

On the inside, young women had to stand as long as fourteen hours at bone-numbing, tedious, and repetitive jobs that often compromised their health. The buildings vibrated with constantly clattering machinery, and the rattle and hammering was deafening. The rooms were hot, damp, and filled with floating lint particles. Sometimes windows were nailed shut to maintain the humidity, which kept yarn from snapping.

As brutalizing as the work could be, it was also the first time unmarried young women had a widespread chance to earn an income. The city gave them opportunities they never had on the farm. They attended plays, lectures, and exhibits; subscribed to newspapers and magazines; and joined literary clubs and lending libraries. One company subsidized a worker-written magazine. Lowell stores were stocked with clothing and other goods unavailable in the small rural communities from which the women came.

The mill owners were as expert about human nature as they were about looms and spindles. To attract a hardworking and loyal labor force, writer Stephen Yafa notes, they devised a way to "repackage the drudgery of factory labor as the chance of a lifetime for self improvement" and would "gain the world's admiration for their efforts."

Despite strict regulation of their lives, these young women retained no small measure of farm-learned pride and independence. They conducted protests over wage cuts and machinery speedups. After 1845, the owners began hiring immigrants. Fleeing harsh conditions in their homelands and desperate for jobs, they accepted lower wages and longer workdays with a minimum of agitation. Beginning with the Irish, a succession of foreign-born men and women came to work in the mills, including French Canadians, Greeks, and Poles. The utopian period faded.

Alan scooped the last remnant of egg on his plate with a piece of seedless rye while I carefully examined the bench.

"Looking for something?"

"Just a crazy notion that Kerouac might have scraped his initials somewhere."

"Kerouac?"

"This was one of his hangouts. Sal Paradise in *On the Road* is named for this place."

We paid for our meals, tossed a few bucks into the tip jar, and dodged a couple of trucks crossing Bridge Street to the bright lawn of Eastern Canal Park, a long, narrow patch of green bounded by the street and canal. It offered a panoramic view of the Massachusetts Mills complex across the Concord River. Two massive brick buildings were joined at right angles, each with symmetrical stair towers and a single tall smokestack behind them.

Turning back toward the diner, my eyes fixed on the monstrous hulking bulk of the Boott Mill behind it. I gazed at the strong brick walls pierced with orderly rows of long windows and an elegant clock tower topped by a golden shuttle weathervane. Kerouac described it as "a Castle high in the air, the king surveyor of all the Lowell monarchial roofs and stanchion-chimneys (O tall red chimneys of the Cotton Mills of Lowell, tall red redbrick goof of Boott, swaying in the termious clouds of the wild hoorah day and dreambell afternoon)." Renovated in the 1980s by a private developer with government aid, a good portion of the complex is now an industrial history museum. A glass case inside contains tangible tokens of the wanderlust that inspired Kerouac's best work—his rucksack and camping gear.

At one end of the park is a small esplanade with benches dedicated to this poet of the mills. Eight granite columns are inscribed with excerpts from his writing. We walked among these pillars of wisdom and read snippets from *On the Road*, *The Dharma Bums*, and *Big Sur*.

"It's strange that a city which had no use for Kerouac during his lifetime would honor him years after his death."

"What's the line about a prophet being without honor in his own country? Besides, Kerouac is now a brand name. He draws tourists. Sells hamburgers. Brings in cash."

Alan and I walked down Merrimack Street, Lowell's main drag, on our way to the Lowell National Historical Park visitor center. The sidewalk was busy with people, and a steady stream of traffic made its way from one stoplight to the next. The storefronts were lively, with fewer of them empty than in many gritty industrial cities. We went past Page's Department Store, Rainbow Shoes, Gary's Ice Cream, and Charo's Bakery, as well as national chains like CVS pharmacy and Dunkin' Donuts. From a visitor's casual glance, it seemed that even if Lowell wasn't exactly thriving, it hadn't slid back toward the desolation of the 1970s.

"There must've been a lot of money here once," Alan said, as we rubbernecked at the substantial architecture on either side of the street. The brick, iron, and stone buildings were alive with artistic details like gargoyles and arches, medallions, balustrades, and brackets that drew the eye. Each glance enticed us with a bright fascination.

"Looks like they were built by people who expected them to last, who wanted to make a statement."

Mungo and his companions had a much different experience trudging through Lowell in 1969. Having weathered the turbulent rapids and falls of the Concord, they landed their canoe behind a taxicab garage, the first place they found where steep walls and chain-link fence did not block their access. With a homemade contraption built from tricycle tires, they wheeled the boat through the center of town. Five years before establishment of Lowell Heritage State Park, and nine before the national park was created, Mungo found "a strikingly 19th-century downtown area but, despite the energetic promotion of the oldest merchants in town, it is slowly corroding as it loses ground to the highway shopping plazas. Life there is sooty." In retrospect, perhaps he was an oddball Paul Revere sounding the alarm at a time when few listened.

As he walked through the city with his canoe, Mungo wondered why Kerouac "came back to Lowell after all those years of making scenes." Tongue-in-cheek, he contemplated whether the King of the Beats would take him and his friends in for a night. He was frustrated that the man stopped writing and "just sat there in crummy Lowell with beer and television." Mungo concludes that Kerouac "must have come back to die." Within days of the end of Mungo's trip, Kerouac would, in fact, be dead at age forty-seven.

The Bon Marché Building at 151 Merrimack rises five stories in tan brick and may be the grandest of all Lowell's retail structures, with its handsome columns, bay windows, and stained glass. I pushed Alan toward Barnes & Noble Booksellers on the ground floor.

"Want to see if they have anything about Lowell?" I asked. I'm not sure Alan cared much for going inside, but over the years he had learned that there were few things I had more difficulty resisting than a bookstore. Protest was useless.

After thumbing through a few shelves of local material ranging from coffee table picture books to scholarly tomes on industrial history, I picked up a paperback copy of a book I had borrowed years ago from my college library and devoured eagerly in just a few sittings though it ran to about five hundred pages. It told the story of a family from a Massachusetts mill city before and during the Second World War. This first novel of Kerouac's, *The Town and the City*, was a paean to family life and to Lowell, though he treated neither idyllically.

At the counter, the clerk handed me a faded photocopy of an ad that had appeared in the *Lowell Telegram* on March 3, 1950. It included a photo of a young Kerouac in jacket and tie and announced that the author of this new "stirring novel" would appear in the Bon Marché bookshop to autograph copies.

"Buying this one was meant to be," I said to Alan, handing him the photocopy.

"I wonder what one of the books he signed that day would fetch on eBay?"

Born in 1922, Kerouac grew up in Lowell as its textile empire crumbled. By the last years of the nineteenth century, it was becoming increasingly apparent that the mills were becoming outdated, yet the owners didn't modernize. Between 1890 and 1895, employment dipped from seventeen thousand to less than fourteen thousand. With the advent of fossil fuels and steam engines, textile plants were no longer tied to waterpower, and owners began to look south where labor and land were cheaper, unions were unheard of, and worker health and safety laws were less restrictive.

Although World War I brought military contracts that created jobs, relief was temporary. In 1926 Hamilton Mills went into receivership, and soon the Suffolk, Tremont, and Massachusetts mills followed. Appleton Mills moved its operations south. By 1936 textile employment had slipped to roughly eight thousand, about what it had been when Thoreau and his brother took their trip.

Several mills were demolished to avoid taxes. Some remained empty and slowly deteriorated. Others were subdivided to accommodate smaller firms. "Parts of Lowell looked like a war-ravaged city," according to the national park handbook. The closures left a wake of misery as families struggled to put food on their tables, children left school to find employment, and some remaining mills took advantage of workers.

With government demands for cloth during World War II, employment and wages shot up dramatically, but the renewed prosperity was short-lived. The Boott and Merrimack mills were shuttered in the 1950s. The grand Merrimack Mill, along with its boarding houses and related structures, was torn down in the name of urban renewal. Employment in textiles dwindled to almost nothing. The remaining mills grew decrepit, and what was once the pride of the city became a grim token of failure that evoked resentment and anger. Kerouac caught this dismal melancholy in his novel *Dr. Sax*, set in Lowell: "There was something wet and gloomy . . . something hopeless, gray, dreary, nineteen-thirty-ish, lostish, broken not in the wind a cry but a big dull blurt hanging dumbly in a gray brown mass of semi-late-afternoon cloudy darkness and pebble grit . . . something that can't possibly come back again in America and history, the gloom of the unaccomplished mudheap civilization."

Continuing down Merrimack Street on our way to the visitor center, I carried Kerouac's first novel under my arm as if it were talisman that would enable us to more clearly see into the very soul of Lowell. Just before turning onto Shattuck Street, we passed between the old city hall and St. Anne's Church, buildings that give Lowell a staid and substantial air, belying the visual cacophony of the many rough and raw neighborhoods we would drive through during our stay. Now used for commercial purposes, the old government building is a long, three-story redbrick structure with decorative medallions and a central gable. The church, built of gray stone excavated during construction of the adjacent Merrimack Canal, has arched gothic windows and doors and a central castellated tower typical of Episcopal architecture.

Ensconced on the ground floor of an old mill, the visitor center is an information mecca, with brochures, a multi-image slideshow, and bookstore. There are exhibits on cloth-making technology, the workforce, the textile business' corporate structure, and other subjects. You can get a tour of old ethnic neighborhoods or downtown architecture. We decided to take a boat ride on the canals.

The presence of uniformed park rangers with Smokey Bear–style campaign hats evoking images of wild places like Yellowstone or landmark structures like the Washington Monument is at first startling in an urban center like Lowell. But this alone gives weight to Lowell's significance. It sends a message even a kindergartener can understand.

The rangers show a contagious enthusiasm for the city. Ambassadors to the past, they bring to life everything from mill power drives with turbines, gearing, flywheels, and belts to the daily routine of Greek immigrant workers a century ago, with stories of how they worked, where they lived, and what they did during their free time. They are interpreters of the politics that has molded and continues to shape the city's sometimes halting revival. Rangers are also guides to contemporary Lowell and can recommend the best place to grab a burger or shop for crafts. They know about concerts and city festivals such as the October Kerouac literary celebration. Park Service employees seem to thrive on questions, and if people better knew what to ask, they would pose queries as eagerly as gamblers feed slot machines. A deep traveler comes armed with questions.

We forked over sixteen dollars each for a canal tour and walked to the trolley stop on the other side of the Merrimack Canal where we waited with a small throng of other tourists. Consistent with our travels on the river, we would have preferred to canoe the canals and explore this ersatz Venice on our own, but the Proprietors of Locks and Canals, which has controlled the system from the beginning, would have had us arrested. Though these artificial rivers seem as much public highways as their macadam brethren, they remain private.

We stood among people reading brochures, fiddling with their cameras, or enjoying a quick ice cream cone. Young couples shared a romantic day, members of an Elderhostel group chatted and joked, and several thirty-something parents wrestled with their children, who wanted a closer look at the water. We were fairly in the stream of Lowell's most important contemporary commerce.

"This is amazing," Alan said, as I looked down the canal where purple loosestrife, Queen Anne's lace, and tree-of-heaven grew between heavy blocks of stone along the dark water.

"For sure," I said, distractedly. "Can you imagine what it must've taken to build this canal network with only hand tools and draft animals?"

"That's not what I meant. What's really amazing are all the people here. In the 1960s when talk started about making Lowell a tourist attraction, the notion that people might come to have fun and vacation here must have seemed less likely than a man landing on the moon."

"I think it took less time from the first Mercury spaceflight to the lunar landing than it did to get that dream of a revitalized Lowell even close to reality."

In the 1960s concepts like "heritage" and "park" were probably considered oxymorons when combined with the word "Lowell." At best, people were ambivalent, with a city in chronic decline and with a past that brought to mind hard-working conditions and rapacious businessmen, if anything. Many people would have just as easily blown up the place and started over. There was even a notion afoot to destroy Lowell's most distinctive feature by filling in the canals, as Manchester, New Hampshire, did, to create more downtown real estate.

By the end of the sixties, visionaries like educator Patrick Mogan and the late Senator Paul Tsongas joined with others to push revitalization based on the city's ethnic heritage, architectural patrimony, and industrial legacy. They decided to use the past to build the future. It took years of tedious debate, thousands of hours of meetings and hearings, development of plans and revisions to plans. A miraculous cooperation emerged among many state, local, and federal agencies; academic institutions; businesses; and social service providers. The coincidence of a strong economy in the late 1970s and early 1980s was fortuitous.

With its bell ringing, an open-car trolley came to a stop and we waited our turn to board. "Rice-A-Roni time," Alan quipped, referring to the old television commercials featuring a ringing San Francisco streetcar.

There were now two miles of trolley track in Lowell, but the cars were reproductions of early-twentieth-century originals that ran on former Boston and Maine rails because the score of track miles that had originally coursed through Lowell streets had been scrapped to help fight the Second World War. The operator was dressed in an old-fashioned navy blue uniform with brass buttons and a bell cap. The car was meticulously kept, with varnished woodwork. It ran slowly between the Merrimack Canal and Dutton Street, carrying tourists wearing shorts and polo shirts on a short ride to Swamp Locks, where the Pawtucket Canal forks to form power canals.

"Seems a little Disneyesque," I said, the train feeling more like an amusement park ride than an old-time streetcar.

"Everyone's smiling. At least it's performing a real function in a real place. With a little imagination you could picture these trolleys on the street."

We boarded the boat beside a long wooden gatehouse for a trip up the canal to the Merrimack River just above the falls. It wasn't far from where Alan and I had dragged our canoe out of the water on the opposite shore. The vessel was a large launch, with seating for about twenty around the edge of the cockpit. As we began motoring upstream, a tall ranger with a rich, booming voice told the story of Lowell's textile and waterpower glory.

The boat glided past steep canal walls of cut stone, both drywall and mortared. Uneven and chinked in some places, the walls were neatly cut in others. The distinctions, the ranger noted, resulted from improved technique, better understanding of hydraulics, and the presence of more money. Soon we were passing the brick Collins and Eggman plant, a factory that follows the curve of the canal. The company twists and dyes thread, one of the last remnants of a once proud textile empire.

"Who said that those who don't study history are destined to be charged admission for it?" I asked, leaning over and whispering to Alan.

"It feels that way sometimes."

"It's weird seeing a place that once produced tangible and useful products now devoted to telling how it used to make the shirt on your back. The city's like a big performance. Just entertainment. Sometimes I feel like we're all a bunch of Peeping Toms leering at the past. I mean, how real can a place full of tourists be?"

"What's the alternative?" Alan shrugged. "Even if it's just a big outdoor museum, at least it's in a city with a lot of other things happening. It's not like Colonial Williamsburg where the whole shtick is frozen in time, or Sturbridge Village which re-creates something that never existed."

"I guess we've seen the alternative. Urban renewal. Just a big jihad on history."

"A lot of cities have tried heritage-based revival strategies, but it usually results in changes to only a building or two, maybe a couple of blocks," Alan began, decades of planning experience stirring his passion and genuine love of places. "They become isolated islands of activity and seem artificial. Often they lose their cachet when the thrill of newness is gone, and you wind up with a spot that looks pretty but lacks street energy. Communities are rarely as successful as Lowell because they typically view renovation and revival as a project or series of projects. They don't look at it organically. A revival strategy has to be ingrained in the city's way of doing business. It's got to be an ongoing fact of public life, like roads and schools."

We entered an old stone lock whose wooden doors closed behind us. Water rushed in from upstream. At first it felt as if we were in rapids, the water rising quickly around us with considerable force.

"The past is only so heroic as we see it," Thoreau wrote in *A Week*. What was critical, it seemed to me, was not to create a mythic and sanitized past mirroring our own needs, longings, and disappointments. We may need help to understand the present and make way for the future, but nostalgia is corrosive. In avoiding Lowell and spending time looking for Indian artifacts, perhaps Thoreau was already trapped by a saccharine hankering for yore. Then again, knowing native ways of sustainable living might be just the next ticket.

It's a deceptive and poisonous Disney Main Street mentality that tricks us into forsaking the present and fearing the future by promoting a fairyland without the dust and mud, poor lighting, and inconveniences of yesteryear. Here was a tourist economy feeding on the carrion shadows of the textile industry. Maybe we should all be made to stand for hours in the Boott weave room on a hot day with the machinery cranking away before being allowed to see the rest of the revitalized city.

The real story is always transformation. With its vaunted factory system, Lowell was America's future in Thoreau's time. Did the city's brand of heritage tourism make it our future today?

The mills were built to last forever, but this was a sad illusion. Even the boosterish Meader, writing in 1869 when Lowell was at the apex of the industrial world, observed that "in another age new and improved monuments may be reared, still testifying to [the Merrimack's] service and its power, long after the chains which now bind it to wheels of monster cotton mills are rusted and decayed and become relics of the past, or the antiquarian may rescue from the debris of its present glory vestiges of the history of its former, but fallen, grandeur."

In a few minutes the boat had risen to the Merrimack's level, and the heavy doors that had kept the water at bay slowly opened. We passed under the wooden building straddling the lock and into an area whose banks bore a more natural appearance, seemed wild almost. Ducks cruised on the placid, dark water and turtles sunned themselves on logs. Trees overhung the canal, casting deep shadows.

"The old industrial landscape may have been decrepit, but it wasn't Hollywood. It was real," I said.

"*Was* real. Not anymore. Not in this time and place. Now tourism is real. This is an age of stories."

"Seems like a dirty trick for a place to be reborn as a theme park."

Lowell evokes conflicting ideas and emotions. The city symbolizes both optimism and despair. It was both the ideal community and a slum for exploitation of workers; the home of industrious, productive

people and an unemployment capital. It has been the epicenter of urban decay and of metropolitan revival. It is a melting pot and a place
of ethnic conflict. It has been known for old-fashioned manufacturing and high-tech industries. It is a model of historic preservation and
an example of the worst abuses of urban renewal. In Lowell we have a
microcosm of the Sturm und Drang of the country's rapid and giddy
industrialization, as well the decades-after hangover. Where was Lowell hurtling to now? Was this the place to catch the next big wave?

The wide Merrimack was a sudden explosion of sun and space as
the boat's pilot—complete with nautical uniform, cap, and sunglasses—slowly crept the vessel close to the edge of the dam where we could
peer over the granite wall built into the bedrock and see the dry, jagged ledges below. Loosestrife grew profusely in cracks where tiny bits
of soil had lodged. Small geysers of water erupted from gaps in the
wooden flashboards sitting atop the masonry dam.

Even the Merrimack is a bit Hollywood here, not a river really, but a
pond tamed to be useful. Upstream, the shore was lined with a green
ribbon of parkland where old men read newspapers on benches, kids
fished, and people frolicked in the water at the edge of a small beach
with a redbrick bathhouse.

Once off the water and back at the trolley stop, we felt the afternoon
grown warm and thick with humidity. Given the tenor of the day, we
repaired for a draught of cold refreshment and a strong dose of authenticity at the Worthen, Lowell's oldest tavern. Built as a single-story
dry goods store in the 1830s, it is a place Henry Thoreau could have
gone to buy supplies for his trip upriver had he been so inclined. A tavern since the 1880s, it now featured a first story of brick and a second
of clapboard below a slate roof.

From bright sun we stepped into the dimly lit barroom, which retains its original trapezoidal floor plan. An elaborate but warped tin
ceiling, tile floor, and dark wainscoting breathe an air of cozy comfort,
of years of conversation and cheer. If the walls could speak, I'm sure
they would have spilled forth a frothy, encyclopedic knowledge of human nature. Above our heads several ceiling fans turned slowly, run
by leather belts attached to a central shaft and powered by an electric
motor. It reminded me of mill power drives.

About half a dozen people sat at the long, narrow bar with its wooden handrail and brass footrest. Classical columns framed the back bar, which had myriad drawers and cabinets. Everyone seemed to know each other and the chesty, blond barmaid. A middle-aged woman sipped red wine while a couple of codgers argued about the Red Sox over beers. Two twenty-somethings appeared to be construction workers with rough hands and soiled jeans.

"Check out the Kerouac poster," Alan said softly, pointing to the wall behind us.

"He used to hang out here with Allen Ginsberg and poet Gregory Corso."

Toward the end of his life, Ginsberg wrote that "Kerouac made Lowell sacred by his attention to it, as Homer did the walls of Troy, as Dante his Florence, as Blake his London . . . so any later illumination of the site flashes with sacred fascination." The inscribed pillars in the park by the canal didn't do much for me, but the Worthen, Paradise Diner, Boott Mills, Bon Marché building, and other spots Kerouac had hung out at or written about were infused with an intrigue other places lacked.

"Is there a bar in Lowell that Kerouac *didn't* haunt?" Alan asked. I shook my head emphatically.

"Nope."

About halfway through my Guinness, the power died and the suddenly silenced television, stereo, air conditioners, and refrigerators left the dim room hushed. Someone laughed nervously, and the barmaid fretted about not being able to use the register. With nothing else to do, we all started yakking with each other, first speculating on the power outage and then on the Red Sox and David Ortiz's uncanny ability to stroke game-winning hits. One of the construction workers had a bad clutch in his pickup, which inspired a rash of transmission tales. Without the air conditioner, the room gradually warmed and weather became a topic of conversation. It didn't matter what we chatted about, the talk was genial and refreshing and seemed to take us back to the dawn of the Worthen's tenure as a bar.

Walking down Worthen Street on our way back to the truck, we passed the strong and handsome stone city hall with its mighty clock tower. On a neatly kept grassy island in front of it, a tall obelisk stood, surrounded by traffic. Crossing over at some risk as cars whizzed by, we read the inscriptions carefully, for here were buried three of the first four casualties of the Civil War. They were killed by a Baltimore mob less than a week after the shelling of Fort Sumter as they made their way south to defend the nation's capital. Luther Ladd, a young man with a baby face, would become a martyr, his haunting image appearing on envelopes and in newspapers to stir anti-southern passion. Remarkably enough, the date of this first Civil War bloodshed was eighty-six years to the day of the shot heard round the world at Concord Bridge, which Josh and I had visited on the first day of our river odyssey.

Fast Lane

The steamship Great Western, arrived at New York, on
Tuesday bringing papers from London and Liverpool
to the 23d and from Bristol to the 24th.

Boston Courier, September 12, 1839

. . . it seems to this newspaper high time for
the resignation of Justice Douglas.

Manchester Union Leader, September 12, 1969

Rollover closes I-93 and 128

Lowell Sun, September 10, 2003

Alan and I got lost in Lowell's labyrinthine streets on our way out of town. We were caught in an area bounded north and west by the Merrimack with the Pawtucket Canal on the south and the Concord River to the east. Most every turn seemed a wrong one. We passed St. Patrick's Church four times before realizing we were circulating like fish in an aquarium. Unfamiliar with the area, we became prey to streets terminating at canals or dead-ending at the North Common. Busy traffic with drivers assuming they owned the road caused havoc with our feeble navigation, and our distracted rubbernecking at people and buildings didn't help.

This frustrating meander took us through neighborhoods where both handsome and decrepit structures stood side by side on sometimes rundown and battered streets. Faded signs from long-gone businesses lingered like ghosts near brightly lit corner stores whose windows glowed with colored neon twists advertising beer and ice cream. Houses with rotting swayback porches and peeling paint stood beside those with flower gardens and vibrant blue or green siding. Everything we saw told stories that left us speculating about the pulse of life and commerce.

Etched in the names of schools, social clubs, eateries, and small groceries was evidence of Lowell's lively polyglot culture. Cruising down Broadway Street we passed the boxy brick Hellenic Cultural Center, the Infante Spanish-American Grocery with its yellow awning attached to a big blue house, Anton's Cleaners, the Acre Pub at the corner of Fletcher, the Mekong Restaurant, Muldoon Gas and its three-bay garage, the Stoklosa Middle School, Yim's Variety, and St. Onge Appliance. We wandered down Waugh Street with its jumble of multi-family houses. School Street featured homes with entryway overhangs having elaborate scrollwork. Nearby were the steep gables and sturdy brick and stone walls of St. George Antiochian Orthodox Church.

On Salem Street we looked into Cote's Market where a sign advertised their "famous salmon pie" and then drove past the Nghi Beauty Salon. Market Street included Club des Citoyens Américains with a mural of small-town Quebec painted on the side. Nearby St. Jean Baptiste Cathedral, a grand castle of stone where Kerouac had been an altar boy, appeared desolate and abandoned.

You didn't have to read books, attend a parade at the annual folk festival, or hear residents' accents to grasp Lowell's essence. The faces of children playing in vacant lots, white-shirted businessmen crossing the street, and old women gingerly making their way down uneven sidewalks in old-fashioned high-waist skirts evidenced a richly textured life. The streets, houses, churches, and corner groceries spoke to us, though often in unfamiliar languages. Not far from the gargantuan mills and federally restored parks and civic buildings, ordinary people were striving as they always had.

Our fascination with these everyday scenes was likely an unexpected by-product of paddling. Days of looking at the world from a different speed and angle, of exploring the universe from a fresh, riverine perspective, had also, perhaps, changed how we saw this typical city neighborhood. We boiled with the same deep traveling questions that had animated our voyage by boat. My mind was still canoeing though we were back in the pickup on patched and potholed macadam.

"I think we're on Dutton Street," Alan said hopefully, as we passed the old steam locomotive displayed at the edge of park headquarters near the trolley stop. Opposite was the yellow and red Club Diner that had served hot coffee and Yankee pot roast since the late 1930s as mills closed around it. Taking furtive glances at the map, Alan looked up just in time to warn me of an impending turn. We barely made our way through a yellow light and around drivers angling right, inciting some modest horn-honking road rage with our unexpected braking even as we cursed the confusing signs.

"You've heard of a planning technique to slow traffic called 'traffic calming'?" Alan asked.

"Yeah. So?"

"Maybe it should include cutting off the middle finger of every driver in America."

Blaring horns were still ringing in my ears when Alan again erupted in a shout. "Right! Go right!" he demanded, gesticulating with his hands for emphasis. Another quick turn found us once again on the broad tongue of pavement known as the Lowell Connector. In moments it joined Lowell with I-495 and other interstate highways that could take us at sixty-five miles per hour anywhere Kerouac headed when the old two-lane blacktops were the country's open road. Of course, now you could go faster, passing in a rushing blur all that Kerouac left Lowell to see.

Before Alan could finish folding the map, we were on I-495 barreling south into Chelmsford in the thick of traffic. Cars whizzed by like bullets, and passing eighteen-wheelers threw our sunny windshield into ominous twilight. I felt like a mouse silhouetted on moonlit snow with an owl's shadow growing larger around me.

Huge, towering light standards stood on the narrow median. Brick hotels and offices peeked through a narrow picket of trees that grew on the road's shoulder as they did on river banks. We passed a Radisson, small clusters of willow trees, a possum flattened and desiccated on the shoulder, a rest area with a squat block toilet building beneath a gable roof.

I held the steering wheel tightly. After the canoe's languid pace, driving felt more like an amusement park thrill ride than a routine means of travel.

I-495 jolted us with an adrenalin shot, like twenty cups of coffee at Arthur's Paradise Diner. Without realizing it, we were quickly up to seventy miles per hour. Despite our speed, vehicles passed us and weaved in and out of traffic like we were on the track at Daytona. Tractor trailers vibrated our small pickup and shook it with their rushing wakes of air. We were now again "fairly in the stream of . . . commerce," as Thoreau put it when his tiny vessel passed through canal locks serving gargantuan boats loaded with lumber and bricks.

Away we sped, knowing we'd be back. Perhaps we'd return many times. A deep traveler always craves more, just as a person satiated with a big meal will get hungry again. Each visit fills us with new experience and deepens our understanding. Deep traveling provokes our interest, foments curiosity.

Familiarity breeds endless questions, which lead to discovery of ever more captivating detail until our vision becomes four dimensional and we see a place not only as it is, but as it has changed and grown over time. We come to know that adaptability makes a place timeless, not what is there on any given day. We visualize buildings and topography as they once existed and come to know people who walked the streets in years past. We imagine how the future might fit into today's space. What endures, endears.

Revisiting infuses a place with the texture of our own memories and binds us further as we see a territory in different seasons, under various fluctuations, and with new experiences we bring with us. We become invested in the landscape. We seek not merely a photo album snapshot or to have seen something and be done with it like amateur ornithologists checking off birds on their life list. Deep travel is as much about reappearance, repetition, and recurrence as it is about exploring new ground.

Through a cluster of trees we snagged a quick glance at houses hard by the right-of-way fence line. Not far ahead cell towers looked as if they could puncture clouds. The median widened with cut grass and a central berm of scraggly pines. A sign listed restaurants at Exit 32: Dunkin' Donuts, Chili's, Boston Market, McDonald's. A second sign announced gas stations: Exxon, Mobil, Gulf. Food and fuel. It was all the same. The only reason to get off the road was to keep moving.

"Look at all these gourmet dinner stops," I said with a smile.

"Doesn't exactly make me salivate," Alan replied sardonically.

"It's food security. At least we won't starve."

"A Hobson's choice, at best."

I found myself aiming the vehicle rather than driving. We were no longer travelers, just racing to cover miles. What we saw and experienced became disconnected from our purpose in leaving home. We were in transit like so much freight, gaining ground, making time. I was following the metal guardrails, the white lines, ticking off the mileposts. In the moment, we weren't anywhere. Rather, we were hurrying back to our offices with cluttered desks, our lawns that needed mowing, our couches and televisions, the familiar sheets on our beds.

I was hypnotized by the road, my thoughts drifting like a front end needing alignment. Though our speed gradually crept up, I had the urge to go still faster, balancing safety with convenience, the risk of getting caught by a trooper with the enticement of movement. Nineteenth-century British critic John Ruskin found fast travel indicative of an inability to enjoy any particular location. Maybe that's the ultimate dirty truth about Americans. We wax nostalgic about places, especially our hometowns, even as we would rather be moving on, not being somewhere—at least not for long. However we feel about them, interstate highways are the epitome of America. Our great works of architecture, monuments, mountains, and rivers are only so many backdrops better seen from behind the wheel.

We retain a frontier mentality even though the distinct line of westward settlement has long been relegated to novels, movies, and collective memory. The frontier is always the next thing we are on to, the next hill we climb. Interstates provide our frontier access as much as the Oregon Trail or the Natchez Trace did in their day. Whether it is a job, a visit to Grandma, or a quick vacation, interstates are increasingly the way to get there. They are our love, our addiction, our never satisfied craving. We let them devour all else even as we curse them. We crave their convenience while we complain.

Red, blue, and yellow strobes flashed where a cop had pulled over a speeder. A swamp crowded with dead trees whizzed by. Deer at the edge of the woods stared at traffic. Littleton 5, Marlboro 22, Taunton 66. A steep slope was tangled with bittersweet and overgrown with Japanese barberry.

After days of paddling I now more than ever imagined the inter-

states as ersatz rivers. They were all about flow, of course—the movement of people and goods. But unlike watercourses, they didn't meander or reflect the gradient and character of the landscape. They were
almost indifferent to all but the grossest topography. Geography sur-
rendered to the engineer's scale and the surveyor's transit. The earth
was flattened to minimize the countryside's flow so vehicles needn't
slow down. Rolls and swales put no strain on the engine, valleys were
filled as much as possible, hills cropped, curves broadened to require
little driving skill. All but the largest rivers slipped beneath the road
undetected.

The landscape moved quickly past the windshield, cinematically.
We were appropriately passive, as if in a theater. Rather than rivers,
maybe the interstates were just "traffic sewers," as New Urbanist planner Andres Duany has called them. Instead of going with the flow of
the landscape, they provided the most direct route for moving the
maximum number of vehicles. They epitomized American life as the
essence of 24/7 motion, but were they getting us anywhere? "Flow,"
Howard Mansfield points out, "is what we mistake for progress."

Interstates made it possible "to drive from New York to California
without seeing a single thing," John Steinbeck lamented. No doubt the
big roads are the antithesis of deep travel, roads to perdition that put
the mind to sleep in a fugue of white-line fever. But while interstates
enable us to go far and fast while noticing little, meeting virtually no
one, and hardly thinking, maybe it doesn't have to be that way. Was it
possible to deep travel on an interstate, or at least soften their effect
with a bit of deep travel doodling? Believing that our means of getting
somewhere is as important as our destination, Alan and I found this
thought worth some dabbling.

With more than 2.8 trillion miles logged annually on the nation's
interstates, the opportunity to improve at least some of our time on
them seemed a good bet. Perhaps mundane highways like I-495 could
be rendered interesting if we understood something about them. As it
was, I easily spent a couple of workweeks of time each year cruising at
sixty-five or creeping in traffic along their paved surfaces, yet knew less
about them than I knew about Spanish politics or anteater biology.

A large phragmites swamp left a gaping opening in the woods.

Plumes swayed in the wind. A handmade roadside cross marked a traffic fatality, plastic flowers hanging from the wood frame and strewn about the ground. "Walden Pond State Reservation" announced a brown sign at Exit 29B. Through the trees we glimpsed a small subdivision.

"Everything's changed since Thoreau's time, but at least he'd know what exit to take," Alan remarked.

"I'm sure he'd enjoy being with the other ten thousand or so solitude seekers on a summer weekend."

"Can't you picture him lying on the sand and slapping on the tanning lotion?" The mental image forced an unexpected hiccup laugh. "No, that's the public beach now," a character from Thomas Pynchon's novel *V.* says "where slobs from Boston who'd be at Revere Beach except for too many other slobs like themselves already there crowding them out, these slobs sit on the rocks around Walden Pond belching, drinking beer they've cleverly smuggled in past the guards, checking the young stuff, hating their wives, their evil smelling kids who urinate in the water on the sly . . ."

I-495 is metro Boston's ring highway, about 121 miles in an interstate system of almost 48,000. Familiar, uniform standards make this road the same as any other: limited access, design speeds up to seventy miles per hour, twelve-foot lane widths, and a ten-foot right and four-foot left paved shoulder. With headlights illuminating only the pavement at night, you can imagine yourself anywhere in the country.

The road's six travel lanes feed traffic to the old Merrimack River mill cities of Lowell, Lawrence, and Haverhill and divert away from Boston vehicles bound to Cape Cod and New Hampshire. Lowell is the busiest part of the road, with an average daily traffic load of more than 124,000 vehicles. But as wide and busy as it is, the three-digit designation indicates that it is merely a half-circle beltway around a city, subservient to I-95, a major interstate route whose odd number indicates it runs north and south.

A vast plain of dried reeds bisected by railroad tracks stretched below us beyond the passenger window. It looked like a textured painting in shades of khaki. Driving in the middle lane, we were simultaneously passed on either side by eighteen-wheelers, and the view changed.

To the right, a load of Fords bounced on a rattling carrier; to the left, a truck hauling for Friendly's restaurants had various foods depicted on the trailer—a gargantuan burger, fries, and Coke. As the walls of moving freight passed us, signs for Exit 28 alerted us to the Fruitlands Museum, Holiday Inn, Dunkin' Donuts, and Exxon.

"What in the world is Fruitlands?" Alan asked wryly, "an apple and orange museum?"

"Actually, it was a utopian community started by some of Thoreau's Transcendental pals. At a time when Lowell was thought to have utopian qualities, Fruitlands was a back-to-the-land anti-Lowell. It didn't last a year."

"Was our buddy Henry a Fruitlander?" Alan asked, barely suppressing a chuckle.

"Are you kidding? He was too much of a loner. Besides, he probably would have irritated the hell out of everyone else, he was so damn brusque and self-righteous."

The country's current highway system was partly inspired by the trek of the first Transcontinental Motor Convoy in 1919, when it took sixty-two frustrating days for an army contingent of eighty-one vehicles to travel 3,251 miles from Washington, D.C., to San Francisco. With virtually all roads outside cities unpaved, the military contended with mud and dust and forded bridgeless streams. They endured heat, breakdowns, and bridge decks that splintered under the weight of their trucks. The rutted roads were bumpy and the vehicles rattled endlessly. Averaging about six miles per hour, they covered approximately fifty-eight miles a day, a distance that took Alan and me less than an hour on I-495. Despite all the difficulties, the trip was considered a resounding success because it proved the country could be crossed with military vehicles. But a young lieutenant colonel who endured the journey wasn't so sure. Dwight Eisenhower determined that the nation needed better roads.

Demand for roads grew as the number of automobiles increased dramatically from four in 1895 to eight thousand in 1900. Roads might lead out of cities or even to state lines, but there was no guarantee they would join to other roads. What connections existed were poorly signed so even careful navigators easily got lost.

Advocacy groups like the American Automobile Association marked utility poles with colored bands to create a network of linked roads, the most famous of which was the Lincoln Highway, which, theoretically at least, ran from New York to San Francisco. By 1925 there were more than 250 named highways, each with its own colored signs.

The Federal Highway Act of 1925 established a numbering system and standardized shield signs for roads crossing state lines. Still used today, these U.S. highways, like Route 1 and Route 66, are now the "blue highways" of legend and lore where many people find the supposedly real and scenic America. This era also birthed parkways—multilane, limited-access roads whose directions of travel were separated by landscaped medians. They featured graceful curves flowing with the countryside and bridges using stone or decorative concrete. They were built for the now lost art of pleasure driving and excluded heavy commercial traffic.

As automobiles increased and became faster, congestion and safety concerns stimulated demand for ever more and better roads. As early as 1938 the federal government evaluated the possibility of toll-financed superhighways, and in 1941 President Franklin D. Roosevelt appointed a committee that recommended a 33,900-mile national expressway system. Meanwhile, the 160-mile Pennsylvania Turnpike connecting Pittsburgh to the state capital at Harrisburg opened in 1940. Although it borrowed from parkways the limited-access concept and wide medians, the turnpike was designed for through traffic with only eleven interchanges, was larger in scale to accommodate heavy trucks, and disregarded the landscape by tunneling through hills and filling valleys. It included straightaways as long as twelve miles.

But the future of the country's roads wasn't experienced only by drivers moving through Pennsylvania's heartland. A network of superhighways was revealed to millions, like my father, who sat mesmerized on the moving benches that wound through Norman Bel Geddes's "Magic Motorways" diorama in the General Motors pavilion at the 1939–1940 New York World's Fair. The United States had about forty million cars.

Dwight Eisenhower campaigned for president against obsolete roads with their "appalling problem of waste, danger and death." He not only remembered the 1919 convoy "through darkest America with truck and tank," but the lightning speed with which he was able to move troops on Hitler's *Autobahnen*. Upon election in 1953, Eisenhower got the federal government to refine its needs assessment, estimate construction costs, determine funding options, and develop construction logistics. After battling with Congress and one failed attempt, passage of the Federal-Aid Highway Act of 1956 established a road-building partnership between the states and the federal government. Washington paid 90 percent of the costs with gas tax revenue for a road to "greater convenience, greater happiness and greater standards of living."

As we passed a green, rectangular sign at the town line for Harvard, Massachusetts, Alan quipped, "Who said it was hard to get into Harvard?" Beer cans, candy wrappers, foam cups, shredded truck recap, and other detritus littered the roadside.

"At this speed we'll graduate without taking a single exam or getting a diploma. Just as well. Thoreau complained that Harvard taught all the branches of learning but none of the roots."

"Good ol' Henry. He might have liked it more if they'd had football back then."

A thick forest of white pine flourished on the west. We counted call boxes on poles while whizzing past them. Outcrops of layered gray rock topped with twisted and spindly pitch pine were common. Cape Cod 81. Mile post 69.

The construction of the interstate highways has been called the grandest public works project the world has ever witnessed. Completed at a cost of more than $100 billion, it would pour enough concrete to build six sidewalks to the moon and move enough dirt and rock to bury Connecticut two feet deep. More than any single action in the mid-twentieth century, this highway program changed the nation. It also fostered a complex economic ecology among construction companies and land speculators, car manufacturers, tire makers, tourist destinations, and oil companies. The politics of routing roads could be brutal.

"Ill conceived and preposterously unbalanced," cautioned social critic Lewis Mumford at the time. Like a stern Old Testament prophet, he warned of "damage to our cities and our countryside, not less to the efficient organization of industry and transportation."

Interstates smashed through cities, destroying whole neighborhoods. They left desolate wastelands beneath massive viaducts and divided communities with concrete chasms where travel lanes coursed below grade. The great roads separated places from their waterfronts and other natural amenities. In the countryside, farms and forests were gobbled up at the rate of more than one hundred acres per mile. Long-standing businesses were bypassed. The roads contributed to disinvestment in cities and promoted sprawling suburbs by stretching the link between home and job.

But interstates also granted average people unprecedented mobility and connectedness. Virtually everyone in the country was within a few days' drive of everyone else. The roads were convenient and offered greater individual freedom for people to go where they wanted, when they wanted. Long-distance trucking increased dramatically and delivered goods across the nation rapidly. The interstates fostered unprecedented economic opportunity for home builders, restaurateurs, hoteliers, and myriad other businesses.

I-495 angled steeply down toward Exit 25 at I-290. A huge clapboard Marriott hotel stood prominently on a rise ahead of us. Over the past decade, this once lonely confluence of three-digit interstates has sprouted offices and shopping malls just beyond the right-of-way. Now it's busy with chain retailers like Best Buy and Borders.

Such places are everyday America, the heart of the country. We may not wax nostalgic, it may not be a postcard image, but here is the real America seen by more people daily than any blue highway heritage attraction. The back roads contain the unusual and the unique, what is pretty and historically interesting. Two-lane blacktops may be authentic America, but so are interstate interchanges. Near ramps funneling traffic on and off the big roads is the America most Americans contend with daily: gas stations, chain stores, and franchise restaurants. We cry for something different, but we crave the comfort of familiarity and vote with our dollars.

"Slow down. There's a cop ahead," Alan warned.

Flashing police strobes reflexively brightened red taillights ahead of us and slowed traffic. I heard the low Bronx cheer of engine-retarding brakes on eighteen-wheelers. A DOT pickup and several dump trucks were gathered to repair guardrails. Traffic merged left and moved at a city creep. I was annoyed. My seventy-miles-per-hour rhythm had been broken. Traveling to begin his Concord and Merrimack voyage in 1969, Mungo experienced similar delays and couldn't "be convinced that Interstate Route 95 will ever be finished." The roads may be complete, but repair and reconstruction are endless.

We passed a succession of dark ledge outcrops banded with lighter rock, big concrete bridge abutments carrying massive I-beam spans, and oak woods with tall white pine enclaves. Enigmatic stone walls on the medians were the truncated remains of long-gone farm field boundaries. A busy cell tower was hung with gratelike antennae, tubes, and dishes.

I-290 connects I-90, the Massachusetts Turnpike, to I-495 and runs through Worcester, the state's second largest city. Little more than twenty miles long, it's heavily traveled, being the quickest route to Maine and New Hampshire from New York and points south. Exits in downtown Worcester carry more than one hundred thousand vehicles a day, while about seventy-one thousand reach I-495.

The road tilted steeply toward long and narrow Lake Quinsigamond. Large buildings stood out on the rugged hillside rising above the opposite shore. Antennae lined the ridge. After crossing the water we climbed toward Worcester and passed a sprawling shopping center and commercial strip parallel to the interstate. Dick's, Lowe's, and Target were among the anchors. The street they fronted was lined with filling stations, McDonald's, and other burger joints, pizza parlors, and doughnut shops, all with familiar logos.

Though engineering and speed conspire to homogenize and flatten the landscape, reducing places to mere scenery, deep travelers are not just tourists, they are explorers. They prize finding interest in the bland and familiar. Beyond the monotony of the pavement, the chatter of wind at the windows, and the constant tick of mile markers, opportunities beckon.

Why couldn't mere movement be as good as a destination? Traveling is a mindset, and the attitude we take from home may be the most important thing we pack. Our experience is shaped more by how we look at things than by the routes of travel or our ports of call. Deep travelers get beyond the funk and fugue of an interstate trip and start inquiring.

Road signs are ubiquitous and a good means for getting a purchase on a place. Town and street names are brimming with tales. A deep traveler grabs an AAA guide or Googles key words to get started. Such shallow information provides the context for questions. Since we see what we look for, we need information enough to focus.

Sometimes deep travelers build an extra fifteen minutes or half hour into an itinerary and take a random exit. They wander back roads that twist along a river and gawk at wetlands or old mill sites. They seek out historical markers, old houses illustrating the period of settlement, and new subdivisions revealing the current nature of a town by lot size and architectural details. They find town centers with Civil War soldier and First World War doughboy monuments. Sometimes deep travelers use a deck of cards to determine turns at intersections, with each suit designated for a cardinal direction. Such means are a delicious serendipity yielding accidental discoveries as important as battlefields or as trivial as an old-time diner. Eventually, deep travelers lose track of individual structures, trees, monuments, and hillsides, finding them quilted together in patterns exposing larger scale mysteries.

You don't even need to get off the interstate to do some modest deep traveling. Contemplate those stone walls on the median, or the cityscape of brick factories and triple-decker houses that flicker past the windshield. Office buildings and stores along the right-of-way give a glimpse into the local economy. Plantings in farm fields and cows pasturing on hillsides speak volumes.

Where is all the freight coming from and going to? Eighteen-wheelers loaded with fruits and vegetables, gasoline, garbage, fuel oil, furniture, hardware, lumber, shoes, and other products come from myriad places and are headed to even more. They stock store shelves, supply construction sites, and fill underground tanks.

Rock outcrops and the landscape's roll are clues to underlying geology, and a companion in the passenger seat can summarize from

James Skehan's *Roadside Geology of Massachusetts* about biotite gneisses, and schists that are tilted and layered along I-495 in Harvard and Stowe. The deep traveler can marvel at the enormous outcrops cut by road builders that illustrate the Assabet River fault at the junction of I-290. Similarly, John and Henry Thoreau read to each other from John Hayward's *New England Gazetteer* about the populations of towns and their principal industries.

Phragmites and purple loosestrife or cattails reveal an area's environmental health. Deep travelers spot fawns at the forest's edge, woodchucks on grassy margins, and beaver lodges in swamps of bleached, standing deadwood. They look for hawks hunting from the top of light standards.

The decrepit silo at the edge of a new subdivision speaks loudly about the past, present, and future. Deep travelers know that the sign for Fruitlands doesn't mark a farm stand but, like the interstate highway system, a utopian dream that failed to meet expectations and left some bitter consequences. Deep travel has its own peculiar ecology, teaching that diverse elements of the human and natural landscapes are connected.

The road took a big bend at the confluence of I-290 and I-190 with a quick glimpse at the geometry of downtown Worcester skyscrapers. The large blue tanks of Peterson Oil came into view. The road headed below grade, and buildings and people looked down on us. Then, like a rollercoaster, we rode up on a viaduct and looked through third-story windows and at rooftop vents and HVAC systems.

On the west, the rail station's twin alabaster towers looked like a Moorish palace. The east side ran close to the stone and concrete Our Lady of Mount Carmel Church, two-thirds of which, like an iceberg, was below the road and out of sight. We got a fleeting glimpse of the colorful artwork in the gable triangle, something hard to see from the ground. On the opposite side of the highway, a billboard atop an Irish pub depicted a full glass with the words "Guinness Refreshes."

The curved brick Worcester Gear Works plant fit neatly into the bend of the road. Moments later a big sign on an old factory proclaimed the home of Rotmans, "New England's Largest Furniture and

Carpet Store." On the other side were Holy Cross College's spotless green sports fields. Brick classrooms and dorms rose on a hill topped with a staid clock tower.

Once while returning from Maine, I got off I-290 for a bite to eat at the Boulevard Diner, which Alan had raved about. A tiny bandbox of an eatery, it has a yellow sheet metal exterior accented in red, and a sign that features a neon-framed clock serving as a crest along the roof's edge. I was starving by the time I got there, having squandered more than an hour totally lost, cruising and cussing Worcester's tangled streets.

Unfortunately, I wasn't merely lacking in direction, but the whole accidental tour of the city was a misbegotten waste because I hadn't yet discovered the often serendipitous ability to deep travel. At the time, two disparate facts were the sum of my Worcester knowledge: the father of modern rocketry, Robert Goddard, hailed from the city, and the first elephant exhibited in the United States had paid a visit there early in the nineteenth century.

I was oblivious to the central mystery of Worcester, something contrary to everything I'd later learn on the Concord and Merrimack— that a major manufacturing city could arise where there was no significant river. The vast range of churches was invisible to me, as were the boxy triplex houses that climbed the many hills. The substantial and handsome buildings of downtown were meaningless. I even went by Mechanics Hall, a classical old stone building, not realizing Thoreau had lectured about John Brown in that very spot. Strangely, it didn't strike me odd that a gritty city should have so many academic institutions although I passed through the campuses of Clark University, Worcester Polytechnic Institute, Becker College, Worcester State College, and Holy Cross College, as well as by the rare manuscript library of the American Antiquarian Society, while making a big fruitless arc around the city.

I was half tempted to head into Worcester now, to see what I might encounter with my deep traveling perceptions so well stropped by my time in Lowell. But we were tired, and Alan would have clobbered me even if I had bribed him with meatloaf or a burger at the Boulevard. I knew now that everything I could see from the road, whether the railroad station, Mount Carmel Church, or the Holy Cross sports fields, told a story.

Suddenly Worcester was behind us in a blur as we looked down on the flat roof of Polar Beverages, where among the stacks and vents sat a large polar bear mascot. There were untold riches of experience to be uncovered in this place I had for years hurried through. Returning was now a necessity.

"Tap the brakes a bit," Alan advised, "so the tailgating truck behind us knows we're getting off for the Mass Pike."

"Finally, the last leg of the journey," I sighed. "I'm beat."

"I can feel the gravity of home already," Alan chimed in.

"We're within striking distance of my coffee pot, mattress, and computer. As far as I'm concerned, we're done traveling. We're just driving back."

At home, we would resume the regular flux and flow of life that deep traveling had interrupted. I would fall back into the pattern of playing catch, hiking, and doing homework with Josh; meals, conversation, and languid nights with Pamela; and Saturday lunches and shared yard work with Alan. But the centrifugal stress of Josh's teen years, the intense magnetism of my relationship with Pam, and the even cadence of time with Alan remained hostage to inexorable and unpredictable forces as diverse as macroeconomics and personal health. At times, it seemed there was more uncertainty at home than on a journey where efforts were so clearly joined and focused. Whatever happened to me and Pam, Alan, or Josh, the events and companionship of the river would stick with us in layers of story and reminiscence. It was a true and lasting possession that could never be taken from us, regardless of life's vicissitudes.

We came to a row of tollbooths, a series of odometer confessionals where an electric eye read the Fast Lane transponder affixed to the pickup's windshield. At 188 miles long, the Mass Pike is the most easterly leg of the more than three-thousand-mile-long I-90, the nation's longest interstate. We traveled to the next exit on what the Turnpike Authority calls the "Main Street of Massachusetts."

The road is a lesson in Massachusetts history, replete with high political intrigue. It's as fresh as a morning headline with charges of corruption and incompetence over construction of the Ted Williams Tunnel to Logan Airport. Recent removal of tolls in western Massachusetts to quell protest that the money funded Boston's Big Dig, to tunnel a highway underground, reaches back to the 1780s when Shays' Rebellion in the rural Berkshires resulted in armed insurrection over a tax system favoring urban eastern Massachusetts.

I accelerated into a tight curve at a steep rock cut and shot out of the exit. Immediately we passed the Dark Brook Reservoir, a large lake split by the road. We went by a small swamp, then a pond.

"No journey is complete," wrote Scott Russell Sanders, "until we carry the stories home." More than that, we are obligated to tell the stories. We have to integrate them into our daily lives so that a worthwhile trip is never over. Successful deep travel changes how we look at where we come from. Home life is renewed by retaining an aspect of the outsider looking in. We are travelers everywhere.

Although Thoreau took a few extended excursions, he was a homebody who "traveled much in Concord," doing his best to question the ordinary and analyze the familiar as a tourist might marvel at an exotic locale. Walden was "a journey taken by staying still and paying attention," scholar W. Barksdale Maynard observed.

Inasmuch as most of us are home most of the year, travel should function as a means to better understand where we live. We should dare ourselves to find something interesting on our doorstep, to look with fresh eyes at our mundane surroundings.

Exploring a place close to home can teach us as much as the farthest reaches of the globe if we travel deeply. Travel is best that inspires us to see anew and become more engaged with our native landscape. It enriches our lives and motivates us to protect nearby areas. Deep traveling fulfills Thoreau's Transcendentalist faith that the entire universe can be found in the most common objects or places, and that ultimately the outer landscape corresponds to the inner one. Nothing could be more satisfying.

SOURCES AND

ACKNOWLEDGMENTS

The sources that gave rise to this work are as manifold as the springs, puddles, wetlands, and seeps that give rise to the Concord and Merrimack rivers. Publications described below are the mainstream influences on this volume, though there are many unnamed and unremembered tributaries of information and inspiration, including snippets of conversation, Internet searches, casually read magazine and newspaper articles, old photographs, and dreams.

Scripture on the subject is, of course, Henry David Thoreau's 1849 *A Week on the Concord and Merrimack Rivers* (Princeton University Press, 1980). Although many editions exist, the 1980 Princeton edition is particularly valuable for its index, historical and textual introductions, and other scholarly apparatus. Exegeses of Thoreau's work can be found in Ray Mungo's *Famous Long Ago* (Citadel Press, 1990), a compilation of three books, including *Total Loss Farm: A Year in the Life*, the first chapter of which is "Another Week on the Concord and Merrimack Rivers"; and in John McPhee's *Uncommon Carriers* (Farrar, Straus, Giroux, 2006), which includes the essay "Five Days on the Concord and Merrimack Rivers" that originally appeared in the December 15, 2003, issue of the *New Yorker*. McPhee's essay was also selected as the introduction to Princeton University Press's 2004 edition of *A Week on the Concord and Merrimack Rivers*. Although it deals only with the Concord River's tributaries, the Assabet and Sudbury, *A Conscious Stillness: Two Naturalists on Thoreau's Rivers* by Ann Zwinger and Edwin Way Teale (Harper and Row, 1982) is central to understanding Thoreau's way with rivers.

Although there is no literature on "deep travel" per se, several works published over the past decade helped prepare me for such a journey. For inspiration and a methodology for looking anew at familiar landscapes, I heartily endorse *Outside Lies Magic: Regaining History and Awareness in Everyday Places* by John R. Stilgoe (Walker and Co., 1998) and *Sight-*

seeking: Clues to the Landscape History of New England by Christopher J. Lenney (University Press of New England, 2003). *Landscape with Figures: Nature and Culture in New England,* by Kent C. Ryden (University of Iowa Press, 2001), is an eye-opening primer on reading cultural landscapes. For looking deeply at a place, William Least Heat-Moon's *PrairyErth (a deep map)* (Houghton Mifflin, 1991) is unparalleled in its detail and ability to make connections among diverse phenomena. The emotional weight of subtle landscape changes are well realized in John Elder's *Reading the Mountains of Home* (Harvard University Press, 1998). The essays in *Understanding Ordinary Landscapes,* edited by Paul Groth and Todd W. Bressi (Yale University Press, 1997), bring fresh insights to the places we see every day and take for granted. The work of John Brinckerhoff Jackson is essential to understanding landscape patterns over time, and his *Discovering the Vernacular Landscape* (Yale University Press, 1984) is a very accessible series of essays.

There are so many fine books about canoeing that it is hard to pick among them. *Threading the Currents: A Paddler's Passion for Water* by Alan S. Kesselheim (Island Press, 1998) is not only well written, but also truly captures the joys and tribulations of paddling. *An Inland Voyage* by Robert Louis Stevenson (1st World Library, 2004) provides an interesting foil to Thoreau's Transcendental musings. Also a first book, it was published in 1878.

Among guides to the subject rivers, *The Concord, Sudbury, and Assabet Rivers* by Ron McAdow (Bliss Publishing Co., 1990) is wonderfully detailed. More general coverage of the Concord and Merrimack rivers is found in the *Appalachian Mountain Club River Guide: Massachusetts, Connecticut, Rhode Island,* 3d ed. (Appalachian Mountain Club, 2000). Both volumes are now in new editions. Historical narratives about the rivers include *The Merrimack* by Raymond P. Holden (Rinehart & Co., 1958), part of the Rivers of America series, and *The Merrimack River* by J. W. Meader (B. B. Russell, 1869).

The complex world of nineteenth-century industrial waterpower is exquisitely explained in *Nature Incorporated: Industrialization and the Waters of New England* by Theodore Steinberg (University of Massachusetts Press, 1991). Steinberg includes much information on Lowell and Manchester, seasoned with references to Thoreau. *Big Cotton: How a*

Humble Fiber Created Fortunes, Wrecked Civilizations, and Put America on the Map by Stephen Yafa (Viking, 2005) is a fast-paced history of textile manufacturing told by a Lowell native. For the workers' perspective on Manchester's mills, read *Amoskeag: Life and Work in an American Factory City* by Tamara K. Hareven and Randolph Langenbach (University Press of New England, 1978). *The Amoskeag Manufacturing Co. of Manchester, New Hampshire* by George Waldo Browne (Amoskeag, 1915) is a detailed company history that was printed and bound in the mills.

The biographical literature on Henry David Thoreau is vast, but among my favorites that represent a range of eras and types of scholarship are *Thoreau* by Henry Seidel Canby (Houghton Mifflin Company, 1939), *Henry David Thoreau* by Joseph Wood Krutch (William Sloane Associates, 1948), and *Henry Thoreau: A Life of the Mind* by Robert D. Richardson Jr. (University of California Press, 1986). *Walden Pond: A History* by W. Barksdale Maynard (Oxford University Press, 2004) is brimming with insights about Thoreau and his Concord and how they relate to our time.

The literature on Concord, Massachusetts, is extensive and includes *Concord in the Days of Strawberries and Streetcars* by Renee Garrelick (Mercantile/Image Press, 1999), *The Great Meadow: Farmers and the Land in Colonial Concord* by Brian Donahue (Yale University Press, 2004), and *Concord's Great Meadows: A Human History* by Carol E. Gupta (Trafford Publishing, 2004).

Much has also been written about Lowell, including *Lowell: The Story of an Industrial City* (Official National Park Handbook, National Park Service, 1992) and *Cotton Was King*, edited by Arthur L. Eno Jr. (New Hampshire Publishing Co., 1976). A highly evocative fictional account is *The Town and the City* by Jack Kerouac (Harcourt Brace and Co., 1950), a novel tracing a Lowell family from the second decade of the twentieth century through World War II.

There is a growing and fascinating literature on children and the outdoors that includes *Last Child in the Woods: Saving Our Children from Nature-Deficit Disorder* by Richard Louv (Algonquin Books of Chapel Hill, 2005), *The Geography of Childhood: Why Children Need Wild Places* by Gary Paul Nabhan and Stephen P. Trimble (Beacon Press, 1995), and *Children at Play* by Howard P. Chudacoff (New York University Press, 2007).

For insight into the development of suburbia, I relied on *Borderland: Origins of the American Suburb, 1820–1939* by John Stilgoe (Yale University Press, 1988) and *Street Car Suburbs: The Process of Growth in Boston, 1870–1900* by Samuel Bass Warner Jr. (Harvard University Press, 1962).

Two books provide details on the Middlesex Canal: *The Old Middlesex Canal* by Mary Stetson Clarke (Hilltop Press, 1974) and *Middlesex Canal Guide and Maps* by Burt VerPlanck (Middlesex Canal Association, 1998).

I owe much to the archives and helpful staff of the Concord Free Public Library and the Billerica Public Library. I am also indebted to the various museums and historic sites I visited. Their docents and rangers were invariably gracious and never seemed to tire of my endless questions. Staffs of the Great Meadows National Wildlife Refuge, various river towns, and the New Hampshire Department of Environmental Services have my gratitude for their eager assistance. Finally, I cannot express enough thanks to the ever helpful staff of my hometown Canton Public Library for their unflagging and cheerful responses to my sometimes obscure and bizarre requests for information.

Living in the Depot: The Two-Story Railroad Station
By H. Roger Grant

Main Street Revisited: Time, Space, and Image Building in Small-Town America
By Richard V. Francaviglia

Mapping American Culture
Edited by Wayne Franklin and Michael C. Steiner

Mapping the Invisible Landscape: Folklore, Writing, and the Sense of Place
By Kent C. Ryden

Mountains of Memory: A Fire Lookout's Life in the River of No Return Wilderness
By Don Scheese

Oneota Flow: The Upper Iowa River and Its People
By David S. Faldet

The People's Forests
By Robert Marshall

Pilots' Directions: The Transcontinental Airway and Its History
Edited by William M. Leary

A Place for Dialogue: Language, Land Use, and Politics in Southern Arizona
By Sharon McKenzie Stevens

Places of Quiet Beauty: Parks, Preserves, and Environmentalism
By Rebecca Conard

Reflecting a Prairie Town: A Year in Peterson
Text and photographs by Drake Hokanson

Rooted: Seven Midwest Writers of Place
By David R. Pichaske

A Rural Carpenter's World: The Craft in a Nineteenth-Century New York Township
By Wayne Franklin

Salt Lantern: Traces of an American Family
  By William Towner Morgan

Signs in America's Auto Age: Signatures of Landscape and Place
  By John A. Jakle and Keith A. Sculle

This Vast Book of Nature: Writing the Landscape of New Hampshire's
  White Mountains, 1784–1911
  By Pavel Cenkl

Thoreau's Sense of Place: Essays in American Environmental Writing
  Edited by Richard J. Schneider